Local Government Law in Scotland: An Introdu

Local Government Law in Scotland: An Introduction

Second Edition

Jean McFadden MA LLB
Former Senior Lecturer in Law at the
University of Strathclyde
Councillor, Glasgow City Council

Tottel publishing

TottelPublishing Ltd, Maxwelton House, 41–43 Boltro Road, Haywards Heath, West Sussex, RH16 1BJ

© Tottel Publishing Ltd 2008

A CIP Catalogue record for this book is available from the British Library.

ISBN: 978 1 84766 269 9

Typeset by Phoenix Photosetting, Chatham, Kent
Printed and bound in Great Britain by M & A Thomson Litho Ltd, East Kilbride, Glasgow

Contents

Preface   vii

Table of Statutes   xi

Table of Cases   xv

Introduction   xvii

Chapter 1 - The development of local government in Scotland and its position in the constitution   1

Chapter 2 - The current structure and functions of local government in Scotland   11

Chapter 3 - Councillors   29

Chapter 4 - Local government general powers and duties   51

Chapter 5 - How councils work   73

Chapter 6 - Financial matters   97

Chapter 7 - The Ombudsman, the Standards Commission and the courts   127

Chapter 8 - Central–local relations post-devolution   149

Appendix - Specific ministerial controls   173

Index   179

Preface

I was first elected as a councillor in 1971, to the Corporation of the City of Glasgow. Following local government reorganisation, I was elected to Glasgow District Council in 1974 and when another reorganisation followed in 1995 I was elected to the City of Glasgow Council. I stood for election (unsuccessfully) to the Westminster Parliament only once, in 1974, but I then decided that I could achieve more for the people of Glasgow by remaining in local government. By then I had become a tremendous enthusiast for local government and I resisted all further invitations to stand for the Westminster and European Parliaments.

In 1992 I became a lecturer in the Law School at the University of Strathclyde and was asked to devise and teach a course in local government law. I have been teaching this ever since and it became part of my mission in life to persuade people, young and not so young, of the importance of local government and the need to become involved in it. It is the tier of government which is closest to the people and it affects people every day of their lives. Unfortunately most people take it for granted – as long as their bins are emptied, the nursery nurses and the teachers are not on strike and the traffic is running freely on roads without potholes.

This book is intended to be an introduction to local government, not just for law students, but also for students of politics and public administration, for local government employees and for people interested in local government generally. As an introduction to a complex and ever-changing subject, it has not been possible to explore the various topics in depth and for that the reader must look elsewhere. For various reasons, the book has been a long time in the making. I first suggested a book such as this in 1999/2000 and had I been able to write it then, it would have been a lot simpler to complete. From 2000 onward, the Scottish Parliament became very active in local government affairs and I have had to take account of a large number of consultation papers and Acts of the Scottish Parliament which deal with what might be described as constitutional issues relating to local government and various new powers and duties. Just after I thought the first edition was finished, the Scottish Parliament passed the Local Governance (Scotland) Act 2004 which amends the law in a number of important areas. For practitioners and students, local government law has become increasingly complicated and there is a crying need for the legislation to be consolidated.

This new edition takes account of the new electoral system for local government which was used for the first time in the council elections of 2007 and the impact which that has had on the governance of Scotland. It also takes account of the new Scottish Administration formed following the third ordinary election to the Scottish Parliament which took place at the same time. In addition, it brings the reader up-to-date on various other changes which have occurred since 2003.

I am grateful to very many people for their help. Chris Young, one of Glasgow City Council's Policy Officers was of enormous assistance in carrying out various pieces of research in his own time and in commenting on the chapters as they were completed. The staff of the Council's Library and Information Services, June Davidson, Jamie Brown and Fiona Hughes, were, as ever, unfailingly helpful. Gail Hepburn, Nikki Loudon, Alannah Bruce and Natasha Lawless at various times provided invaluable secretarial and moral support.

I have pestered the life out of many officers of Glasgow City Council and I am particularly grateful to: George Black, the Chief Executive of Glasgow City Council; Ian Drummond, the Solicitor to the Council; Iain Scott, Assistant Solicitor to the Council; Annemarie O'Donnell, Head of Governance, Dr Kenneth Meechan, Fiona Simpson and Linda Welsh Senior Solicitors.

For the chapter on financial matters (a fiendishly complicated subject), I am indebted to: Don Peebles of the Chartered Institute of Public Finance and Accountancy; Lynn Brown, Director of Financial Services of GCC Morag Johnston, the Depute Director, and their staff. I also acknowledge the permission given by Her Majesty's Stationery Office to reproduce the map on page 19. I am of course, solely responsible for any mistakes or omissions in the text.

Various people went to great lengths to find a suitable copy of the quirky photograph used on the cover of the first edition, including Kitty Bell who tracked a copy down in the People's Republic of China, Bailie Alan Stewart who was prepared to climb the statue of the Duke of Wellington and replace the traditional parking cone on its head, Craig McArthur of GCC's Public Relations and Marketing Department and Victoria Hollows and George Inglis of Glasgow Museums. I am glad to see that the Duke of Wellington continues to grace the cover of the new edition, albeit from a different angle. I leave the reader to work out its significance.

Many of my councillor colleagues helped in various ways and I am particularly grateful to Bailie Alan Stewart for attempting to photograph the statue under circumstances which might have led to his arrest, to Councillor Alistair Watson for information on transport, to Councillor Tom McKeown for information on planning and to the many who responded to my frantic e-mail with the information that it was Hartlepool which had elected a man dressed in a monkey suit as mayor.

The Scottish Parliament has made many changes to the legal framework under which local authorities operate, many of them welcomed by councillors and officers alike. However, the proximity of the Scottish Ministers, the MSPs and the civil servants, located in Edinburgh and much more accessible than their predecessors in the Scottish Office, has resulted in a change of attitude towards local government. Ministers, MSPs and civil servants seem to feel that they are better able to run local government services than locally elected councillors. There appears to be little understanding of the workload involved in being a councillor and of the many calls that are made on their time, day and sometimes night. The high calibre of officers and their dedication to local government is seriously underestimated and the parity of esteem recommended by the McIntosh Commission at the start of the Scottish Parliament's life is far from being achieved. I hope that this little book might go some way to increasing understanding of the value of local government, of how it works and how important it is to all the people of Scotland.

In the preface to the first edition I said that I was rather less optimistic about the future of local government in Scotland than I was when I first started out on this work. Despite a period of relative calm in terms of primary legislation affecting local government since 2004, I remain somewhat pessimistic, particularly as it seems that, under the new Scottish Government's proposals, councils' ability to raise local taxes is to be removed. That will undermine its status as local *government* and, in my view, that would be a matter for great regret.

Jean McFadden

August 2008

Table of Statutes

[All references are to paragraph number]

Abolition of Domestic Rates etc
  (Scotland) Act 1987 ...... 6.12
Burghs and Police (Scotland) Act
  1833 .... 1.5
Children and Young Persons
  (Scotland) Acts 4.21
Civic Government (Scotland) Act
  1982 .... 4.21
  s 112–116 .... 4.26
  117 .... 4.26
  117(6) 4.28
  118 .... 4.26
Compensation Act 2006
  s 2 .... 7.16
Countryside (Scotland) Act 1967: 4.21
Data Protection Act 1998 ... 5.2, 5.39,
                      5.41, 5.42
Disability Discrimination Act
  1995 .... 4.16
District Courts (Scotland) Act
  1975 .... 3.21
Education (Scotland) Act 1872 .. 1.8
Education (Scotland) Act 1980 .. App 15
  s 23(1A), (3A) 2.27
Equal Pay Act 1970 .... 4.16
Ethical Standards in Public Life
  etc (Scotland) Act 2000
  (asp 7) 3.26, 3.29, 5.47,
               6.35, 6.37, 7.20,
               7.40, 7.41, 8.22,
               8.37, App 6
  s 1 .... 7.21
  6 .... 17.36
  7 .... 3.28, 7.23, App 6
  8–10 .... 7.34
  12–14 .... 7.34
  17, 18 .... 7.35
  19 .... 3.13
  21 .... 7.37
  22 .... 7.38
  29 .... 3.16, 7.38
  33 .... 6.38
  34, 35 .... 4.36

Freedom of Information (Scot-
  land) Act 2002 (asp 13) .. 3.33, 5.2,
                    5.36, 5.37,
                    5.39, 5.40
Glasgow Corporation Water
  Works Act 1859 .... 1.9
Highland Regional Council
  (Harbours) Order Confirma-
  tion Act 1991 .... 4.29
House of Lords Act 1999 ...... 3.2
Housing (Scotland) Act 1987 ... App 7
  s 20(3) 3.31
Housing (Scotland) Act 2001
  (asp 10) 6.30
Human Rights Act 1998 .... 5.45
  Sch 1
  Art 6 .... 5.45, 7.33,
                  7.40, 7.47
  8 .... 5.45
  10 .... 5.49
  11 .... 5.45
  14 .... 5.45
  First Protocol, art 1 .... 5.45
Labour Exchange Act 1909 .... 1.7
Licensing (Scotland) Act 1976 .. 2.32
Licensing (Scotland) Act 2005
  (asp 16) 2.32
Local Authorities (Admission of
  the Press to Meetings) Act
  1908 .... 5.29
Local Governance (Scotland) Act
  2004 (asp 9) 2.39, 3.6, 3.7,
              8.17, 8.19, 8.20,
              8.24, 8.26, 8.40
  s 1 .... 8.36
  2 .... 8.35
  4 .... 2.36, 2.37
  7 .... 3.9, 3.10,
               3.42, 8.35
  8 .... 3.8, 3.42, 8.35
  9 .... 3.12, 3.42,
              5.49, 8.35
  10 .... 3.18, 5.46, 8.35

Local Governance (Scotland) Act
   2004 – *contd*
  s 11 .... 3.36, 8.35
    12 .... 3.13, 8.35
    13 .... 3.36, 8.35
Local Government (Access to
   Information) Act 1985 . . . 3.32, 5.2,
                       5.29, 5.33
  s 2 .... 3.33
  Sch 1 .... 3.33
Local Government Act 1972
  s 111 .... 4.5
Local Government Act 1974 ... 7.3
Local Government Act 1986 ... 2.4
  Pt 2 (ss 2–6) 4.32
  s 2 .... 4.33, 4.35
   2A 4.36, 8.22
Local Government Act 1988: 4.13, 4.32
  s 17–19 .... 4.39
    28 .... 4.36
    29 .... 7.8
    35 .... 6.47
Local Government Act 1992 ... 4.13
  s 1 .... 6.47, 6.48
   5, 6 .... 6.34
Local Government Act 2000
  s 2, 3 .... 4.10
  Pt II (ss 10–48) 5.23
  s 10, 11 .... 8.34
Local Government Act 2003 ... 4.36
Local Government and Housing
   Act 1989 .... 3.12, 5.48, 5.49
  s 1–3 .... 3.11, 5.49
   4, 5 .... 5.5
   15 .... 3.32, 5.12
   16 .... 3.32
   32 .... 7.11, 7.18
Local Government and Planning
   (Scotland) Act 1982 ...... 2.3
Local Government (Contracts)
   Act 1997 .... 4.6
  s 2(1) 4.6
   5(3) 4.6
   6, 7 .... 4.6
Local Government etc (Scotland)
   Act 1994 .... 2.15, 2.19, 2.20,
              2.22, 2.23, 2.28,
            3.21, 5.10, App 1
  Pt I (ss 1–61) 7.45
  s 2 .... 3.1
   4 .... 3.20
   5(3) 3.4
   20 .... 2.24
   22 .... 2.32

Local Government etc (Scotland)
   Act 1994 – *contd*
  s 23 .... 2.16
    27 .... 2.27
    30 .... 3.29
    31 .... 5.13
    32(2), (3) 2.27
    33 .... 2.27
    34 .... 2.25
    35 .... 2.25
    36 .... 2.25
    40 .... 2.26
    58 .... 2.25
    60 .... 7.45
  Pt II (ss 62–126) 4.37
  s 170 .... 6.47
  Sch 13, para 92(5) 2.38
Local Government Finance Act
   1992 .... 6.7, 6.12
  s 70 .... 6.12
    77 .... 6.13
    94 .... 6.21
   112 .... 3.30, 6.20
  Sch 7 .... 6.21
Local Government (Gaelic Names)
   Act 1997 .... 2.15, 2.38
Local Government (Goods and
   Services) Act 1970 .... 4.39
Local Government in Scotland
   Act 2003 (asp 1) ... 4.8, 6.26, 6.45
  Pt 1 (ss 1–14) 4.15
  s 1 .... 6.40
   (1) 4.15
   (2) 4.15, 6.40
   (3) 4.15, 6.40
   (4), (5) 4.15
   2 .... 6.40, App 2
   3 .... 6.41, 6.49
  ss 3–6 .... 4.17
  s 4 .... 6.49
   7 .... 4.39
   8 .... 4.39
   11 .... 4.38
   13 .... 6.48
   (2) 6.48
  Pt 2 (ss 15–19) 4.18
  s 15, 16 .... 4.19
   18 .... App 2
   20 .... 8.15
   (1), (2) 4.9
   (4) 4.9
   21 .... 4.9, 8.15, App 2
   22 .... 8.15
   (1) 4.10

Local Government in Scotland
  Act 2003 – *contd*
s 22(4), (5) 4.10
   (7), (8) 4.10
   (9). 4.10
ss 23-27 . . . . App 16
s 23(1), (2) 6.42
 24 . . . . 6.42
 26(1), (2) 4.10
 27 . . . . 4.10
 35 . . . . 6.3
 43 . . . . 3.42
Local Government (Scotland)
  Act 1889 . . . . 1.2, 1.10
Local Government (Scotland)
  Act 1929 . . . . 1.13, 1.14
Local Government (Scotland)
  Act 1947 . . . . 1.14
Local Government (Scotland)
  Act 1973 . . . . 1.22, 1.23, 1.24,
                2.1, 2.23, 2.31,
                5.2, 5.9, 5.10
s 4(3). 3.21
 12 . . . . 2.34
 22 . . . . 4.31
 23 . . . . 2.38
 28 . . . . 2.36
 29 . . . . 3.7, 3.8
 31 . . . . 3.9, 3.10, 3.13
 32 . . . . 3.14
 33 . . . . 3.15
 33A 3.29
 35 . . . . 3.16, 7.36, 7.38
 37 . . . . 3.17
 38–40 . . . . 7.17
 50A 3.33, 5.29, 5.32
 50B–50K 3.33, 5.29
 51–55 . . . . 2.30
 56 . . . . 4.28, 5.6, 5.14
  (5) 2.24
  (6) 5.5, 6.20
 57 . . . . 5.6, 5.13
  (4) 5.11
 58–62 . . . . 5.6
 62A 2.24
 62B 2.25
 63 . . . . 5.6
 64 . . . . 5.46
 67 . . . . 3.18
 69 . . . . 4.5, 4.39
  (1), (2) 6.26
 70 . . . . 4.38
 71 . . . . 4.38
 73 . . . . 4.38

Local Government (Scotland)
  Act 1973 – *contd*
s 75 . . . . 4.38
 81 . . . . 4.39
 82 . . . . 4.30
 87 . . . . 4.37
 88 . . . . 4.32, 4.33
 94 . . . . 6.3, 6.26
 95 . . . . 6.1
 97 . . . . 6.33
 97A 6.47
 99 . . . . 6.34
 101 . . . . 6.35
  (4) 6.34
 102 . . . . 6.38
  (3) 6.35
 103 . . . . 6.37, 6.38
 103B 6.35
 103D 6.35
 103E 6.37
 103F 6.39
 103F(2) 6.38
 103F(3) 6.39
 103G(1), (2) 6.39
 103J 6.39
 104 . . . . 6.37, 6.38
 122A 6.47
 189 . . . . 7.43
 201 . . . . 4.21
 202 . . . . 4.21, App 8
 203, 204 . . . . 4.21
 209 . . . . App 13
 210 . . . . App 14
 211 . . . . App 15
 231 . . . . 3.29, 7.45
Sch 6 . . . . 2.37
Sch 7A 3.33, 5.29, 5.31
Local Government (Scotland)
  Act 1975 . . . . 7.3
Pt II (ss 21–32) 7.14
Lothian Region (Edinburgh
  Western Relief Road) Order
  Confirmation Act 1986 . . . . 4.29
Management of Offenders etc
  (Scotland) Act 2005 (asp
  14) 5.27
National Assistance Act 1948 . . 4.10
National Health Service Reform
  (Scotland) Act 2004 (asp 7): 5.26
National Insurance Act 1911 . . . 1.7
Orkney County Council Act
  1974 . . . . 4.29
Parliamentary Commissioner Act
  1967 . . . . 7.3

Poor Law (Scotland) Act 1845:   1.7
Prevention of Corruption Act
    1906 .... 3.24, 7.17
Prevention of Corruption Act
    1916 .... 3.24, 7.17
Private Legislation Procedure
    (Scotland) Act 1936 ......   4.30
Public Bodies (Admission to
    Meetings) Act 1960 .... 3.32, 5.29
Public Bodies Corrupt Practices
    Act 1889 .... 3.24, 7.17
Public Finance and Accounta-
    bility (Scotland) Act 2000
    (asp 1) 6.34
Public Health (Scotland) Act
    1867 ....   1.6
Public Health (Scotland) Act
    1897 .... 1.6, 4.21
Race Relations Act 1976 ......   4.16
Regulation of Investigatory
    Powers Act 2000 ....   5.45
Representation of the People Act
    2000 .... 3.2, 3.3
Representation of the People
    (Equal Franchise) Act 1928:   1.2
Requirements of Writing
    (Scotland) Act 1995 .....   3.1
School Education (Ministerial
    Powers and Independent
    Schools) (Scotland) Act
    2004 (asp 12) ...... 8.40, App 16
Scotland Act 1998 .... 1.28, 1.29,
                    4.16, 7.5, 8.9
    s 91 ....   7.4
    Sch 5 .... 1.28, 6.12
    Sch 5, L2 ....   4.16
    Sch 5, Pt III, para 1 ....   1.28
Scottish Borders Council (Jim
    Clark Memorial Rally) Order
    Confirmation Act 1996 ....   4.29
Scottish Local Government (Elec-
    tions) Act 2002 (asp 1) 3.5
    s 2 ....   8.16
    5 ....   8.16

Scottish Public Services Ombuds-
    man Act 2002 (asp 11) 7.5
    s 1 ....   7.5
    2 ....   7.6
    (2) 7.13
    5 ....   7.6
    7, 8 ....   7.7
    9, 10 ....   7.8
    11–14 ....   7.9
    15 ....   7.10
    16 ....   7.11
    17 ....   7.13
    22 ....   7.13
    Sch 2 ....   7.6
    Sch 4 ....   7.7
Sex Discrimination Act 1975 ...   4.16
Social Work (Scotland) Act
    1968 ....   1.15
Tenants' Rights etc (Scotland)
    Act 1980 ....   6.30
Tourist Boards (Scotland) Act
    2006 (asp 15) 2.20
Town and Country Planning Act
    (Scotland) 1972
    s 4A 2.27
Town and Country Planning
    (Scotland) Act 1997 ...... App 4
    s 5 ....   2.27
    18 .... App 5
    47 .... App 10
    130 .... App 10
    238, 239 ....   7.33
Transport (Scotland) Act 2005
    (asp 12) 2.26, 8.40
Water Industry (Scotland) Act
    2002 (asp 3) 2.20
Western Isles Islands Council
    (Berneray Harbour) Order
    Confirmation Act 1986 ....   4.29
Western Isles Islands Council
    (Vatersay Causeway) Order
    Confirmation Act 1987 ....   4.29
Zetland County Council Act
    1974 ....   4.29

Table of Cases

[All references are to paragraph number]

A

Aberdeen Bon-Accord Loyal Orange Lodge 701 v Aberdeen City Council
2002 SLT (Sh Ct) 52 .... 5.45
Advocate (Lord) v City of Glasgow District Council 1990 SLT 721 .... App 15
Ahmed v United Kingdom (2000) 29 EHRR 1, [1998] HRCD 823, ECtHR .. 5.49
Associated Provincial Picture Houses Ltd v Wednesbury Corporation [1948] 1
KB 223, [1948] LJR 190, 177 LT 641, [1947] 2 All ER 680, CA 4.3, 7.47
Attorney-General v Great Eastern Railway Company (1880) 5 App Cas 473,
(1880) 42 LT 810, HL 4.4
Attorney-General v Fulham Corporation [1921] 1 Ch 440, (1921) 90 LJ Ch
281, (1921) 125 LT 14, (1921) 85 JP 213 .... 4.3

B

Battelly v Finsbury Borough Council (1958) 56 LGR 165, (1958) 122 JP 169 .. 5.8

C

Commission for Local Authority Accounts in Scotland v City of Edinburgh
District Council 1988 SLT 767, 1988 SCLR 553, Ct of Sess (2 Div) .. 4.32, 6.35
Commission for Local Authority Accounts in Scotland v Grampian Regional
Council 1994 SLT 11209 .... 4.35, 6.35
Commission for Local Authority Accounts in Scotland v Stirling District
Council 1984 SLT 442 .... 2.4, 6.35
Council of Civil Service Unions v Minister for the Civil Service [1985] AC
374, [1984] 3 All ER 935, [1984] 1 WLR 1174, HL9 .... 4.3, 7.47
County Properties Ltd v Scottish Ministers 2002 SC 79 .... 7.33
Credit Suisse v Allerdale Borough Council [1997] QB 306, [1996] 4 All ER
129, [1996] 3 WLR 894, CA 4.5, 4.6
Credit Suisse v Waltham Forest London Borough Council [1997] QB 362,
[1996] 4 All ER 176, [1996] 3 WLR 943, CA 5, 4.6

D

D and J Nicol v Dundee Harbour Trustees 1915 SC (HL) 7, 1914 2 SLT 418 . 4.4
Dumfries and Galloway Council v Baldwick (10 March 1998, unreported) .. 3.15

G

Glasgow Corporation v Flint SC 108; sub nom Secretary of State for Scotland
v Glasgow Corporation 1966 SLT 183, Ct of Sess (2 Div) 4.4
Graham v Glasgow Corporation 1936 SC 108, 1936 SLT 145 .... 4.4

H

Hazell v Hammersmith and Fulham London Borough Council [1992] 2 AC 1,
[1991] 1 All ER 545, [1991] 2 WLR 372, HL 4.5

L

Lloyd v McMahon [1987] AC 625, [1987] 1 All ER 1118, [1987] 2 WLR 821,
HL 2.4

M

McColl v Strathclyde Regional Council 1983 SC 225, 1983 SLT 616, Ct of
Sess (OH) 4.5
Manton v Brighton Corporation [1951] 2 KB 303, [1951] 2 All ER 101, 115
JP 377 . . . .   3.32
Meek v Lothian Regional Council 1980 SLT (Notes) 61 . . . .   4.5
Meek v Lothian Regional Council 1982 SC 84, 1983 SLT 494 . . . .   4.32
Morgan Guaranty Trust Company of New York v Lothian Regional Council
1995 SLT 299, 1995 SCLR 225, Ct of Sess (IH) 4.5
Moss' Empires Ltd v Glasgow Assessor 1917 SC (HL) 1, 1916 2 SLT 215 . .   4.2

O

Oxfordshire County Council v R (on the application of Khan) [2004] EWCA
Civ 309, [2004] HLR 706, [2004] LGR 257, (2004) 7 CCLR 215, [2004]
All ER (D) 322 (Mar) 4.10

P

Parker v Yeo (1992) 90 LGR 645, (1992) The Guardian, October 20, CA 3.8

R

R (Alconbury Developments Ltd and Others) v Secretary of State for the
Environment, Transport and the Regions; R (Holding and Barnes plc) v
Secretary of State for the Environment, Transport and the Regions;
Secretary of State for the Environment, Transport and the Regions v Legal
and General Assurance Society Ltd [2001] UKHL 23, [2003] 2 AC 295,
[2001] 2 All ER 929, [2001] 2 WLR 1389, HL 7.33
R v Port Talbot Borough Council, ex p Jones [1988] 2 All ER 207, (1988) 20
HLR 265 . . . .   5.7
R v Secretary of State for the Environment, ex p Hillingdon London Borough
Council [1986] 2 All ER 273, [1986] 1 WLR 807, (1986) 130 SJ 481,
CA 5.7
Roberts v Hopwood [1925] AC 578, [1925] All ER Rep 74, 94 LJKB 542, 133
LT 289, 89 JP 105, 41 TLR 436, 69 Sol Jo 475, 23 LGR 337, HL 6.37

S

Secretary of State for Scotland v Glasgow Corporation. See Glasgow
Corporation v Flint
Short v Poole Corporation [1926] Ch 66, [1925] All ER Rep 74, 95 LJ Ch 110,
134 LT 110, 90 JP 25, 42 TLR 107, 70 Sol Jo 245, 24 LGR 14, CA 7.47

W

West Dunbartonshire Council v Harvie 1997 SLT 979, Ct of Sess (OH) 4.38
Wishart Arch Defenders Loyal Orange Lodge 404 v Angus Council 2002 SLT
(Sh Ct) 43 . . . .   5.45

Introduction

Local government touches the lives of every one of us, literally from the cradle to the grave. Our births, marriages and deaths are registered in the local registration office. Most Scottish children are educated in schools run by the local authority; many of us live in council houses. Our bins are emptied and our streets swept and lit by the council. Home helps are provided for the elderly and disabled, sports centres and swimming pools for the more active. Scottish local authorities have large budgets, running into hundreds of millions of pounds and employ about one-quarter of a million people in Scotland. Yet most people take local government for granted – until something goes wrong.

In constitutional terms, local councils are subordinate bodies. They were created by an Act of the UK Parliament[1] and could be abolished by another Act of Parliament. However, since the establishment of the Scottish Parliament in 1999, all constitutional aspects of local government, with the exception of the right to vote in local government elections, and most of its functions have been devolved to the Scottish Parliament and, in practice, the fate of local government lies in the hands of the MSPs.

Despite its subordinate nature, local government is important for a number of reasons. The members of local authorities (the councillors) are directly elected by and accountable to the local people whom they serve[2]. This democratic basis sets it apart from and raises it to a level above other administrative bodies.

Local authorities also have an important local dimension. Until May 2007, Scotland was divided into 1,222 single-member wards, each of which elected its own councillor. The wards were grouped into 32 councils. The Local Governance (Scotland) Act 2004[3] brought in multi-member wards, of which there are 353, each one represented by either three or four councillors. The total number of councillors in Scotland remains at 1222 and there are still 32 councils. The introduction of large multi-member ward dilutes the local link between a councillor and his or her electorate.

The councils vary considerably in terms of geographical areas and populations. Highland Council, for example, is responsible for the largest territory geographically of any United Kingdom local authority, extending to 10,000 square miles, while its population is only around 200,000. Glasgow City Council, on the other hand, has a population of around 600,000 and covers a relatively small area geographically. When there were single-member wards, the individual wards were relatively small (less so in rural areas). With the introduction of multi-member wards, the new wards are considerably larger both in terms of population and geographical area but attempts have been made to ensure as far as possible that communities with local links are grouped together[4].

Local councils are also political bodies in the sense that most of the councillors are elected on a party political ticket.

Another important feature of local government is that it has tax-raising powers[5]. The current local tax is the council tax which is paid by the majority of the adult inhabitants of an area. However, the Scottish Government[6] formed after the election in 2007 announced that it was their intention to replace the council tax with a nationally set 'local' income tax.

The money raised from the council tax (or a local income tax) does not fund local government services in their entirety as much of local government funding comes from the Scottish Government but the power to levy a local tax gives local authorities an opportunity to provide services tailored to local needs. Again the tax-raising power differentiates local authorities from other public bodies which generally have the power to charge customers only for services actually consumed. Only the Parliament of the United Kingdom, the Scottish Parliament and local government have the power to raise a general levy from part of the general population to pay for the provision of general services and where the amount payable by an individual is not related to the number or kind of services actually consumed.

These two features, direct elections and tax-raising powers, are what makes local government 'government' rather than local administration.

Scottish local authorities are major players in Scotland with a significant role in most areas of economic and cultural life. In 2006-7 Scottish local authority expenditure amounted to around £ 18.9 billion. As they employ around a quarter of a million people, they are very influential in the local labour market and many Scottish local authorities are the largest employers in their areas. In the field of culture local authorities support a large number of the arts organisations which flourish in Scotland, including the Royal Scottish National Orchestra, Scottish Opera, Scottish Ballet, the internationally renowned Citizens Theatre in Glasgow, most of the major museums outside Edinburgh and a huge range of smaller bodies.

Another distinguishing feature of local government is the wide range of functions which it discharges. Most public bodies or government agencies are responsible for the provision of one kind of service or a group of related services. The Scottish Qualifications Agency and the National Health Service are good examples of such bodies. Local authorities, on the other hand, discharge a wide range of functions which do not seem to have much connection other than public utility. There are few public services for which local government does not have some responsibility. Many of these are so taken for granted that the public is hardly aware of who their provider is.

The powers of local government are conferred by Acts of either the UK Parliament or the Scottish Parliament and by statutory instruments made by the Parliaments. It is a well-established principle of law that a statutory body has no power to do anything which it is not required or authorised to do by the statute or statutes under which the body was established or which otherwise govern its activities. So if a local authority does something which it is not authorised to do, it is acting ultra vires (outwith its powers) and may find its action challenged in court. A recent Act of the Scottish Parliament has relaxed the rigour of this rule to a considerable extent[7].

Local government is important in other less concrete ways. An influential report on local government, published in 1986[8], identified the value of local government as stemming from its three attributes of pluralism, participation and responsiveness. Pluralism means that political power is not concentrated in one organisation of the state but is dispersed, providing a system of political checks and balances and a restraint on arbitrary government. Local government contributes to pluralism by providing a number of points where decisions are taken by people of different political beliefs, thus spreading political power. Participation by the public is provided by local government in a number of ways: first, in that people are able to stand for election to the council in their own local area; and, second, by offering opportunities for the public to share in decision-making in various ways through, for example, consultation, membership of community councils and local lobbying. Local government, by being close to the people it represents, is also able to be more responsive to local needs than a non-elected system of local administration.

The following chapters deal with various aspects of local government in Scotland, including its position in the UK constitution, its current structure and functions, the roles, duties and rights of councillors, local government's general powers and duties, how councils work, local government finance, relations with central government (mainly with the Scottish Executive and Scottish Parliament) and various external controls. The book does not deal in detail with the law relating to function and readers who wish more information on functions should consult specialised texts.

1 The Local Government etc (Scotland) Act 1994 is the Act which established the current structure of local government in Scotland.
2 For local elections, see ch 3.
3 Local Governance (Scotland) Act 2004, s 1
4 the term Scottish Government was introduced in 2007. Prior to that the term used was the Scottish Executive
5 For the current structure of local government, see ch 2.
6 For local government finance, see ch 6.
7 For the ultra vires rule and its development, see ch 4.
8 *Report of the Committee of Inquiry into the Conduct of Local Authority Business* (the Widdicombe Report) (Cmnd 9797) (1986).

Chapter 1

The development of local government in Scotland and its position in the constitution

1.1   Before we examine the various aspects of modern local government, let us take a very brief look at the development of local government in Scotland[1].

Local government has existed in some form or another since the twelfth century when Scottish burghs emerged as local administrative units during the reign of King David I (1124–1153). The burghs were mainly concerned with law and order and the regulation of trade and were given representation in the old Scottish Parliament. Burghs were incorporated by charters granted by the king or by other feudal superiors; and royal burghs had more extensive privileges than those created by feudal superiors. From a very early stage, there was a distinction between burghs and rural counties or landward areas. In the counties sheriffs were appointed by the king to carry out military, financial and administrative tasks. Many of these sheriffdoms were created in the twelfth and thirteenth centuries and, because of the different conditions prevailing at the times when the country was thus divided up, the division into counties does not seem to have any logic or uniformity either in terms of population or of geography. Nevertheless the county was to become the most important unit of local government until the latter part of the twentieth century.

1 For more information on the historical development of local government in Scotland, see *SME Reissue* Local Government, paras 16–47.

1.2   The other important unit in Scottish local government was the parish. Parishes were originally founded by the medieval church and were areas within a diocese large enough to support a church or a clergyman. The parish and its council were important because the provision of certain services, such as education and poor relief, were seen as important works of Christian charity and the administration of these were handled at parish level.

Such local government as existed was not democratically elected as most men did not have the right to vote until various nineteenth century Representation of the People Acts gradually enfranchised them. Some women were given the vote for local government elections by the Local Government (Scotland) Act 1889 but women were not fully enfranchised until 1928[1].

1 Representation of the People (Equal Franchise) Act 1928.

1.3   While Scotland remained a rural country with only a few major centres of population, there was not the demand for the range of local government services provided today. However, the Industrial Revolution and the development of large towns and cities in the nineteenth century changed all this. The growth of industry brought about huge shifts in population from rural areas to the towns and cities. Between 1841 and 1911 the population of Glasgow rose from 275,000 to 748,000 and population growth in Edinburgh, Aberdeen and Dundee was similar.

1.4   The huge population growth combined with low wages and insecure employment led to the creation of slum conditions in the towns and cities. Housing conditions were appalling and conditions in the cities led to epidemics of cholera and typhus. There were no mechanisms in place, either public or private, which could deal with the problems of slum housing and public health that were brought about by the rapid growth of industry based on coal. Linked to the housing and public health problems were concerns about law and order among the middle classes who feared that the slum-dwellers might revolt against their miserable living and working conditions.

1.5   The Burghs and Police (Scotland) Act 1833 was a very important and enlightened piece of legislation which empowered the inhabitants of various burghs to establish a system of policing and to elect police commissioners. The 1833 Act also provided powers for the construction of drains and sewers, the supply of water, for paving, lighting and cleaning the streets and for the provision of fire engines in the burghs. A form of local tax or charge was imposed on local householders to meet the costs of the services provided. These powers were gradually extended by various Acts to all 'populous places'[1].

1 A populous place was one with a population of 700 or more.

1.6   Public health problems were tackled by the Public Health (Scotland) Act 1867 which gave powers in both the burghs and the rural areas for the prevention and mitigation of disease, the removal of nuisances, the regulation of common lodging houses and the provision of sewerage, drainage and water supply services. The Public Health (Scotland) Act 1897 established a Local Government Board for Scotland with powers of compulsion and incentives through grants to promote a more integrated public health service. This Local Government Board was the early predecessor of the present Scottish Executive Health Department which is responsible for the NHS in Scotland. The 1897 Act also provided for the establishment of hospitals, the provision and maintenance of mortuaries and the regulation of the fitness of buildings for human habitation. The nineteenth century also saw the introduction of legislation to deal with specific aspects of public health, such as infectious diseases, vaccination, food and milk standards, animal diseases, river pollution and the abatement of smoke nuisance from chimneys.

1.7   The problems of the poor and the unemployed have also posed enormous difficulties over the centuries. Various Acts were passed in attempts to secure the relief of the poor and to deal with beggars and 'vagrants'. These culminated in the Poor Law (Scotland) Act 1845 which was not repealed until 1948. The Poor Law Act gave parishes various duties in the relief of poverty including the duty to lodge the insane poor in asylums. The Labour Exchange Act 1909 was the first attempt to deal with the problems of unemployment on a national scale, while the National Insurance Act 1911 introduced a scheme under which people who earned a wage were required to contribute to an insurance scheme which would guarantee benefits in certain situations.

1.8　　For centuries education was by and large provided by the churches with the parish being the basic unit of provision. The Education (Scotland) Act 1872 introduced an integrated system of elementary education for children of school age (at the time 5–13 years of age). Responsibility for schools was given to parochial boards and you will still see today, on older school buildings, engravings in the stone work proclaiming the establishment of a school by a long-gone Parish School Board[1]. Later, in 1893, education committees were established in the counties and the cities to administer and co-ordinate secondary education, their members elected by county or town councils and school boards. These committees and the school boards were replaced in 1918 with 33 ad hoc education authorities which were independent of the local authorities but which were democratically elected.

1 For example, on Downhill Primary School in Glasgow, 'Downhill Public School, Govan Parish School Board'.

1.9　　As important as the Acts of Parliament, which were passed to deal with the social and economic problems caused partly by the Industrial Revolution, was the determination of certain councillors to improve the living conditions of the people they represented. To achieve their goals they had to persuade their councils to promote private Acts of Parliament[1]. Glasgow Corporation was the pioneer in the municipal provision of services. In 1859, the Glasgow Corporation Water Works Act enabled fresh water to be piped into the city from Loch Katrine and the benefits of this were clear when cholera hit Glasgow again in 1864–5 as only 53 Glaswegians died compared with 4,000 who died in the 1853 outbreak. Glasgow's forward-looking programme of municipalisation also included the provision of gas, tramlines, fever hospitals, laundry services, public baths and washhouses. Dundee and Edinburgh Corporations followed Glasgow's lead in the provision of municipal services during the second half of the nineteenth century but local public service provision remained limited in the other Scottish towns and in the countryside.

1 For private Acts of Parliament, see ch 4.

1.10　　In the 1890s, it was recognised that there was a need to bring some cohesion to the variety of bodies which were delivering services. This led to a series of Acts of Parliament. Many boards which had been set up to deal with specific services were replaced by a smaller number of multi-purpose authorities and a more systematic structure of local government began to emerge. The Local Government (Scotland) Act 1889 established 33 county councils, democratically elected by ratepayers (including women), which were given extensive powers. In the towns and cities most of the powers were given to the burgh councils. Nevertheless, the structure was far from satisfactory. In 1900, there were 33 county councils, 200 burgh councils, 860 parish councils, more than 1,000 school boards and numerous other bodies such as Burgh Police commissioners, County Road Boards and County District Committees. One significant change that came about as a result of the legislation passed in the 1890s was that the provision of many local authority services became mandatory: in other words the local authorities were obliged to provide them. Previously, the legislation had given local authorities discretionary powers.

1.11   Prior to the 1914–18 War, there were very few council houses although councils had some regulatory powers in relation to overcrowding and slum clearance. The condition of the housing in which the working classes lived was very poor and poor housing contributed to poor health. In 1900, 122 out of every 1,000 children born alive died within their first year. In 1917 a Royal Commission[1] set up to investigate housing conditions in Scotland reported that the private housing sector could not solve the crisis and that a massive programme of public sector house-building was required. This led to a series of Housing Acts and from the 1920s the local authorities began a huge programme of council house provision which lasted well into the 1970s.

1 *Royal Commission on Housing in Scotland* (the Ballantyne Commission) (Cmnd 8731) (1917).

1.12   During the early twentieth century there was considerable growth in the provision of public services generally with the provision of public parks and public libraries and the extension of sewerage and public hospitals to areas which had not had the benefit of the municipalisation of the late nineteenth century.

1.13   However, the structure of local government was still cumbersome and more fundamental reform was required. This came in the form of the Local Government (Scotland) Act 1929. Under this Act, the counties became the main unit of administration, regardless of their size, but they were divided into districts which provided minor services on a local basis. Burghs continued to operate and were classed as large burghs (if they had a population of 20,000 or more) or small burghs, with their powers varying according to their classification. The cities of Aberdeen, Dundee, Edinburgh and Glasgow became counties of cities and were separate all-purpose units of local government. The functions of the education authorities were transferred to the counties and the cities. Parish councils were abolished.

1.14   The Local Government (Scotland) Act 1929 created a fivefold structure:

- 4 counties of cities
- 33 counties
- 21 large burghs
- 176 small burghs
- 196 districts (within counties).

This structure remained largely in place until the reorganisation of 1974–75[1].

1 The Local Government (Scotland) Act 1947 repealed and replaced the 1929 Act but made no change to the structure put in place by that Act.

1.15   By the 1960s both the type and the scale of services provided by local government had changed dramatically since 1929. For example, the requirement for personal and social services had grown considerably and, in response to this, the Social Work (Scotland) Act 1968 established social work departments within local authorities to co-ordinate the provision of such services.

1.16   In addition, the proliferation of local authorities caused serious problems for large-scale economic and land use planning and for major redevelopment projects backed by central government. A much more rational system of local government was required with fewer and larger local authorities.

THE WHEATLEY COMMISSION AND THE 1974–75 REORGANISATION

Introduction

1.17   In 1963, the Conservative Government published a consultation paper, *The Modernisation of Local Government in Scotland*, which proposed a two-tier system with about 15 combined counties forming the top tier and between 50 and 60 burgh or rural councils forming the lower tier. The change of government in 1964 led to that proposal being shelved in the meantime. What the new Labour government did was to establish, in 1966, Royal Commissions to investigate and report with recommendations on local government reform in both Scotland and England. The Scottish Commission was chaired by Lord Wheatley, the English Commission by Lord Redcliffe-Maud.

1.18   The Wheatley Commission consulted widely and its report, which was produced in 1969, remains the most comprehensive study of Scottish local government[1]. Although the reforms which followed the Wheatley Report were dismantled in 1995–96 and the Wheatley Report may seem to be ancient history, many of its conclusions are still valid today.

1 *Report of the Royal Commission on Local Government in Scotland* (the Wheatley Report) (Cmnd 4150) (1969).

1.19   The very first paragraph of the Report went straight to the heart of the problem:

'Something is seriously wrong with local government in Scotland. It is not that local authorities have broken down, or that services have stopped functioning. The trouble is not so obvious as that. It is rather that the local government system as a whole is not working properly . . . at the root of the trouble is the present structure of local government. It has remained basically the same for forty years while everything around it has changed. There is ample evidence to show that local authorities on the whole are too small. The boundaries pay little heed to present social and economic realities. Services are often being provided by the wrong sorts of authorities and over the wrong areas[1]....'

1 *Report of the Royal Commission on Local Government in Scotland* (the Wheatley Report) (Cmnd 4150) (1969), paras 1, 2, 3.

1.20 In Wheatley's view local government has two main purposes, namely to supply local services and to provide government at a local level in the sense that there should be real local control over services and an element of choice and local self-expression.

Reorganisation of local government should secure four objectives:

Power. Local government should be enabled to play a more important, responsible and positive part in the running of the country, to bring the reality of government nearer to the people.

Effectiveness. Local government should be equipped to provide services in the most satisfactory manner, particularly from the point of view of the people receiving the services.

Local democracy. Local government should constitute a system in which power is exercised through the elected representatives of the people and in which those representatives are locally accountable for its exercise.

Local involvement. Local government should bring the people into the process of decision-making as far as possible and enable those decisions to be made intelligible to the people[1].

1 The Wheatley Report, para 128.

Recommendations

1.21 The Wheatley Commission recommended that the existing structure of over 400 units should be abolished and replaced by a two-tier system of local government, with seven regional authorities with populations of over 200,000 providing large-scale, strategic services and 37 district authorities providing more local services. The three island groups – Orkney, Shetland and the Western Isles – should not be accorded special status but should be part of a Highlands and Islands Regional Authority. The district authorities were not to be seen as under the control of the regional authorities. They were to be independent of the regions although, in the case of some services, there was a clear case for mutual consultation and co-operation between the two tiers. The Report also recommended the creation of community councils throughout the districts, with no service delivery functions and no power to levy any form of local tax but with the object of expressing the voice of a neighbourhood.

The main large-scale strategic services for which the regional authorities were to be responsible were identified as strategic planning, personal social services (education, social work and housing), protective services (police, fire and civil defence), refuse disposal, roads and transportation, water and sewerage. The more local services which were to be allocated to the district authorities included local planning, cleansing and refuse collection, regulation and licensing of taxis, cinemas and theatres, parks and recreation, museums, art galleries and libraries.

1.22   Although there was a change of government from Labour to Conservative in 1970, the new government broadly accepted the recommendations of the Wheatley Commission but some significant changes were made during the legislative process of what became the Local Government (Scotland) Act 1973. The number of regions was increased from seven to nine and the number of districts from 37 to 53. The three islands groups were given individual single-tier status.

The populations of the regions ranged from 2.3m in Strathclyde Regional Council to 103,000 in the Borders region. The district council populations ranged from 689,000 in Glasgow District to 10,420 in Nairn District.

1.23   The distribution of functions broadly followed the Wheatley recommendations, but housing was made a district and islands function thus separating it from strategic planning and from the other personal social services. Refuse disposal also became a district and islands function along with cleansing and other environmental services. Because of the sparsity of population in some rural areas the district councils lying within the Highlands, the Borders and Dumfries and Galloway regions did not have responsibility for libraries, building control and local planning. Instead these functions were carried out by the regional councils. The island councils, which were given single-tier status under the 1973 Act, did not have sole responsibility for the police and fire services as they did not have large enough populations or geographical areas to sustain these services. These were shared with Highland Regional Council.

1.24   The first election of councillors to the new local authorities took place in May 1974 and they served for a 'shadow' year alongside the councillors of the local authorities which were due to be abolished. The changeover to the new system took place in May 1975. The Local Government (Scotland) Act 1973 made provision for the staggering of elections to the district councils and the regional councils in the early years to establish the rotation of district councils in leap years and the regional and islands councils in the even-numbered years in between. In other words, the system settled down to a position where each tier of local government was elected for a four-year term but an election to one or other tier was held every two years.

1.25   The allocation of powers of the regional and district councils can be seen in the table below. There was a degree of overlap in the case of some functions such as industrial promotion and development.

Table 1

Regional Council functions	District Council functions
Roads including traffic regulation and road safety	Building control
	Liquor licensing
Public transport	Miscellaneous licensing and registration
Ferries, piers and harbours	
Water supply	Housing
Sewerage	Local planning
Flood prevention	Tourism
Coast protection	Libraries
Police service	Museums and art galleries
Fire service	Leisure and recreation
Public processions	Environmental health
Certification of sports grounds	Cleansing
Registration of births, marriages and deaths	Refuse collection and disposal
	Allotments
Trading standards	Burial grounds and crematoria
Education	District courts
Social work	Markets and slaughterhouses
Children's reporter and children's panels	Control of stray dogs
Strategic planning	
Industrial promotion and development	

1.26   After the creation of the two-tier system in 1975–76, it looked as if the structure of local government in Scotland was settled for the foreseeable future. However, that was not to be the case[1].

1 For developments in the 1990s, see ch 2.

THE CONSTITUTIONAL POSITION OF LOCAL GOVERNMENT

1.27   Local government rests firmly on statute[1]. Local authorities were created and reorganised by Acts of the UK Parliament and derive virtually all their powers from statute. Acts of Parliament prescribe who may and may not be elected to local councils and how local elections are to be conducted. Acts also regulate in some detail the way in which local authority business is conducted, the forms of internal organisation and the form of local taxation. Local government functions are not found in any one Act of Parliament but in a vast range of statutes – Education Acts, Roads Acts, Planning Acts and so on.

It is well known that the United Kingdom does not have a written constitution in the sense of a single document with special legal status enforceable by the courts. The only sovereign body in the United Kingdom is the UK Parliament (although that sovereignty is somewhat undermined by the United Kingdom's membership of the European Community). Although local government originated long before the doctrine of parliamentary sovereignty emerged in the seventeenth century, it does not have independent status. None of the local government statutes gives local government any constitutional guarantees of its continued existence nor can they as that is impossible under the doctrine of parliamentary sovereignty. Many other countries which do have written constitutions protect the status of their important political institutions, including local government, so that they cannot be abolished by a simple majority of the legislature. That is not the case in the United Kingdom. However, as the Widdicombe Report of 1986 pointed out, this does not mean that the summary abolition of these institutions would be constitutionally acceptable. The sovereignty of Parliament is underpinned by custom and convention as to the manner in which that sovereignty is exercised[2].

1 See further Appendix, p 173.
2 *Report of the Committee of Inquiry into the Conduct of Local Authority Business* (the Widdicombe Report) (Cmnd 9797) (1986) paras 3.3–3.4.

1.28   With the advent of devolution, the constitutional position of local government has changed to a considerable extent and the sovereignty of the UK Parliament has become less relevant. Under the Scotland Act 1998 (SA 1998) which established the Scottish Parliament, reserved matters, that is matters which the United Kingdom has kept under its control, are listed in Schedule 5. Matters not listed are devolved to the Scottish Parliament. The only reference to local government in Schedule 5 is to the franchise (the right to vote in local elections). Thus it would appear that all other aspects of local government have been devolved to the Scottish Parliament. However, the position is more complicated than that. Local government has had allocated to it a number of functions which are themselves reserved to the UK Parliament. Examples of such matters include consumer protection, weights and measures, the administration of housing benefit and the reception of asylum seekers. The 1998 Act defines public bodies whose functions include a mixture of reserved and devolved matters as 'Scottish public authorities with mixed functions'[1] and makes it clear that the constitution, establishment and dissolution of such bodies is devolved to the Scottish Parliament as well as the conferring and removal of functions which are not reserved. Thus the powers of the Scottish Parliament in relation to local government are very wide.

1 Scotland Act 1998, Sch 5, Pt III, para 1.

1.29   Prior to the passing of the Scotland Act 1998, the Scottish Constitutional Convention[1] had recommended that the SA 1998 should contain a section committing the Scottish Parliament to secure and maintain a strong and effective system of local government, embodying the principle of subsidiarity so as to guarantee the role of local government in service delivery[2]. However, the SA 1998 contains no such section. The position, therefore, is that the existence of Scottish local government is not guaranteed. Theoretically, the entire system could be swept away by an Act of the Scottish Parliament. However, as Lord Wheatley pointed out in his Report of 1969:

'We are convinced that local government of some kind is absolutely indispensable in this country. No alternative that we could conceive of could administer the whole range of local services satisfactorily, while still retaining the principles of democracy'[3].

This is probably still the position but, as we shall see, there have been fears in local government circles for some time that the Scottish Executive (now the Scottish Government) has been encroaching too far on the present powers and functions of local government in Scotland[4].

1 The Scottish Constitutional Convention was a cross-party group, with involvement of a wide spectrum of Scottish life, which between 1989 and 1995 drew up various documents which they hoped would be a blueprint for a Scotland Act.
2 Scottish Constitutional Convention Scotland's Parliament: Scotland's Right (1995) p 17.
3 *Report of the Royal Commission on Local Government in Scotland* (Cmnd 4150) (1969) para 122.
4 For further discussion of the relationship between the Scottish Parliament, the Scottish Executive/Government and local government, see ch 8 below. Note that from May 2007, the Scottish Executive has been known as the Scottish Government. Where the term Scottish Executive is used in the text, it refers to actions, decisions etc. taken before May 2007.

Chapter 2

The current structure and functions of local government in Scotland

2.1   The two-tier system of local government introduced by the Local Government (Scotland) Act 1973 took some time to settle down. At first people were confused as to which tier was responsible for the various functions. This problem was exaggerated to some extent by those who yearned for the old days of a single-tier structure (which, of course, had not existed previously except in the four cities of Aberdeen, Dundee, Edinburgh and Glasgow). In practice, a person who contacted the wrong council was redirected to the correct one. If someone went to the surgery of a district councillor to complain about a matter which was the responsibility of the regional council or vice versa, the councillor either dealt with the matter or passed it on to his or her regional or district colleague.

2.2   In some areas, particularly the cities, some minor resentments were felt by the councillors of one tier against the other. District councillors resented the fact that regional councillors considered themselves to be the senior tier, while regional councillors resented the fact that the district councils retained the regalia of the former burghs and the title of Provost or Lord Provost. At the operational level, however, it soon became clear that strategic planning, roads and transportation and, to some extent, industrial promotion were being dealt with more effectively at regional level and that the regional authorities, by virtue of their size, large tax base and big budgets, were able to tackle social problems much more successfully than their predecessors by concentrating social work and educational resources in areas of deprivation.

2.3   Nevertheless, the fact that the two tiers shared some functions did cause some confusion and the government set up a Committee of Inquiry in 1980, chaired by Anthony Stodart, to review the working relations between the two tiers. The terms of reference did not allow the Committee to recommend major changes to the basic structure. Nevertheless, councillors in the four cities of Aberdeen, Dundee, Edinburgh and Glasgow used the opportunity presented by the existence of the Stodart Committee to press their case (unsuccessfully) for all-purpose status for their cities. The Stodart Committee concentrated on a rationalisation of the distribution of functions while maintaining the viability of the existing two-tier structure. The Committee reported in 1981[1] and its recommendations concentrated on tidying up concurrent and overlapping functions, mainly in the areas of environmental health, industrial development, the provision of leisure facilities, tourism, the countryside and planning. Many of the Stodart Committee's recommendations were implemented in the Local Government and Planning (Scotland) Act 1982.

There was also established an inquiry into the functions and powers of the islands councils under the chairmanship of Sir David Montgomery. This reported in 1984[2] but its recommendations did not lead to legislative change.

1 *Report of the Committee of Inquiry into Local Government in Scotland* (Cmnd 8115) (1981).
2 *Report of Inquiry into the Functions and Powers of the Island Councils of Scotland* (Cmnd 9216) (1984).

THE REORGANISATION OF 1995–96

2.4   Local government was not popular with central government during the years of Mrs Thatcher's premiership. Many of her government's measures promoted centralisation in the guise of giving power to the people but the overall effect was a massive increase in the power of central government and a decline in local government autonomy. Many councils were controlled by Labour and the Labour councillors saw themselves as front-line troops in the 'war' against Thatcherism. They did their best to thwart many of the Conservatives' measures to reduce local government expenditure and powers and more than one council found itself in court[1]. Protecting jobs and services became their battle-cry. The Greater London Council, under the leadership of a left-wing councillor, Ken Livingstone, became a particular thorn in Mrs Thatcher's flesh. Of course, local authorities, being subordinate bodies, could not win any war against central government and, in 1983, the government announced that the Greater London Council and the metropolitan authorities of England were to be abolished. This took place under the Local Government Act 1986. The metropolitan authorities were roughly the equivalent of the Scottish regional councils and it might have been expected that they too would be abolished. However, no action was taken against them at that time.

1 See eg *Commission for Local Authority Accounts in Scotland v Stirling District Council* 1984 SLT 442; *Lloyd v McMahon* [1987] AC 625 (Liverpool Council).

2.5   However, after Mrs Thatcher's resignation in 1990, a new reorganisation agenda appeared. The Minister responsible for local government in England and Wales announced a wide-ranging review of local government structure south of the border. This was followed in March 1991 by an announcement by the then Secretary of State for Scotland, Ian Lang, that the government was minded to abolish the two-tier system and replace it with a system of unitary or single-tier authorities in Scotland. Unlike the reorganisation of the 1970s which was preceded by a comprehensive Royal Commission report, there was to be no Commission on this occasion, only an exercise in public consultation. The government's proposal was seen by many as a political exercise designed to get rid of the large regional authorities in the central belt whose electors had consistently returned Labour-controlled administrations. The Prime Minister of the day, John Major, had publicly described Strathclyde Regional Council as 'a dinosaur', although it was a reasonably successful local authority.

2.6   The first consultation paper entitled *The Structure of Local Government in Scotland: The Case for Change* was published in June 1991[1].

It was a flimsy little document, running to only 21 pages, long on assertion but short on evidence of the need for change. The arguments which the government advanced were as follows:

- the two-tier system was not readily understood and there was confusion in the public mind as to which tier was responsible for what. This had led to a clouding of accountability;
- old allegiances to the old counties and county towns lived on;
- some of the regional authorities were seen as too large and too remote from the local communities they served;
- the two-tier system had resulted in a measure of duplication and waste, delays and friction.

It was further argued that government policies relating to local government had changed the way in which local authorities discharged their statutory functions and organised themselves administratively. The emphasis was on the enabling role of local government rather than on direct service provision.

1 *The Structure of Local Government in Scotland: The Case for Change* (HMSO, June 1991).

2.7   The arguments in favour of single-tier authorities were basically a mirror image of the above:

- a single-tier system is simple to understand and removes confusion in the public mind as to where responsibility within local government lies. Therefore it clarifies accountability;
- it removes the potential for duplication, waste, delay and friction;
- it allows free scope for sensible and imaginative co-ordination of functional activity;
- it increases the capacity of authorities to operate as enablers;
- it facilitates a flexible response and allows best use to be made of scarce financial and human resources.

2.8   The consultation paper set out the following principles on which the new single-tier system should be based:

- the new system should be firmly rooted in the democratic tradition;
- the new system should not be based exclusively on either of the existing tiers;
- the new units need not be of uniform size;
- the new units should reflect local loyalties and allegiances and be truly representative of them;
- the new units should be strong, cost-effectively resourced and capable of discharging their statutory functions effectively and efficiently;
- the new units should be clearly accountable to their electorate;
- the new units should be capable of effective management of services and resources and of seeking better and more cost-effective methods of service delivery which reflect local needs, wishes and circumstances;
- the new units should demonstrably provide value for money across the range of statutory functions;
- the new units should be able to recruit sufficient staff of appropriate calibre and to train and manage them effectively.

2.9   An analysis of the responses to the consultation revealed that 27.4 per cent of the respondents unequivocally supported the proposal to replace the two-tier structure with a single-tier system[1]. Many respondents made their support conditional on the establishment of a Scottish Parliament, a proposal to which the Conservative government was implacably opposed.

1 Unit for the Study of Government in Scotland, Edinburgh University 'An Analysis of Submissions to the Scottish Office Consultation Paper The Case for Change' (1992).

2.10   The government issued a second consultation paper in October 1992. It was entitled *The Structure of Local Government in Scotland: Shaping the New Councils*[1]. It was clear that the government had decided on single-tier structure of local government in Scotland. On the number of councils in the new structure the government remained open-minded. The consultation paper contained four illustrative maps:

- a 15-unit structure;
- a 24-unit structure;
- a 35-unit structure;
- a 51-unit structure.

1 *The Structure of Local Government in Scotland: Shaping the New Councils* (HMSO, October 1992).

2.11   The consultation paper concentrated heavily on the effects of structural change on the provision of each of the services for which local government is responsible and considered the extent to which each of these might require special mechanisms, such as joint arrangements, to ensure the delivery of effective services.

Again the responses to this consultation paper were lukewarm on the change to single-tier local government. The most common response was to question the need for any kind of change at all[1].

1 Unit for the Study of Government in Scotland, Edinburgh University 'An Analysis of Non-Local Authority Submissions to the Scottish Office Consultation Paper: Shaping the New Councils' (1993).

2.12   A parallel consultation was carried out on the future of the water and sewerage services which were at that time the responsibility of the regional and islands councils. The consultation paper entitled *Investing for our Future*[1] set out the necessity to raise standards and increase investment and proposed a series of possible options for the future administration and management of these services ranging from the use of the new councils, through appointed public bodies, to privatisation. This proved to be extremely controversial as the vast majority of the Scottish people were opposed to any possibility of water supply being privatised[2].

1 *Investing for our Future* (HMSO, November 1992).
2 Strathclyde Regional Council carried out a referendum on the government's proposals. 1,720,940 postal ballots were issued of which 1,230,328 were returned (71.5 per cent). 94 per cent were against any form of privatisation.

2.13   In July 1993, the Secretary of State for Scotland presented to Parliament a White Paper entitled *Shaping the Future – The New Councils*[1].

This set out the government's proposals for reorganisation. There were to be 25 new unitary authorities on the mainland of Scotland. The suggested boundaries of some of the new councils further fuelled suspicions that the exercise was politically driven in that they appeared to be drawn in such a way as to enhance the possibility of Conservative-controlled administrations being returned in some of the smaller councils such as Stirling and East Renfrewshire. In addition, four of the new councils were to have the same boundaries as former regional councils – the Borders, Dumfries and Galloway, Fife and Highland – only one of which had been under Labour control.

The three islands councils were to remain in existence. Elections were to be held in 1995 with the new authorities taking over full responsibility on 1 April 1996 after a 'shadow' year during which they were to co-exist with the regional and district councils. The White Paper contained proposals to remove the administration of the children's reporter system from local government and set up a national service with a new unelected body or quango responsible for providing the reporter service to children's hearings throughout Scotland. Most controversial of all was the proposal that water and sewerage services should be taken out of local government control and passed to three new water authorities whose members would be appointed by the Secretary of State.

1 *Shaping the Future – The New Councils*, (Cmnd 2267) (July 1993).

2.14   The Local Government etc (Scotland) Bill was introduced into the House of Commons in December 1993. It provided for 28 local government areas as proposed in the White Paper with certain minor adjustments to boundaries of Glasgow, Dundee and the Lothians. The Bill had a protracted passage through Parliament as the opposition parties sought to frustrate the government's intentions. There was intensive lobbying by various district and regional councils as well as local groups to change the boundaries of some of the local government areas proposed and to form additional councils. During the Commons stages of the Bill the number of local government areas rose from 28 to 32. Ayrshire was split into three (North, South and East Ayrshire Councils) instead of the original North and South Ayrshire Councils. Inverclyde was removed from the proposed West Renfrewshire Council to form a separate Inverclyde Council. Clackmannan was split off from the proposed Clackmannan and Falkirk Council to form a separate Clackmannan Council with a population of only about 48,000. In the Lothians the original proposal was to have a Lothians Council consisting of West Lothian and Midlothian and to include East Lothian with Berwickshire. By the time the Bill left the Commons, separate councils for East, West and Midlothian had emerged and Berwickshire had been included in the Borders Council.

2.15   The Bill received royal assent in November 1994. Elections to the new councils were held in 1995 and the new councillors served a 'shadow' year alongside the members of the soon to be abolished regional and district councils. The Local Government etc (Scotland) Act 1994 came into full force and effect on 1 April 1996. The entire two-tier system on mainland Scotland was swept away and replaced by the new structure comprising 29 unitary authorities. The structure of the three islands authorities remained unchanged.

Thus there are now 32 local authority areas in Scotland. The new local government areas with the estimated populations in 2006 and the corresponding former regional and district councils are as follows:

Table 1

New local area	Former regional council	Former district council(s)	Population 2006	Area by government sq. km.
City of Aberdeen*	Grampian	Aberdeen	206,880	186
Aberdeenshire	Grampian	Banff & Buchan, Gordon, Kincardine and Deeside	236,260	6,318
Angus	Tayside	Angus plus Monifieth & part of Sidlaw from Dundee District Council	109,320	2,181
Argyll and Bute	Strathclyde	Argyll & Bute plus Helensburgh and part of Loch Lomondside from Dumbarton District Council	91,390	6,930
East Ayrshire	Strathclyde	Kilmarnock & Loudon, Cumnock & Doon Valley	119,290	1,252
North Ayrshire	Strathclyde	Cunninghame	135,490	884
South Ayrshire	Strathclyde	Kyle and Carrick	111,670	1,202
The Borders*	Borders	Berwickshire, Ettrick and Lauderdale, Roxburgh, Tweeddale	110,240	4,734
Clackmannan*	Central	Clackmannan	48,900	157
Dumbarton & Clydebank*	Strathclyde	Clydebank and Dumbarton District Councils (minus Helensburgh and part of Vale of Leven)	91,240	162
Dumfries and Galloway	Dumfries and Galloway	Annandale and Eskdale, Nithsdale, Stewartry, Wigtown	148,030	6,439
East Dunbartonshire	Strathclyde	Bearsden and Milngavie, Strathkelvin (minuspart of Chryston)	105,460	172
City of Dundee*	Tayside	City of Dundee minus Monifieth and parts of Sidlaw	142,170	65
City of Edinburgh	Lothian	City of Edinburgh	463,510	262
Falkirk	Central	Falkirk	149,680	299

New local area	Former regional council	Former district council(s)	Population 2006	Area by government sq. km.
Fife	Fife	Dunfermline, Kirkcaldy, North East Fife	358,930	1,323
City of Glasgow*	Strathclyde	City of Glasgow minus Rutherglen, Fernhill, Cambuslang, Halfway and parts of King's Park and Toryglen	580,690	175
Highland	Highland	Badenoch & Strathspey, Caithness, Inverness, Lochaber, Nairn, Ross & Cromarty, Skye & Lochalsh, Sutherland	215,310	25,784
Inverclyde	Strathclyde	Inverclyde	81,540	162
North Lanarkshire	Strathclyde	Cumbernauld and Kilsyth, Monklands, Motherwell District Councils, plus part of Chryston from Strathkelvin District Council	323,780	474
South Lanarkshire	Strathclyde	Clydesdale, Hamilton, East Kilbride District Councils plus Rutherglen, Fernhill, Cambuslang, Halfway and parts of King's Park and Toryglen from City of Glasgow District Council	307,670	1,771
East Lothian	Lothian	East Lothian	92,830	678
Midlothian	Lothian	Midlothian	79,290	356
West Lothian	Lothian	West Lothian	165,700	425
Moray	Grampian	Moray	86,750	2,238
Perth and Kinross	Tayside	Perth and Kinross District Council, plus part of Sidlaw from City of Dundee District Council	140,190	5,311
East Renfrewshire	Strathclyde	Eastwood District Council and Barrhead (from Renfrew District Council)	89,290	173
Renfrewshire	Strathclyde	Renfrew minus Barrhead	169,590	261
Stirling	Central	Stirling	87,810	2,196

Table 2

Island local authority areas	Population	Area by sq. km.
Orkney Islands Council	19,770	992
Shetland Islands Council	21,880	1,438
Western Isles Council*	26,350	3,134

The councils marked * have changed their names since the LG(S)A 1994 was passed. The Cities of Aberdeen, Dundee and Glasgow Councils changed their names to Aberdeen City Council, Dundee City Council, and Glasgow City Council respectively. The Borders Council changed its name to the Scottish Borders Council, Clackmannan Council to Clackmannanshire Council and Dumbarton and Clydebank Council to West Dunbartonshire Council. The Western Isles Council utilised the provisions of the Local Government (Gaelic Names) Act 1997 to change its name to Comhairle Nan Eilean Siar and is now known simply as Eilean Siar.

THE NEED FOR DECENTRALISATION SCHEMES

2.16   Although one of the criticisms which the government had levelled at the two-tier structure was that some of the regional authorities were seen as too large and too remote from the local communities they served, some of the new unitary authorities are co-terminous with former regional authorities[1]. The new Highland Council, in particular, is geographically very large with a land area of 25,784 sq km, roughly the size of Wales which has 22 councils. Under the two-tier system, there had been eight district councils within the area of Highland Regional Council which made local government more local. In order to avoid the criticism of remoteness being levelled at them in turn, the government included in the LG(S)A 1994 a duty to prepare decentralisation schemes[2]. Each council had to prepare a draft scheme before 1 April 1997, publish the scheme, consult community councils in its area and, after considering representations, adopt a scheme. The scheme had to contain the council's proposals for the administration of local government functions within the whole of the council's area. The scheme could include:

- arrangements for holding meetings of the council, its committees or sub-committees at particular places within the area of the council;
- the establishment of area committees and the delegation to those committees of specified functions of the council;
- the location of council offices locally staffed by employees who had been given certain delegated functions;
- the provision of local centres providing advice on council functions.

1 Borders, Dumfries and Galloway, Fife and Highland Councils.
2 Local Government etc (Scotland) Act 1994, s 23.

2.17   Guidance issued by the government identified three key objectives:

- to bring services and decision-making closer to the public where this would result in an improvement to services;

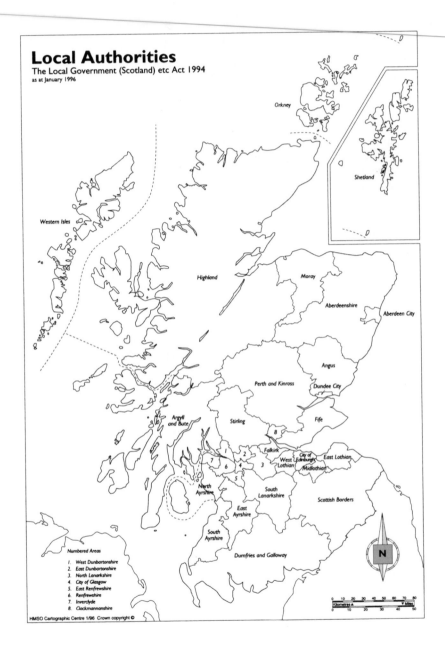

Local Authorities
The Local Government (Scotland) etc Act 1994
as at January 1996

Orkney

Shetland

Western Isles

Highland

Moray

Aberdeenshire

Aberdeen City

Angus

Perth and Kinross

Dundee City

Argyll and Bute

Stirling

Fife

Falkirk

West Lothian

City of Edinburgh

Midlothian

East Lothian

North Ayrshire

South Lanarkshire

Scottish Borders

East Ayrshire

South Ayrshire

Dumfries and Galloway

Numbered Areas
1. West Dunbartonshire
2. East Dunbartonshire
3. North Lanarkshire
4. City of Glasgow
5. East Renfrewshire
6. Renfrewshire
7. Inverclyde
8. Clackmannanshire

HMSO Cartographic Centre 1/96 Crown copyright ©

N

- to enable the public to influence and shape the design of these services and the way in which the council serves its community; and
- to provide more effective and responsive local government.

The decentralisation schemes which were adopted by the councils vary in character and scale but there are three broad forms which can be combined:

- political decentralisation which involves area committees with or without community representatives as members of these committees and groups such as community forums which give community representatives improved access to councillors and other decision-makers;
- physical decentralisation which provides for example 'one-stop shops' which deal with enquiries about council services; and
- managerial decentralisation which locates local managers with decision-making powers nearer to the point at which services are provided.

2.18   The fact that a statutory duty to prepare decentralisation schemes was imposed on councils indicates one of the flaws of the reorganisation of 1995–96. The district councils which in many areas were truly local were abolished and area committees and offices were thought to go some way to fill the gap. In a sense, the decentralisation arrangements restore a lower tier of local government, or at least local administration, in the areas of each of the unitary councils.

FUNCTIONS REMOVED FROM LOCAL GOVERNMENT

2.19   The tables above[1] shows that nine of the new mainland councils and the three island councils have populations of under 100,000. The Wheatley Commission[2] had recommended that the minimum size of local authority for an acceptable standard in certain services should be around 200,000 and only eight of the new unitary authorities have populations of more than that figure. Various other local authority functions also require a fairly large geographical area. Because of the small populations of many of the new councils and the small geographical areas of others it was not possible for the entire range of local government functions to be allocated to them[3]. The government's response to this was twofold: to remove some functions from local government control entirely and to make arrangements for other functions to be handled by means of joint arrangements.

1 Tables 1 and 2, see pp 16–18 above.
2 See ch 1.
3 For the functions of local government prior to the commencement of the Local Government etc (Scotland) Act 1994, see Table 1 in ch 1, p 8 above.

2.20   The functions removed from local government control by the Local Government etc (Scotland) Act 1994 were:

- responsibility for water and sewerage. This responsibility was transferred to three water and sewerage authorities whose members were initially appointed by the Secretary of State for Scotland and after 1999 by the Scottish Ministers[1];

- responsibility for the children's reporter system. This was transferred to the Scottish Children's Reporter Administration whose members were also appointed by the Secretary of State for Scotland and after 1999 by the Scottish Ministers;
- responsibility for tourism. This was transferred to area tourist boards established by the Secretary of State for Scotland. Local authority representatives may be appointed to the area tourist boards but must not form a majority of the membership[2].

1 The three water and sewerage authorities were replaced by a single authority, Scottish Water, by the Water Industry (Scotland) Act 2002.
2 The 14 area tourist boards were replaced by two network boards in 2005. These were abolished by the Tourist Boards (Scotland) Act 2006 and replaced by a national body called VisitScotland. Local authorities still have some powers to carry out various tourism-related activities.

2.21   The removal of some functions from local authorities might be seen as inevitable, given the structure of local government which the government had decided to adopt, but it would have been possible for them to remain as local government functions and be handled by joint arrangements. Their removal was seen by supporters of local government as a further attempt to undermine its importance.

THE NEED FOR JOINT ARRANGEMENTS

2.22   With the exception of the functions discussed above, for which special provisions are made by the Local Government etc (Scotland) Act 1994, each of the new councils has all the functions in relation to its area which had been exercised by the regional, district or islands councils which had existed in its area prior to 1 April 1996[1].

The Wheatley Report[2] had recommended that the minimum size of local authority for an acceptable standard of education and social work services should be around 200,000 and, as we have seen, only 8 of the 32 unitary authorities have populations of more than that figure. Various other local authority functions such as police, fire and aspects of planning also require a fairly large population or geographical area.

1 See Table 1 in ch 1 above for the functions of the regions and the districts.
2 See ch 1.

2.23   When the government announced its firm plans to dismantle the two-tier system in its White Paper of 1993, it recognised that the new local authorities would have to consider, to a greater extent than in the recent past, the need to provide services or parts of services in conjunction with other local authorities as some of the new authorities would be too small to provide the complete range of services on their own. There were already provisions in the Local Government (Scotland) Act 1973 which enabled local authorities to enter into joint arrangements but a more flexible legal framework was required. This was provided in the Local Government etc (Scotland) Act 1994.

2.24   The two most visible forms of joint arrangements are joint committees and joint boards.

The Local Government (Scotland) Act 1973 allows two or more local authorities to discharge any of their functions jointly either by a joint committee or by an officer of one of them[1]. A joint committee may appoint sub-committees. A joint board differs from a joint committee in that it has a separate legal personality. Prior to the passing of the Local Government etc (Scotland) Act 1994, a joint board could be established only where there was a specific statutory power to do so. An Act would normally authorise the appropriate minister to create a joint board by an order requiring the approval of Parliament. This order would establish the board as a body corporate with a common seal, perpetual succession, power to hold land, to sue and be sued. The LG(S)A 1994 amends the LG(S)A 1973 to remove the need for a specific Act of Parliament to establish a joint board[2]. The situation now is that local authorities which have appointed or propose to appoint a joint committee to discharge certain functions may apply in writing to the Scottish Ministers for the incorporation of the joint committee as a joint board. The local authorities must advertise the proposal in a local newspaper to allow representations to be made and include in their application to the Scottish Ministers a statement of their consideration of any representations made. The Scottish Ministers may then issue an order establishing a joint board and delegating various functions to it.

1 Local Government (Scotland) Act 1973, s 56 (5).
2 LG(S)A 1973, s 62A (added by the Local Government etc (Scotland) Act 1994, s 20).

2.25 The Local Government etc (Scotland) Act 1994 also gives the Scottish Ministers the power to take the initiative in the establishment of a joint board where they consider it to be necessary and after consulting the relevant local authorities[1].

Another aspect of the flexible legal framework provided in the LG(S)A 1994 to enable small authorities to ensure the delivery of local government services is to be found in section 58 of that Act. A local authority or a joint board (in this context known as 'the contracting authority') may agree with another local authority or joint board (in this case known as 'the supplying authority') that the supplying authority is to carry out any activity or service which the contracting authority is required to or may legitimately carry out.

The government decided not to leave the formation of joint arrangements for police and fire services to the discretion of local councils and made provision in the LG(S)A 1994 for statutory joint boards to be established. In the White Paper, *Shaping the Future: The New Councils*[2], it was made clear that the existing eight police forces and fire brigades should remain in place[3]. In the case of Fife and Dumfries and Galloway, where the new councils' boundaries are co-terminous with those of the former regional councils, the existing police forces and fire brigades became the police forces and fire brigades of the new councils. In the rest of Scotland, amalgamation schemes were made by the Secretary of State for Scotland and joint boards were established, with their members coming from the various councils in each scheme[4]. For example, the joint boards of the Strathclyde police and fire services have representatives of the 12 councils which lie in the area of the former Strathclyde Regional Council in membership.

1 Local Government (Scotland) Act 1973, s 62B (added by the Local Government etc (Scotland) Act 1994.
2 (Cmnd 2267) (1993).
3 Police and fire services had been regional functions under the two-tier system, but in the case of Lothian and Borders Regional Councils, there was a combined police force and a combined fire brigade. Highland Regional Council and the Islands Councils also had a combined police force and a combined fire brigade.
4 Local Government etc (Scotland) Act 1994, ss 34–36.

2.26   In the case of public transport, the Local Government etc (Scotland) Act 1994 established the Strathclyde Passenger Transport Authority to which all the functions, staff and property of the former Strathclyde Regional Council as a Passenger Transport Authority were transferred[1]. In 2006, the authority was renamed the Strathclyde Partnership for Transport following the passing of the Transport (Scotland) Act 2005. The Authority consists of councillors appointed by the 12 councils within the area of the former Strathclyde Regional Council and up to seven appointed members from a professional transport background.

1 Local Government etc (Scotland) Act 1994, s 40.

2.27   Under the Local Government etc (Scotland) Act 1994, each council is a valuation area[1] but the Secretary of State for Scotland (now the Scottish Ministers) was given the power to establish joint valuation boards[2]. Ten such joint boards have been established. Four councils are valuation authorities on their own[3].

Structure planning was the responsibility of the regional and islands councils under the two-tier system. The LG(S)A 1994 amended the Town and Country Planning legislation then in force to give the Secretary of State for Scotland (now the Scottish Ministers) the power to designate structure plan areas[4]. Where a structure plan area extends to the district of more than one planning authority (that is, council), they must form a joint committee. Seventeen structure plan areas were designated, six of which require joint working. Education was also the responsibility of the former regional and islands councils. A consequence of the reorganisation of 1995–96 was that in some areas secondary schools were located in a local authority area different from that of some of their feeder primary schools. The LG(S)A 1994 gives an education authority power to make arrangements with another education authority ('the provider authority') for the provision of education for pupils belonging to their area in an educational authority under the management of the provider authority. Special arrangements were also made to ensure that in such a situation siblings were not discriminated against[5].

1 Valuation is the process which establishes the band into which houses and other domestic property are placed for council tax purposes and the rateable value of non-domestic property for the payment of rates.
2 Local Government etc (Scotland) Act 1994, s 27.
3 Glasgow, Fife, Scottish Borders and Dumfries and Galloway Councils.
4 Town and Country Planning Act (Scotland) 1972, s 4A (added by the LG(S)A 1994, s 33). See now Town and Country Planning (Scotland) Act 1997, s 5.
5 Education (Scotland) Act 1980, s 23(1A) and (3A) (added by the LG(S)A 1994, s 32(2), (3)).

2.28   The Local Government etc (Scotland) Act 1994 thus makes considerable statutory provision for joint working but the local authorities have had to go further. A large number of joint committees have been formed. A good example is the arrangement which has had to be made in the West of Scotland to provide an archaeological service. Under the two-tier system such a service had been provided by Strathclyde Regional Council. After the reorganisation of 1995–96, none of the new councils was large enough to provide an archaeo-logical service on a cost-effective basis, so a West of Scotland Joint Archaeological Committee was formed, the members of which come from the 12 councils which make up the area of the former Strathclyde Region.

Falkirk, Stirling and Clackmannanshire Councils, all of which have relatively small populations, have formed a number of joint committees and made other joint arrangements to enable them to provide specialist services in various areas of service provision such as education and social work.

2.29   The Convention of Scottish Local Authorities[1] (COSLA) carried out a survey of joint arrangements made by local authorities between 1996 and 1998 and found that a total of 333 joint arrangements had been established.

Joint committees, boards and other arrangements are not new. They were used extensively in Scotland before the introduction of the two-tier system in 1974–75 when there was a cumbersome structure of over 400 local authorities. Joint arrangements, however, have their drawbacks and have been described as notoriously ineffective. The councillors from the smaller councils tend to feel dominated by their colleagues from larger councils, they tend to be officer-led rather than member-led and, since the councillors of the joint committees and boards are appointed by the relevant councils and are not directly elected, they lack democratic legitimacy and direct accountability to the electorate.

1 The Convention of Scottish Local Authorities is the body which represents most of the Scottish Local Authorities.

COMMUNITY COUNCILS

2.30   The Wheatley Commission, having proposed a local government structure in which the pre-1975 local authorities, many of them very small and local, would be dissolved and replaced by much larger authorities, felt that there should still be some unit which would allow for local self-expression. What they proposed was the community council and a scheme for the establishment of such councils was embodied in the Local Government (Scotland) Act 1973[1].

Although they are elected bodies, community councils do not have the status of local authorities and are not to be regarded as a third tier of local government. The general purpose of a community council is:

‘ … to ascertain, co-ordinate and express to the local authorities for its area, and to public authorities, the views of the community which it represents … and to take such action in the interests of the community as appears to it to be expedient and practicable’[2].

Initially, every islands and district council was required to submit to the Secretary of State for Scotland before 16 May 1976 a scheme for the establishment of community councils for its area. There was a requirement on the councils to invite suggestions from members of the public as to the areas and composition of proposed community councils. After the Secretary of State had approved a scheme, the islands or district council had to publicise the approved scheme by way of an exhibition and invite electors to apply to the council for the establishment of community councils. A minimum of 20 electors in each area was required and, if that number was reached, the local authority was required, within six weeks, to organise elections for the establishment of a community council. So it lay (and still lies) in the hands of the electors in each community council area to decide whether to requisition a community council.

1 Local Government (Scotland) Act 1973, ss 51–55.
2 LG(S)A 1973, s 51.

2.31   The Local Government (Scotland) Act 1973 makes provision for schemes to be reviewed and amended from time to time to meet changing circumstances, again after public consultation. A decision to do so must be made by a resolution of the local authority, passed by not less than two-thirds of the members at a meeting of the council specially convened for that purpose.

2.32   The Local Government etc (Scotland) Act 1994 continues existing schemes for community councils but gives the new local authorities the power to revoke a scheme affecting their area and replace it with a new one[1]. The need for the approval of the Secretary of State for Scotland or the Scottish Ministers is removed.

In addition to the broad remit to be 'the voice of the community', legislation has also conferred some specific powers on community councils. For example, the Licensing (Scotland) Act 1976, now the Licensing (Scotland) Act 2005, requires that relevant community councils are notified of applications to sell alcohol, while planning legislation requires local authorities to consult community councils on planning applications affecting their area. In addition, councils had to consult community councils on their draft decentralisation schemes[2].

1 Local Government etc (Scotland) Act 1994, s 22.
2 For decentralisation schemes, see pp 18–20 above.

2.33   There are around 1,200 functioning community councils in Scotland. The extent to which they can take action on behalf of their communities varies from community to community and largely depends upon the individuals involved as community councillors and the extent of the assistance in cash and kind which they receive from the local authorities in whose areas they are situated. Local authorities have a discretionary power to make them grants or loans and provide them with accommodation, equipment and staff. Some may provide a resource centre. Community councils rely on such assistance as they have no power to levy a local tax. In general, most local authorities (and other public authorities) have well-established lines of communication with community councils, thus ensuring that their views are heard on important local issues before action is taken. There is an Association of Scottish Community Councils which acts as their collective voice.

CHANGES IN LOCAL AUTHORITY BOUNDARIES, ELECTORAL ARRANGEMENTS AND NAMES

Boundaries and electoral arrangements

2.34   Frequent large-scale reorganisations of local government are undesirable because of the disruption they cause to the public and to the people who work in local authorities. However, there must be some provision for minor adjustments to take account of changing circumstances such as shifts in population. A local authority cannot unilaterally change its boundaries and is not permitted to promote a private Act of Parliament to alter its area, its status or its electoral arrangements or to form or abolish a local government area. Those tasks are allocated to the Local Government Boundary Commission for Scotland which was established by the Local Government (Scotland) Act 1973[1]. The functions of the Commission are to:

- carry out statutory reviews of electoral and administrative arrangements;
- monitor electoral arrangements; and
- respond to requests for ad hoc reviews of electoral or administrative arrangements.

1 Local Government (Scotland) Act 1973, s 12.

2.35   The Commission may make proposals to the Scottish Ministers for:

- the alteration of a local government area;
- the constitution of a new local government area;
- the abolition of a local government area; and
- a change of electoral arrangements.

2.36   'Electoral arrangements' means the number of councillors on a council, the number and boundaries of the electoral wards into which a local government area is divided, the designation of any electoral wards, and now, with the introduction of multi-member wards and STV, the number of councillors for each electoral ward[1]. The primary criterion to be applied by the Commission is what is in its opinion desirable in the interests of effective and convenient local government.

The Commission also has a duty to carry out periodic reviews of all local government areas. The next of these reviews was due to be carried out between 2004 and 2008 and thereafter at intervals of not less than eight and not more than 12 years from the date of the last review. However, under the Local Governance (Scotland) Act 2004, which introduced the Single Transferable Vote (STV) as the electoral system for local government, the Boundary Commission had to conduct a review of electoral arrangements and formulate proposals for multi-member wards in time to take effect at the local government election in 2007[2].

1 Local Government (Scotland) Act 1973, s 28 (as amended by the Local Governance (Scotland) Act 2004, s 4.
2 Local Governance (Scotland) Act 2004, s 4.

2.37   The Commission may at any time on its own initiative review all or any part of a local government area and make proposals to Ministers. Normally, however, the Commission will do this in response to a request from a local authority or from someone who has an interest in the area in question. The Scottish Ministers may also direct the Commission to carry out such reviews.

Electoral arrangements must also be reviewed at intervals of not less than eight and not more than 12 years. In considering changes to electoral arrangements, the Scottish Ministers and the Commission must observe the two main rules[1].

1   Having regard to the change in number or distribution of electors likely to take place over the ensuing five years, the number of electors calculated by dividing the number of electors in each ward by the number of councillors to be returned, shall be, as nearly as may be, the same.

    The strict application of this rule may be departed from in any area where special geographical considerations appear to make a departure desirable.

2   Regard must be had to the desirability of fixing boundaries which are and will remain easily identifiable, such as rivers, railway lines and major roads, but also to any local ties which would be broken by fixing any particular boundary. In the case of conflict, local ties are to be given greater weight.

1 Local Government (Scotland) Act 1973, Sch 6 as amended by the Local Governance in Scotland Act 2004, s 4.

Changing names

2.38   Before the passing of the Local Government etc (Scotland) Act 1994, a council which wished to change its name had to obtain the consent of the Secretary of State for Scotland[1]. The LG(S)A 1994 removed this requirement. The law now is that a council can change its name by a resolution passed by a two-thirds majority at a meeting of the council specially convened for that purpose and with notice of the purpose given to the public. Notice of the name change must be given to the Secretary of State (now the Scottish Ministers), the Director General of the Ordnance Survey and the Registrar General of Births, Marriages and Deaths[2].

There is also the Local Government (Gaelic Names) Act 1997 which enables a council to change its name into Gaelic.

1 Local Government (Scotland) Act 1973, s 23.
2 The Local Government etc (Scotland) Act 1994, Sch 13, para 92(5).

AN EVALUATION OF THE PRESENT STRUCTURE OF LOCAL GOVERNMENT

2.39   The present structure of local government is not ideal. As has been noted above, some of the councils are very small in terms of population, with more than 10 having populations of less than 100,000. They are thus forced into forming joint arrangements with neighbouring councils to provide some specialist services. Joint committees and boards dilute accountability to the electorate as the members are not directly elected to them but appointed by the member councils.

In some cases, notably Glasgow and Dundee, some areas which are the natural suburbs of the respective cities lie outside the cities' boundaries. The cities, which provide many services used by the inhabitants of the suburbs such as roads, street lighting, libraries, museums, art galleries and leisure facilities, do not receive the suburbanites' council tax and thus the financial burden of the provision of these services falls unfairly on the cities' residents.

However, in 2002 the then Scottish Executive ruled out a review of local authority boundaries in the foreseeable future, on the grounds that many councils were still feeling the effects of the 1995–96 reorganisation and needed a period of stability to allow them to concentrate on the task of efficient and effective service delivery[1]. The SNP-led Scottish Government formed in 2007 gave a commitment that there would be no structural reform of Scottish local government during the 4-year term of the Parliament elected in 2007[2].

However, the provision in the Local Governance (Scotland) Act 2004 to introduce the Single Transferable Vote system for local government elections from 2007 has caused a major political upheaval throughout Scotland as the council areas were reorganised into multi-member wards[3]. The Single Transferable Vote system also enabled candidates from smaller political parties to win seats. This has led to changes of political control in a large number of councils. In the majority of councils no one party has overall control, which can cause a degree of instability in the administration of the councils' concerned[4].

1 *Renewing Local Democracy: The Next Steps*, (March 2002) para 6.
2 Concordat between the Scottish Government and the Convention of Scottish Local Authorities, November 2007. See further ch 8.
3 See ch 3.
4 See ch 8.

Chapter 3

Councillors

3.1   Every local government area must have a council consisting of a convener (chairman or chairwoman) and councillors, who are also known as members. The council for each area is a body corporate[1] called 'The Council' with the name of the relevant area added, (for example Stirling Council) and has a common seal which is used to authenticate documents[2]. Each local authority area is divided into electoral wards and each ward returns either three or four councillors. There are at present 353 wards in Scotland with electorates varying from over 23,000 in Edinburgh and Glasgow, and around 2000–3000 in the islands councils[3].

1 The council as a body corporate is a legal person with a separate existence from the councillors themselves.
2 Local Government etc (Scotland) Act 1994, s 2. The Requirements of Writing (Scotland) Act 1995 has made the use of the seal somewhat redundant.
3 Prior to 2007, there were 1222 councillors in 1222 single member wards with electorates ranging from over 6,000 in Glasgow and Edinburgh to fewer than 1000 in the islands.

THE RIGHT TO VOTE IN LOCAL GOVERNMENT ELECTIONS

3.2   Councillors are elected by the local government electors for the area. The law relating to the right to vote is found in the Representation of the People Act amended by the Representation of the People Act ~~2000.~~ To be entitled to vote at a local government election, a person must be: 1983

- registered in the register of local government electors for an area;
- a qualifying[1] Commonwealth citizen, a citizen of the Republic of Ireland or a citizen of the European Union;
- not subject to any legal incapacity;
- of voting age (currently 18 or over) on the day of the election[2].

Legal incapacity means that a person is disqualified from voting by reason of being an alien (that is, not a British, Irish, qualifying Commonwealth or EU citizen), a convict in detention or unlawfully at large, an offender detained in a mental hospital or unlawfully at large, or a person guilty of certain electoral offences in the previous five years.

Members of the House of Lords, who are not entitled to vote in elections to the House of Commons, have the right to vote in local government elections as are hereditary peers who are no longer eligible to sit in the House of Lords[3].

1 'Qualifying' means qualified to be in the United Kingdom in terms of immigration law.
2 In 2008, the Scottish Government announced its wish to have the voting age lowered to 16, but as matters relating to the franchise are reserved to the UK Parliament, it does not have the power to do so unilaterally.
3 The House of Lords Act 1999 removed all but 92 hereditary peers from membership of the House of Lords.

3.3 Prior to the Representation of the People Act 2000, to be entitled to vote, a person had to be resident in the local government area on 'the qualifying date' which in Scotland was 10 October in the year prior to the publication of the annual register. The 2000 Act gives greater flexibility, allowing registration once resident on any date. It also extends the right to vote to homeless persons who have no fixed address through a 'declaration of local connection'. The declaration of local connection must give an address (such as a hostel) to which election correspondence can be delivered or contain a statement that the homeless person is willing to collect such correspondence from the electoral registration officer's office. It would appear that few homeless people have availed themselves of this new right.

THE TIMING OF ELECTIONS

3.4 When the two-tier system of local government was in operation in Scotland between 1974–75 and 1995–96, the elections settled into a pattern where the elections for the regional and islands councils and for the district councils were staggered so that there was an election for one or other tier every two years on the first Thursday in May, with the councillors for each tier elected for a four-year term. The Local Government etc (Scotland) Act 1994, which abolished the two-tier system and replaced it with the present 32 unitary councils, changed the electoral cycle to a three-year cycle[1]. However, that was not to last for very long.

1 Local Government etc (Scotland) Act 1994, s 5(3).

3.5 On 1 May 1999, the first Scottish Parliament was elected for a four-year term. Local government elections were held on the same day, the councillors being elected for a three-year term. The next set of elections would have been in 2002 for local government and 2003 for the Scottish Parliament. In 1998 the Secretary of State for Scotland had set up a Commission (the McIntosh Commission[1]) to examine relations between the Scottish Parliament, the Scottish Executive and local government and one of the issues it considered was the relationship between the two electoral cycles. It recommended that local government should be moved back to a four-year term. The Scottish Executive accepted this recommendation and the Scottish Parliament passed the Scottish Local Government (Elections) Act 2002 which provides that local government elections are to be held on the day of the ordinary general election to the Scottish Parliament. The term of the councils which were elected in 1999 which should have come to an end in May 2002 was extended to 2003.

There was some concern about the Scottish Parliament elections and the local government elections being held on the same day. While it was argued that this would increase the turnout of voters for the local government elections (which usually had been very low) the concern was that local government issues would be overshadowed by Scottish Parliament issues. Indeed, the Scottish media concentrate almost entirely on Scottish parliamentary issues. However, calls for the elections to be "decoupled" were rejected by the then Scottish Executive[2].

However, the problems which arose at the 2007 joint elections are very likely to lead to change. The problems were caused by the introduction of a new electoral system (STV) for the local government elections and a re-design of the Scottish Parliament ballot papers. These resulted in a great deal of voter confusion and thousands of ballot papers (mainly for the Scottish Parliament) were declared invalid.

Following the wide-ranging concerns about the conduct of these elections, the Electoral Commission decided to hold a full expert review. It was chaired by Ron Gould, a well-known elections expert from Canada. A number of recommendations were made covering many aspects of the conduct of the elections[3]. In relation to the combined Scottish Parliamentary and local government elections, the Report concluded that the combined elections were not only a disservice to the local councils and candidates but also to the electorate. It recommended that the elections should be separated, preferably by a period of about two years.

As a result, there is a strong possibility that the elections will be decoupled. At the time of writing, the most likely scenario is that the local government term will be extended temporarily to five or six years and that eventually there will be a two year difference between the Scottish Parliament elections and the local government elections as recommended by Gould.

1 This Commission was called the McIntosh Commission after the name of its chairman, Neil McIntosh. *The Report of the Commission on Local Government and the Scottish Parliament* was published by the Scottish Office in June 1999. The recommendations of the Commission are considered in more detail in ch 8.
2 "Decoupled" means that the elections would be held on separate days or in different years
3 The Scottish Elections Review Report (the Gould Report), 2007.

THE ELECTORAL SYSTEM

3.6   For many years, the electoral system used for elections to Scottish local authorities was the relative majority or first-past-the post system. The McIntosh Commission examined this system and alternatives to it and recommended that a system of proportional representation should be introduced for local government elections by the Scottish Parliament. The McIntosh Commission did not indicate a preference for any particular system and, in July 1999, the Scottish Executive established a working party to investigate, among other things, the most appropriate system for local government. This working group was known as the Renewing Local Democracy Working Group and was chaired by Richard Kerley who had himself served as a local councillor in Edinburgh. The Group reported in June 2000 and the recommendation of the majority was that the system of proportional representation for local government should be the Single Transferable Vote[1].

The Single Transferable Vote (STV) system involves the formation of multi-member wards, each returning several councillors. The voter expresses his or her preferences for candidates in numerical order that is by marking 1, 2, 3 etc... against candidates' names. The system is controversial because it breaks the member–ward link which was valued by most councillors.

Proportional representation is favoured by most of the smaller political parties, who argue that it is a fairer system (and would give them more seats) and opposed by many in the Labour Party who argue that it leads to instability because of the unlikelihood of a majority party administration (and would lose them seats, particularly in the central belt of Scotland).

Despite these concerns within the Labour Party, the Partnership Agreement made between the Labour Party and the Liberal Democrat members of the Scottish Parliament in May 2003 contained a commitment to introduce STV for the local government elections due in 2007. The Scottish Executive wasted little time in putting this proposal onto the statute book.

The Local Governance (Scotland) Act 2004 now provides for council elections to be held under the Single Transferable Vote (STV) system and for the number of councillors per ward to be either three or four[2].

1 See further ch 8.
2 For the impact of the introduction of STV on local government, see para 8.35.

STANDING FOR ELECTION

3.7   As the law stands at present, a person is qualified to be nominated as a candidate or to be elected as a member of a local authority if he or she:

- is 18 years of age or over;
- is a British, or other qualifying Commonwealth citizen, a citizen of the Irish Republic or a citizen of the European Union; and
- is not subject to any legal incapacity[1].

The Local Governance (Scotland) Act 2004 provided for the reduction of the age for standing for election from 21 to 18[2]. This brought Scotland into line with most other European countries. Several candidates under the age of 21 stood for election in 2007 and three were elected. One of these, aged 18, was appointed as the Depute Provost in Aberdeen City Council.

1 Local Government (Scotland) Act 1973, s 29.
2 Local Governance (Scotland) Act 2004, s 8.

3.8   In addition to the above, there must be some local connection. The aspiring councillor must also:

1   be a local government elector for the area on the day of nomination as a candidate; or
2   have been the owner or tenant of land or other premises in the local authority area for the whole of the 12 months prior to the day of nomination; or
3   have had his or her principal or only place of work in the area of the authority in the 12 months prior to the day of nomination; or
4   have resided in the area of the authority for the whole of the 12 months prior to the day of nomination[1].

The case of *Parker v Yeo*[2] raises an interesting point as to what the word 'work' means in the English equivalent of head 3 above. Mr Yeo was elected to Exeter City Council. His sole qualification was that he was managing director of a business within the council area. In 1990 he retired and devoted himself to council duties and stood for re-election at the next election. This was challenged on the ground that he had no qualifying local connection as working solely on council duties was not 'work' in the sense that the law intended. However, the Court of Appeal held that this was too restrictive an interpretation and allowed Mr Yeo's appeal. This means that a councillor who no longer lives or is employed within a local authority area is qualified to stand for re-election. It is likely, however, that the political parties would impose their own rules on their candidates and require more of a local connection.

1 Local Government (Scotland) Act 1973, s 29.
2 (1992) 90 LGR 645.

Disqualifications

Local government employees

3.9   Under s 31 of the Local Government (Scotland) Act 1973, as originally enacted, a person may be disqualified from being nominated as a candidate, from being elected or from being a member of a local authority for a number of reasons.

The provision which affects the largest number of people is that which disqualifies a person, if he or she holds any paid office or employment (other than the office of convener or depute convener) or other place of profit in the gift or disposal of the local authority or of any joint committee or joint board whose expenses are defrayed by the authority[1]. Until recently this disqualification meant that anyone who was a local government employee was unable *to be nominated* to stand for election to the council which employed him or her, let alone stand or be a member. Such a person had to resign his or her post in order to be nominated. This was a rather risky proposition as the person might fail to be elected and find himself or herself without a council seat and without a job. This disqualification meant that a large number of local people were unable to take full part in the civic life of their area as the local council is often one of the largest employers in the area. In the days of the two-tier system, a person who was an employee of a regional council was able, if qualified, to stand for election to a district council and vice versa and quite a number of people did so. Employees of the islands councils did not have this option, thus depriving the elected part of the council of much talent. Under the unitary system, the only way in which local government employees could become councillors was to live in or have another relevant local connection with a different local authority from the council which employed them. The main reason for this disqualification is to maintain something akin to a separation of powers between the elected members and the officers of local government[2].

3.9 *Councillors*

Until recently, a person was also disqualified if his or her business partner held any paid office or employment in the local authority. This was abolished by the Local Governance (Scotland) Act 2004[3].

1 Local Government (Scotland) Act 1973, s 31.
2 This means, broadly, that there should be no overlap between the elected members and the officers who work for the council.
3 Local Government (Scotland) Act 1973, s 31, amended by LG(S)A s 7.

3.10 The trade unions which represent local government employees argued over many years that this disqualification eroded the civil rights of the employees involved. The McIntosh Commission consulted on this issue and recommended that, subject to appropriate safeguards, employees other than the most senior and those in politically sensitive posts should be permitted to stand for election and serve as elected members[1].

There still remained some unease at the prospect of local government employees being at the same time local government councillors because of the possibility of conflicts of interest. Eventually a compromise position emerged – that local government employees should be able to be nominated and stand for election and should be required to resign only if successfully elected. The Local Governance (Scotland) Act 2004 embodies this compromise by amending section 31 of the Local Government (Scotland) Act 1973, to the effect that a successfully elected employee must resign on the first working day following the declaration of election. The disqualification relating to business partners was also repealed[2].

In the elections of 2007, a number of local government employees stood for election to their employing councils. Several were elected and resigned immediately from their employment. Such a resignation takes effect immediately notwithstanding any contrary provision in their terms and conditions of employment, such as a period of notice

1 The Report of the McIntosh Commission June 1999 paras 147–152.
2 Local Governance (Scotland) Act 2004, s 7.

Politically restricted posts

3.11 There is another disqualification which affects some but not all local government employees, that is people who hold what are known as 'politically restricted posts'. This concept was introduced by the Local Government and Housing Act 1989 following the concern of the government of the day about 'twin-tracking', the practice (relatively uncommon in Scotland) whereby the holder of a senior post in one local authority was a senior elected member of another local authority. Sections 1–3 of the 1989 Act disqualify:

- chief officers and their deputes;
- a council's monitoring officer;
- assistants to political groups;
- persons whose duties include giving advice on a regular basis to councillors or speaking to the media on behalf of the council on a regular basis.

from becoming or remaining a councillor in *any* local authority in Great Britain. People holding politically restricted posts are also barred from taking part in certain political activities such as acting as an election agent, canvassing for candidates standing for election and holding office in a political party.

3.12   The Local Government and Housing Act 1989, as originally enacted, also deemed employees earning a salary at the level of Spinal Column Point 44 and above, to be holders of politically restricted posts. The local government trade unions lobbied on this issue ever since it was introduced and in 2002 the Scottish Executive consulted on the possible relaxation of the restrictions[1]. There was general support for removing the disqualification based on a salary threshold and the Local Governance (Scotland) Act 2004 removes such posts from the politically restricted category, thus allowing such post-holders to take part in political activities and to stand for election[2].

1 *Renewing Local Democracy: The Next Steps*, (March 2002).
2 Local Governance (Scotland) Act 2004, s 9 and see further, ch 5.

Other disqualifications

3.13   Persons in the following categories are also disqualified from being nominated for election, from being elected and from being a member of a local authority:

- a person whose estate has been sequestrated by a court in Scotland or who has been adjudged bankrupt elsewhere than in Scotland. This disqualification ceases when the sequestration is recalled or reduced or when the bankruptcy is discharged;
- a person who has, within the previous five years, been convicted in the United Kingdom, the Channel Islands, the Isle of Man or the Irish Republic of a criminal offence which has resulted in a term of imprisonment (whether suspended or not) for a period of not less than three months without the option of a fine;
- a person who has been found guilty of certain electoral offences[1];
- a person who has been disqualified by the Standards Commission for Scotland[2].
- in addition, under the Local Governance (Scotland) Act 2004, a person who ceases to be a councillor and accepts a severance payment will from then on be disqualified for standing for election[3].

1 Local Government (Scotland) Act 1973, s 31.
2 Under the Ethical Standards in Public Life etc (Scotland) Act 2000, s 19. See ch 7.
3 Local Governance (Scotland) Act 2004, s 12. For severance payments, see ch 8.

3.14   Proceedings against a person on the grounds that he or she is disqualified from being nominated as a candidate can be instituted before the sheriff principal by any opposing candidate at the election. Proceedings against a person on the ground that he or she has acted (or claimed to be entitled to act) as a member of a local authority while disqualified can be brought before the sheriff principal either by the local authority concerned or by four or more local government electors for the area[1]. If the disqualification is proved, the sheriff principal may declare the office vacant in which case a by-election would be held to fill the vacancy. The Local Government (Scotland) Act 1973 provides that the acts of a person elected and subsequently disqualified are not to be considered invalid.

1 Local Government (Scotland) Act 1973, s 32.

RESIGNATION AND VACATION OF OFFICE

3.15   If a councillor wishes to resign from office, he or she can do so at any time by giving written signed notice to the proper officer (the returning officer who is usually the Chief Executive) and the resignation will take effect after the lapse of three weeks or such earlier time as is stated in the notice[1]. It is essential that the notice is delivered to the proper officer and not to the convener of the council or any other council official[2].

1 Local Government (Scotland) Act 1973, s 33.
2 *Dumfries and Galloway Council v Baldwick* (10 March 1998, unreported).

3.16   There are few legal sanctions against a lazy councillor although if he or she is a member of a political party there may be political repercussions in that the party may refuse to endorse the councillor for future elections. A councillor cannot be forced by the council to resign. However, if a councillor fails to attend any meeting of the local authority during a period of six consecutive months, he or she ceases to be a member of the authority unless the failure to attend was due to some reason, such as illness, which has been approved by the council or because he or she has been suspended by the Standards Commission[1]. There is a fairly wide definition of what constitutes attendance at a meeting of the authority. Attendance as a member at a committee, a sub-committee, a joint committee or joint board counts as does attendance as a representative of the council at a meeting 'of any body of persons'. This would include attendance at a local Housing Association meeting or a community council meeting or any of the myriad outside bodies to which councils appoint councillors as representatives. There is a special provision exempting members of the armed forces and certain others when employed during war or any emergency such as the Falklands conflict of 1982 or the war against Iraq which started in 2003.

1 Local Government (Scotland) Act 1973, s 35 (amended by Ethical Standards in Public Life etc (Scotland) Act 2000 s 29). See ch 7.

3.17   Casual vacancies may arise for reasons other than resignation or the vacation of office described above. A councillor may deliberately fail to make the declaration of acceptance of office or become disqualified for some reason such as sequestration of his or her estate, or even die in office. Further, an election may be declared void as a result of an election petition alleging electoral malpractice and the seat is then declared to be vacant. Normally, casual vacancies must be filled by an election (commonly called a by-election) held within three months of the vacancy occurring and the person elected holds office until the day of the next ordinary election[1]. However, if the next ordinary election is due to be held within six months of the casual vacancy occurring, the vacancy is not filled until that ordinary general election takes place. This is to save the expense and inconvenience of two elections being held within a relatively short time. There is one exception to this and that is where the casual vacancy results in the total number of vacancies exceeding one-third of the total number of councillors. In that case an election or elections must be held to bring the total back to over one-third.

1 Local Government (Scotland) Act 1973, s 37.

3.18   Previously, when a councillor gave up office in a local authority for whatever reason, he or she was disqualified from being employed by that local authority for a period of 12 months after ceasing to be a member[1]. This restriction could cause real difficulties for retiring councillors seeking employment in an area where the council is a major employer. In the case of teachers and social workers, the council may be virtually the only employer. The Local Governance (Scotland) Act 2004 provided for this to be amended to a period of three months, except for appointment to politically restricted posts and for ex-councillors who have been involved in the appointment of officers to politically restricted posts, where the 12-month restriction remains[2].

1 Local Government (Scotland) Act 1973, s 67.
2 Local Governance (Scotland) Act 2004, s 10.

CONVENER AND DEPUTE CONVENER

3.19   Before looking at the roles, duties and rights of councillors generally, we will consider the positions of a council's 'first citizens': the convener and depute convener.

3.20   The first business of a local authority after an ordinary election is the election of the person who is to be the chairman or chairwoman of the council[1]. In Scotland the non-sexist term 'convener' is generally used for this office. However, the conveners of each of the city councils of Aberdeen, Dundee, Edinburgh and Glasgow must be known as the 'Lord Provost', regardless of whether the holder of the office is a man or a woman. In the case of the other councils in Scotland, the council may decide what title to confer on the convener but cannot use the title 'Lord Provost' without the consent of the Scottish Ministers. In many cases, the council decides to use the title 'Provost'.

1 Local Government etc (Scotland) Act 1994, s 4.

3.21   Prior to the passing of the Local Government etc (Scotland) Act 1994, a convener held office for the full term of the council and it was not possible for him or her to be sacked by the members of the council. In the 1980s this was a matter of controversy in Glasgow District Council when the Lord Provost fell out of favour with his fellow councillors who were unable to replace him until after the next ordinary election when his term of office came to an end. The LG(S)A 1994 now enables a council to make provision in its standing orders both for the duration of the term of office (which may not extend beyond the next ordinary election) and for the early removal from office of the convener[1]. Thus a council could in theory decide to elect a new convener every year but in practice the convener holds office for the full term of the council and is eligible for re-election as long as he or she remains a councillor.

Councils must elect a convener and may, if they so wish, elect a depute convener from amongst the members. Until 2007, conveners and depute conveners were paid such allowances as the council thought fit, to enable them to meet the expenses of their offices. From 2007, the amounts paid to 'civic heads' (conveners) are set in regulations made by Scottish Ministers. A council may have only one civic head and thus a depute convener would have to be designated as a Senior Councillor in order to receive enhanced remuneration[2].

In some councils the office of convener is quite distinct from the post of council leader. The convener is the ceremonial leader of the local authority while the council leader is the political leader. The distinction is somewhat similar to the distinction between the Queen and the Prime Minister. In addition to chairing the meetings of the full council, the convener will host civic lunches and dinners, meet visiting dignitaries, attend the parade on Remembrance Day, visit local authorities abroad with which the council is twinned, attend charitable functions and so on.

In addition, the Lord Provosts of Aberdeen, Dundee, Edinburgh and Glasgow are the Lord-Lieutenants of their respective cities. The Lord-Lieutenant is the representative of the Queen within the area and has various duties in relation to royal visits, visiting heads of state, the armed forces, medals and honours and (until 2007) justices of the peace. The Lord-Lieutenant also arranges for messages of congratulation to be sent on behalf of the Queen to couples who celebrate their sixtieth, sixty-fifth and subsequent wedding anniversaries and to people celebrating their hundredth, hundred-and-fifth and subsequent birthdays.

The office of bailie existed up until 1975. A bailie was a local magistrate and sat as the judge in the local burgh police courts. That role was taken over by justices of the peace under the District Courts (Scotland) Act 1975 and the office of bailie was abolished. However, Glasgow District Council and subsequently Glasgow City Council decided to retain the title and bestow it on various senior councillors. Their role is purely ceremonial and consists of standing in for the Lord Provost at civic functions.

1 Local Government (Scotland) Act 1973, s 4(3).
2 See further paras 3.36–3.37 below.

THE COUNCILLOR'S ROLES

3.22   Councillors have a number of roles. First, and in the eyes of many the most important, is the 'constituency' role in which the councillor represents the individual electors and residents in his or her ward. A councillor is expected to represent and be accessible to them regardless of whether they voted for the councillor or not. It is now generally expected, certainly in urban areas, that councillors will hold 'surgeries' or 'clinics' locally in schools or other suitable premises on a regular basis at which residents can consult them about problems with the delivery of council services or other matters connected with the functions of the local authority. In addition, people who have business premises in the area but who are not resident there may wish to consult the councillor about applications for planning permission, business development and other issues relating to the business. There is no legal requirement on a councillor to hold surgeries but a councillor who fails to make himself or herself available to constituents may encounter punishment at the ballot box at the next election. Moreover, if a councillor is a member of a political party, the party may impose requirements as to the holding of surgeries before endorsing him or her for re-selection. The Code of Conduct for Councillors[1] sets out as part of its general principles the duty to be accessible to all the people of the councillor's ward.

1 For the Code of Conduct for Councillors, see ch 7.

3.23   The second role is the 'corporate' role in which the councillor makes decisions on a corporate basis, along with all the other members of the council, at meetings of the council and its committees and sub-committees. A good example of the corporate role was the decision of Glasgow District Council in the 1980s to instigate the Glasgow's Miles Better campaign to improve the image of the city at home and abroad. More mundane but important corporate decisions include such matters as the setting of the council's annual budget, the refurbishment of schools, the consideration of planning applications and literally thousands of other decisions taken to try to ensure the smooth running of the council's functions.

3.24   A third role which an increasing number of councillors have is the political role. Fewer than 20 per cent of councillors are elected as independents. Although the number of independents elected rose slightly from 204 in 1999 to 230 in 2003, the number fell to 192 in 2007. The remainder are elected as candidates of political parties which will have issued manifestos setting out their policies for local government in the area. Such councillors will be expected to attend private party group meetings where the group line on certain issues will be decided which the members of the group are expected to support.

The law makes no distinction between these different roles and in law the councillor is free to vote and act in whatever way he or she thinks appropriate.

THE COUNCILLOR'S DUTIES

Conduct

3.25   Until recently, there was no comprehensive statutory definition of the duties of an elected member of a local authority but it was accepted that a councillor's overriding duty was to the whole local community in general and to his or her constituents in particular. As far as the law was concerned, once he or she had been duly elected and had made the declaration of acceptance of office, then provided he or she attended at least one meeting every six months and did not incur any of the statutory disqualifications or commit some offence which resulted in the forfeiture of office, he or she remained a member until the day of the next ordinary election. A member's task was and still is essentially voluntary and he or she is under no *legal* obligation to perform it, (minimal attendance at meetings apart). A member is regarded as being accountable to the electorate and if neglectful or incompetent may expect to lose votes at the next election.

Councillors are, of course, subject to the law and if found guilty of fraud or theft will be punished appropriately. There are also statutory codes which deal specifically with bribery in public authorities. These are contained in the Public Bodies Corrupt Practices Act 1889, the Prevention of Corruption Act 1906 and the Prevention of Corruption Act 1916. These Acts make it an offence corruptly to give, solicit or receive any gift, reward or other advantage as a reward for or an inducement to a member, officer or servant of a public body including a local authority to do or not do something concerned with the functions of the body.

However, in the course of their council work, councillors may find themselves in less clear situations where their private interests might conflict with their public duties without being criminal. Attempts have therefore been made over the years to regulate aspects of the conduct of members[1].

1 For a more detailed discussion, see ch 7.

3.26   The most recent and most comprehensive attempt to regulate the conduct of elected members is to be found in the Code of Conduct for Councillors established under the Ethical Standards in Public Life etc (Scotland) Act 2000, one of the first Acts passed by the Scottish Parliament.

The key principles of the code of conduct, some of which are specifically referred to as duties, are:

- **Duty**: a duty to uphold the law and act in accordance with the law; to act in the interests of the council as a whole and all the communities served by it; a duty to be accessible to the electorate and to represent their interests conscientiously;
- **Selflessness**: a duty to take decisions solely in terms of public interest and not to act to gain financial or other benefit for family or friends;
- **Integrity**: the necessity of avoiding placing oneself under any obligation to any individual or organisation which might reasonably be thought to exert influence in the performance of the councillor's duties;
- **Objectivity**: the requirement to make decisions solely on merit including making appointments, awarding contracts and recommending people for rewards and benefits;
- **Accountability and stewardship**: the duty to consider issues on their merits, taking account of the views of others and ensuring that the council uses its resources prudently and in accordance with the law;

- **Openness**: the duty to be as open as possible about decisions and actions, giving reasons for decisions and restricting information only when the public interest clearly demands;
- **Honesty**: any private interests relating to public duties must be declared and steps must be taken to resolve any conflicts in a way which protects the public interest;
- **Leadership**: there is a duty to support the principles by leadership and example and to maintain and strengthen the public's trust and confidence in the integrity of the council and its councillors in conducting public business;
- **Respect**: councillors must respect other councillors and all council employees, treating them with courtesy at all times.

Councillors are expected to apply the principles of the code in informal dealings with council employees, party political groups and others as scrupulously as at formal meetings of the council and its committees.

3.27   Various principles of general conduct are set out in the Code as follows:

- a duty to follow the Protocol for Relations between Councillors and Employees contained as an annex to the Code;
- a duty to comply with the rules for payment of remuneration, allowances and expenses;
- detailed guidance as to the acceptance of gifts and hospitality along with a duty to ensure that all are recorded in a document available for public inspection;
- a duty to respect all present during council or committee meetings and to comply with rulings from the chair;
- a duty to observe any confidentiality requirements;
- a duty to use council facilities for council duties only;
- a duty to observe the rules of the Code of Conduct in carrying out the duties of any partner organisation to which a councillor is appointed;
- a duty not to seek preferential treatment in any dealings with the council on a personal level, such as council taxpayer, tenant, applicant for a licence etc;
- a duty to avoid indebtedness to the council.

There is nothing which is new in the various duties listed in the Code. What the Code does is to draw together in one document what has long been regarded as good practice for elected members in any tier of government. Every council is under a duty to promote high standards of conduct and assist councillors in observing the Code. Because of the disciplinary powers given to the Standards Commission to enforce the Code[1], members will probably be more aware of what is expected of them than perhaps was the case in the past.

1 For the powers of the Standards Commission, see ch 7.

Registration and declaration of interests

3.28   The Ethical Standards in Public Life etc (Scotland) Act 2000 also makes new provision for each council to set up, maintain and make available for public inspection a register of the interests which a councillor must register under the Code of Conduct[1]. Councillors are required to register their interests within two months from the date of election. If an item of council business involves a matter in which a councillor has a financial interest, the councillor should declare that interest, take no part in discussion and voting on the issue and leave the room until discussion of the item of business is concluded. The position regarding non-financial interests is less clear and is discussed in more detail in chapter 7.

1 Ethical Standards in Public Life etc (Scotland) Act 2000, s 7. For the details of the seven categories of registerable interests, see ch 7.

Declaration of acceptance of office

3.29   Since 1990, a person elected as a councillor must make a declaration of acceptance of office before he or she can act in that office[1]. The wording of the declaration is:

'I ... having been elected to the office of Councillor for the ... ward of ... council, declare that I accept that office and that I will duly and faithfully fulfil the duties of it according to the best of my judgement and ability. I undertake to meet the requirements of the Councillors' Code issued under the Ethical Standards in Public Life etc (Scotland) Act 2000 in the performance of my functions in that office'[2].

The declaration is made before two members of the local authority concerned, the proper officer of the council, a sheriff or a justice of the peace. The declaration must be made within two months of the election and, if the declaration is not made in time, the office of the councillor becomes vacant. However, where the declaration is not made in time as a result of ignorance rather than neglect of duty, it is possible for the omission to be cured by an application to the sheriff[3]. This procedure was used by Kirkcaldy District Council in 1993 when it came to light that 40 councillors elected in 1992 had failed to make the declaration of acceptance of office because no one had told them of this requirement. The sheriff's order in this case prevented the cost and inconvenience of a mass by-election.

L.G.H A 1989

1 ~~The Local Government etc (Scotland) Act 1994, s~~ 30, (adding Local Government (Scotland) Act 1973, s 33A).
2 For the Ethical Standards in Public Life etc (Scotland) Act 2000 and the Councillors' Code, see ch 7.
3 LG(S)A 1973 contains a section entitled 'Application to the sheriff in cases of difficulty' (s 231) which can cover a multitude of circumstances. See ch 7.

OTHER RESTRICTIONS ON VOTING

3.30   In addition to the restrictions on voting imposed by a declaration of interest, there are other more specific restrictions on voting. If a councillor is at least two months in arrears in payment of council tax and any matter relating to the setting of the council tax or related issues arises at a meeting at which the member is present, he or she must disclose the fact of the arrears and must not vote on the matter. Interestingly, the legislation does not prohibit the member from speaking on the matter and does not require the member to leave the meeting. So an eloquent councillor could sway the votes of colleagues while not being able to vote personally. A councillor who is in arrears and fails to disclose the fact commits a criminal offence[1].

1 Local Government Finance Act 1992, s 112. Similar rules applied to arrears of the community charge (poll tax).

3.31 Another restriction on voting and one which seems to undermine the councillor's representative role is in relation to the allocation of council housing. If such a decision is to be taken and either the house in question is situated, or the applicant for the house is resident, in the member's ward then the member is barred from taking part in the decision[1].

1 Housing (Scotland) Act 1987, s 20(3).

THE COUNCILLOR'S RIGHTS

3.32 A councillor has the right to attend every meeting of the full council, unless he or she has declared an interest which requires the member to leave the council chamber, in which case the councillor withdraws only during consideration of the item concerned. Councillors are also under a general obligation to observe the standing orders of the council and respect the authority of the convener in the chair. If a member fails to do so or acts in a disorderly manner, he or she may be excluded from the remainder of the meeting and required to leave the room.

The member's right to attend committee meetings, however, is a qualified right. He or she has no statutory right to demand membership of a particular committee or indeed any committee and there is no redress if the council, however unreasonably, refuses to appoint him or her to any committee of the council.[1] Most local authorities will make specific provision in their standing orders for the size and composition of their committees and sub-committees. Members may be able to indicate preferences for membership of particular committees. In England and Wales there are statutory provisions which require councils to allocate seats on committees and sub-committees to the members of different political groups in proportion to each group's membership on the council[2]. These provisions are not yet in force in Scotland.

Once appointed to a committee or a sub-committee, a councillor has the right to attend all meetings and speak and vote subject to the restrictions mentioned above in relation to meetings of the council. The right of councillors to attend meetings of committees and sub-committees of which they are not members is not so clear-cut. They may attend as ordinary members of the public where members of the public have the right to do so[3]. A councillor may have a common law right to attend a meeting of a committee or sub-committee if he or she has a 'need to know' in the sense of a legitimate interest as a councillor in the subject matter under discussion and could not otherwise obtain the information. Any other rights to attend, speak and possibly vote will be contained in the council's standing orders.

1 *Manton v Brighton Corporation* [1951] 2 All ER 101.
2 Local Government and Housing Act 1989, ss 15, 16.
3 Under the Public Bodies (Admission to Meetings) Act 1960 and the Local Government (Access to Information) Act 1985.

Access to information

3.33   Under the Local Government (Access to Information) Act 1985[1], members of local authorities, committees and sub-committees have statutory rights of inspection of various documents related to business to be transacted by the authority unless the documents disclose certain types of 'exempt information'[2]. To gain access to exempt information, the councillor would have to rely on the common law 'need to know'. However, the right of access to information does not authorise the member to disclose 'confidential information' which is defined as information disclosed to the local authority by the government on a confidential basis and information the disclosure of which is prohibited by statute or by a court order. Members are also expected to maintain the confidentiality of information disclosed at any part of a meeting from which the press and public are excluded.

Councillors may also use the provisions of the Freedom of Information (Scotland) Act 2002 to access information[3].

1 For further information, see ch 5.
2 The Local Government (Scotland) Act 1973, ss 50A–50K and Sch 7A (added by the Local Government (Access to Information) Act 1985, s 2, Sch 1). Schedule 7A contains 14 categories of exempt information, including information relating to particular employees and information relating to adoption and fostering of particular children.
3 See further paras 5.36–5.40.

The right to requisition a council meeting

3.34   An individual member (other than the convener or depute convener) has no right to call a meeting of the council or demand that one be called, but has the right to join with others in requisitioning a special meeting. The requisition has to be signed by at least one-quarter of the councillors and must be held within 14 days of the requisition being delivered to the proper officer of the council. There is no similar statutory right to requisition a special meeting of a committee or sub-committee, but the council's standing orders may allow for this to happen.

Remuneration of councillors

3.35   Remuneration has been a thorny issue for councillors for many years. Many of them work very hard as councillors. A survey carried out by COSLA in 2003 found that full-time councillors spent an average of 42.9 hours per week on council business, while those who had another job averaged 27.2 hours.

Before the reorganisation of local government in 1974–75, councillors received no allowances at all, apart from travelling and subsistence, although a councillor who was in employment could claim loss of earnings incurred in carrying out council duties. In 1975, an attendance allowance of £10 was introduced for attendance at various specified meetings. The amount was the same whether the meeting lasted for five minutes or five hours and only one allowance could be claimed per day. In 1980, a scheme of special responsibility allowances was introduced with maximum amounts, depending on the population and type of council (region, islands or district) set out in regulations. The amounts set were not generous and it was estimated that the leader of Glasgow District Council in the 1980s was paid approximately 2 pence per hour more than the council cleaners, on the basis of a 40-hour week. In 1989, a basic allowance per councillor was introduced and in 1994–95 the government removed the statutory limits on special responsibility allowances and gave councils the freedom to set their own amounts. Despite this freedom, few councillors received more than £20,000 per annum. Compare this figure with the salaries paid to chief officers which in the larger councils may be around £100,000 per annum. In addition, there was no pension scheme for councillors and those who have spent many years working more or less full-time on council duties have found themselves financially disadvantaged when they retired.

The Renewing Local Democracy Working Group[1] (the Kerley Group) examined the whole issue of members' remuneration and recommended that the basic allowance should be raised to £12,000 per annum and that the number of councillors receiving a special responsibility allowance should be cut down considerably to between eight and five per council, depending on size. It also recommended that the leaders of Glasgow and Edinburgh City Councils should receive the same amount of remuneration as backbench MSPs (around £50,000 per annum) with other leaders remunerated on a proportional basis and that future increases in remuneration should be linked directly to increases in MSPs' remuneration. In response to the Kerley recommendations, the Scottish Executive announced in 2002 that it was committed to changing the current system of allowances for councillors and establishing some form of pension provision.

1 See ch 8.

The Scottish Local Authorities Remuneration Committee

3.36　　The Local Governance (Scotland) Act 2004 enabled the Scottish Ministers to make new regulations relating to councillors' remuneration and allowances and (for the first time) pensions. The 2004 Act also established an independent Scottish Local Authorities Remuneration Committee to give advice to Scottish Ministers on these matters[1].

The Scottish Local Authorities Remuneration Committee made its first report in 2006 [2].

Its main recommendations were:

- The abolition of the basic allowance and the Special Responsibility Allowance and their replacement by a new salary structure for all councillors;
- A basic salary for all councillors;
- Enhanced salaries for council leaders;
- Enhanced salaries for a limited number of senior councillors in each council, the number to be based on the population of the council area;
- All councillors to have a role description, participate in a training needs assessment and have a personal development plan;
- The Standards Commission to be able to direct that a councillor's salary should be reduced if that councillor has been suspended;
- A pension scheme for councillors.

The Scottish Executive accepted the majority of SLARC's recommendations[3].

1 Local Governance (Scotland) Act 2004, ss 11, 13.
2 Review of Remuneration Arrangements for Local Authority Councillors – www. Scotland.gov.uk/ Publications/2006/01/25090631/0
3 www.scotland.gov.uk/Topics/Government/local-government/16340/SLARCletter.

The new scheme of Councillors' Remuneration

3.37   Following the elections of 2007, a new scheme of remuneration came into effect. The main aspects of the scheme are as follows[1]:

- The basic allowance and the special responsibility allowances were abolished and replaced with a new salary structure. The basic salary for councillors is the same in all councils and was set at £15,452. Councils are not able to vary this figure, although a councillor may choose to renounce all or part of this.
- The salary levels for Council Leaders are on a banded system based on the population of the council area. For Council Leaders in Band A, the figure was set at £25,754 (inclusive of the basic salary); in Band B, £30,905; in Band C, £36,005: and in Band D £46,357[2].
- The salary levels for Civic Heads (normally the Provost or Convener) are left to the discretion of the local authority concerned, up to a maximum of 75% of the remuneration of the Leader of the Council. For Band A, the maximum figure is £19,316; Band B, £23,179: Band C, £27,041; Band D, £34,768 (also inclusive of the basic salary).
- In addition to the Council Leader and the Civic Head, councils may have a maximum number of Senior Councillors. Senior Councillors should hold a significant position of responsibility in the Council's political management system but it is up to the councils to decide which posts should be deemed to be Senior Councillor posts and also the level of salary, provided it is within the overall budget set by Scottish Ministers. A Senior Councillor may not be paid more than 75% of the salary paid to the Leader. The maximum number of Senior Councillors ranges from 8 in Clackmannanshire and Midlothian, to 24 in Edinburgh and Glasgow.

1 Local Governance (Scotland) Act 2004 Regulations (Remuneration) 2007 (SSI/2007/183). See also Councillors' Remuneration: salary, allowances, and expenses – Interim Guidance, 2007.

2 Councils in Band A have populations up to 100,000; in Band B, between 100,001 and 200,000; in Band C between 200,001 and 400,000; and in Band D over 400,001 (only Glasgow and Edinburgh City Councils).

Allowances and reimbursement of expenses[1]

3.38   The only allowance provided for under the new Regulations is for mileage by private car, motorcycle or bicycle while a councillor is carrying out an approved duty. The Scottish Ministers have set mandatory rates.

Civic Heads may be reimbursed for actual and receipted expenditure incurred in carrying out civic duties up to maximum amounts set by Scottish Ministers for each of the four Bands.

Where a councillor is required to carry out council business outwith their own ward or outwith council offices, the actual cost of reasonable expenses incurred for meals may be reimbursed on production of receipts. Upper limits have been set by the regulations. Councillors may also be reimbursed for actual receipted costs for overnight accommodation when they are carrying out council business away from home. Again, upper limits are set by the regulations.

Councils are expected to provide councillors with the equipment necessary to carry out their roles, such as mobile phones, computers and fax machines and some telephone costs may be reimbursed.

1 The Local Government (Allowances and Expenses) (Scotland) Regs (SSI/2007/108).

Pensions

3.39   From 2007, the Local Government Pension Scheme became available to councillors[1]. Councillors who were first elected before 2007 are allowed to opt in to an arrangement that would allow them to buy pension entitlement in respect of previous year service, limited to 1995. Members contributions have been set at 6%, the same as other members of the scheme, and normal employers' contributions apply, with calculations based on career average rather than final salary.

1 The Local Government Pensions Etc. (Councillors and Visit Scotland) (Scotland) Amendment Regs 2007 (SSI/2007/71).

Job descriptions

3.40   All councillors must now have a job description, participate in a training needs assessment and have a personal development plan. Councils have to publish a list of councillors who have undertaken training when they publish information about councillors' salaries, allowances and expenses.

The Standards Commission now has the power to direct that a councillor's salary be reduced if, after a hearing, the councillor has been suspended form carrying out any part of his role.

WIDENING ACCESS TO COUNCIL MEMBERSHIP

3.41   The remit of the Renewing Local Democracy Working Group (the Kerley Group) included consideration of ways in which council membership could be made more attractive to a wider cross-section of the community and councils could become more representative of the make-up of the community. The Kerley Report included a chapter devoted to widening access to council membership[1]. Its recommendations included the following:

- the publication of role descriptions to make clear to the public what councillors do;
- a review by councils of their business arrangements to ensure that the majority of councillors can carry out their role effectively on a part-time basis;
- a review by councils of the impact of their management arrangements on councillors' travelling time (a particular problem in rural areas);
- a review of the time councillors are required to spend in meetings and on preparation for meetings;
- discussions with representatives of employers and employees about making it easier for people in employment to act as councillors;
- a review by councils of the administrative support provided to councillors;
- a review by councils of arrangements to facilitate and encourage participation by councillors and potential councillors with a disability;
- a review by the Scottish Executive of the legislation which hinders councils from using information and communication technologies to streamline the conduct of council business;
- training for people interested in becoming councillors and for newly-elected councillors;
- a review by councils of their organisational arrangements with a view to increasing participation by women;
- an action plan by the Convention of Scottish Local Authorities and people from ethnic minority backgrounds to increase participation by ethnic minorities;
- the reduction of the age for standing for election from 21 to 18 years of age.

Many councils carried out the reviews suggested by the Kerley Group to make council membership more attractive.

However, a survey of councillors elected in 2003 found that the average Scottish councillor was white, male, aged 55, owned his house and a car, had a degree or professional qualification and worked in a professional or managerial job[1]. Only 21.8 per cent were women, just over 1 per cent were under 30 years of age and 34 per cent were over 60; only 14 out of 1,222 came from an ethnic minority background, and people with disabilities were significantly underrepresented on councils[2].

1 Report of the Renewing Local Democracy Working Group (2000) ch 3.
2 Scottish Local Government Information Unit, Convention of Scottish Local Authorities Report (2004).

3.42   As noted above, the Scottish Parliament reduced the age for standing for election to 18 and removed the political restrictions on most local government employees[1]. The Scottish Parliament also provided for what is called 'remote participation and calling of meetings'[2]. Thus meetings can be called by email and councillors can participate by video-conferencing. The latter is particularly useful for councillors who represent the islands and other remote areas. Improved remuneration and pension arrangements were also thought to encourage more people to consider becoming councillors, (although a drastic reduction in the number of special responsibility allowances might be a disincentive.)

1 Both are now provided for in the Local Governance (Scotland) Act 2004, ss 7, 8, 9.
2 Local Government in Scotland Act 2003, s 43.

3.43   Two surveys of the councillors elected in May 2007 were carried out in the year following the elections, one on behalf of the Convention of Scottish Local Authorities and the Scottish Government[1], the other by the Electoral Reform Society[2].

The survey for COSLA and the Scottish Government was based on a response rate of 61.8% (755 councillors). It found that, despite the changes made to make serving as a councillor more attractive, little had changed. The average councillor is white, male, married, aged 54, owns his own house and works in a professional or managerial job. 22.4% are women, 2.6% are under thirty years of age and 35% are sixty or over. Just under 2% appear to come from ethnic minority groups and 18% said they suffer from long term health problems or disabilities which limit their activities in some way. (The comparable figure for 2003 was 9%).

The survey by the Electoral Reform Society appears to be based on information about the total number of councillors (1222). It concentrates more on the party political results under the STV system, compared with First Past the Post, but has some information about the age, sex, and ethnicity of councillors elected. Its figures are probably more accurate than those of the Cosla/Scottish Government survey.

According to this report, the total number of women elected was 263 (21.6%). down six from 2003. The number of councillors aged below 30 is 28 (2.33%), three of whom are 18–21 year-olds. Nine councillors come from an ethnic minority background, (0.75%), all from an Asian background. There is no information about older people or people with disabilities.

1 Scotland's Councillors 2007, Cosla and the Scottish Government, April 2008.
2 Local Authority Elections in Scotland, Electoral Reform Society, November 2007.

3.44   So while some progress has been made in terms of representation of younger people, the representation of women and ethnic minorities seems to have decreased. Some people expected that the change in the electoral system to STV would, of itself, increase the number of women and ethnic minority councillors. However, STV alone cannot achieve this. Political parties also have a major role to play in widening participation by the underrepresented groups. Over 80 per cent of councillors represent a political party and it is the political parties which select them as candidates. The parties could review their selection procedures to ensure that more young people, women, ethnic minorities and people with disabilities are selected as candidates for winnable seats.

Local authorities too can make service as an elected councillor more attractive to under-represented groups by continuing to review the recommendations of the Kerley Report such as those relating to the way in which they organise business and the support they provide to councillors.

Chapter 4

Local government general powers and duties

4.1   This book does not cover the law relating to the various functions of local government. For this the reader should refer to specialised texts on each. In this chapter, the broader powers and duties of local government will be considered.

THE ULTRA VIRES DOCTRINE

4.2   It is a well-established principle of law that a statutory body has no power to do anything which it is not authorised or required to do by statute. This is known as the ultra vires principle[1]. This principle is the basis for judicial review and the fact that it applies to local authorities in Scotland was confirmed in a case in 1916 in which Lord Kinnear stated that the Court of Session had the power to set aside an 'excess of power' by 'any administrative body'[2]. The strict effect of this principle is that a local authority (including a joint committee, joint board or other body exercising local authority or local authority-related powers) may not do anything for which it cannot point to a statutory authority. However, the courts developed a rule known as the 'incidental' rule which considerably relaxed the rigour of the ultra vires principle. As we shall see, the Scottish Parliament has recently relaxed the rule even further by giving Scottish local authorities a power to advance well-being.

1 'Ultra vires' is a Latin phrase which literally means 'beyond its powers'. The phrase 'intra vires' means 'within its powers'.
2 *Moss' Empires Ltd v Glasgow Assessor* 1916 2 SLT 215.

4.3   There are few local government cases on the ultra vires principle in the strict sense, largely due to the operation of the incidental rule. One example is the English case of *Attorney-General v Fulham Corporation* in which it was held that the Corporation, which had express powers to provide public wash-house facilities, was acting ultra vires in providing a full-scale laundry service[1].

To prevent the abuse of the discretionary powers conferred on local authorities and other bodies, the courts have broadened the scope of the ultra vires principle. So an action may be ultra vires, not because the local authority did not have the power to act but because of the way the power was exercised or the use to which it was put. This is 'abuse of power' rather than 'excess of power'. This wider sense of ultra vires was discussed in depth by Lord Greene in the *Wednesbury* case[2] and more recently by Lord Diplock in the *GCHQ* case where he defined the grounds of judicial review as illegality, irrationality and procedural impropriety[3].

1 [1921] 1 Ch 440.
2 *Associated Provincial Picture Houses Ltd v Wednesbury Corporation* [1948] 1KB 223.
3 *Council of Civil Service Unions v Minister for the Civil Service* [1985] AC 374. It is known as the *GCHQ* case because the civil servants involved were employed at Government Communications Headquarters.

THE INCIDENTAL RULE AT COMMON LAW

4.4   The functioning of local authorities would have been severely restricted if explicit statutory authority were required for every single action which a council proposed to take. So it was necessary to develop the 'incidental' rule. The principle was first defined in a case concerning a railway company[1] in which it was held that the courts should not hold actions to be ultra vires which could be fairly regarded as incidental to or consequential upon existing statutory powers.

Various examples have arisen to illustrate what can and cannot be regarded as incidental. In *D and J Nicol v Dundee Harbour Trustees*[2] it was held that running pleasure trips was not incidental to the statutory function of running ferry services on the River Tay. In *Graham v Glasgow Corporation*[3], on the other hand, the establishment by the Corporation of a printing department was considered to be fairly incidental to its statutory functions, as many of these required stationery and printing facilities. If the Corporation had been manufacturing paper or producing schoolbooks, these would probably not have been regarded as incidental to the Corporation's functions. In the later case of *Glasgow Corporation v Flint*[4] it was held that payment by the Corporation for the installation and billing of telephones for councillors, for the purpose of strengthening links between councillors and members of the public, was not fairly incidental to any of the Corporation's functions (although such payments were not ultra vires if made from the Common Good Fund[5]).

1 *Attorney-General v Great Eastern Railway Company* (1880) 5 App Cas 473 HL.
2 *D and J Nicol v Dundee Harbour Trustees* 1914 2 SLT 418.
3 *Graham v Glasgow Corporation* 1936 SLT 145.
4 *Glasgow Corporation v Flint* 1966 SLT 183.
5 The common good is property held by former burgh councils for the good of the community as a whole. These funds were transferred to the district and islands councils in 1975 and to the unitary authorities in 1996.

THE INCIDENTAL RULE IN STATUTE

4.5   The incidental rule was embodied in section 69 of the Local Government (Scotland) Act 1973[1]. Thus local authorities have the subsidiary statutory power

> ' ... to do anything ... which is calculated to facilitate, or is conducive or incidental to, the discharge of any of its functions'.

Cases based on this statutory provision give further examples of what may or may not be regarded as incidental. In *Meek v Lothian Regional Council*[2] it was decided that there was sufficient doubt about the application of section 69 to the council's decision to allow some employees paid leave to attend a national lobby of Parliament to make Meek's petition for interdict a matter for further enquiry. The court seemed to accept that 'incidental to' was to be interpreted more strictly than 'in connection with'. In *McColl v Strathclyde Regional Council*[3], it was decided that the council's statutory duty to provide wholesome water did not empower it to add fluoride to the water supply for the purpose of improving dental health.

Several cases arose in relation to local government finance which highlighted the limits of councils' incidental powers. Both Scottish and English courts have held that profit-seeking interest swap deals were ultra vires and not justifiable under the incidental rule[4]. In *Credit Suisse v Allerdale Borough Council*[5], the council established a company to finance the construction of a leisure pool with time-share accommodation and guaranteed a loan to the company. When the bank sought repayment of the loan, the council argued that it had no statutory authority to enter into the contract of guarantee. The Court of Appeal agreed and dismissed the bank's claim that the contract could be justified under the incidental rule. The contract was therefore ultra vires, void and unenforceable. In a similar case, *Credit Suisse v Waltham Forest London Borough Council*[6], the council established a company to provide housing for homeless persons and guaranteed a loan to the company. When the bank sought to enforce repayment from the council, the Court of Appeal held that the council's incidental powers could not be used to imply powers to provide housing as detailed statutory provisions relating to housing were already in place.

1 A similar power was included in the Local Government Act 1972, s 111 which extends to England and Wales.
2 *Meek v Lothian Regional Council* 1980 SLT (Notes) 61.
3 *McColl v Strathclyde Regional Council* 1983 SLT 616.
4 *Hazell v Hammersmith and Fulham London Borough Council* [1992] 2 AC 1; *Morgan Guaranty Trust Company of New York v Lothian Regional Council* 1995 SLT 299.
5 *Credit Suisse v Allerdale Borough Council* [1997] QB 306.
6 *Credit Suisse v Waltham Forest London Borough Council* [1997] QB 362.

THE LOCAL GOVERNMENT (CONTRACTS) ACT 1997 AND THE ULTRA VIRES RULE

4.6 In Scotland, where a contract is declared void because it is ultra vires, recovery of money is possible through the principle of restitution. However, no such principle exists in English law and financial institutions became wary of lending to local authorities. The government decided that it was necessary to provide a mechanism to protect those who entered into contracts with local government. This led to the Local Government (Contracts) Act 1997 which permits councils to enter into contracts of guarantee of the kind involved in the *Credit Suisse* cases and provides for a scheme of certification for contracts. Once a contract is properly certified, it will have effect as if the local authority had the power to enter into it and a decision by the courts that a certified contract is ultra vires will not necessarily make the contract void[1]. The Act also provides for compensation if a certified contract is held to be void[2], it does not, however, abolish the ultra vires rule in relation to contracts.

1 Local Government (Contracts) Act 1997, ss 2(1) and 5(3).
2 LG(C)A 1997, ss 6 and 7.

A POWER OF GENERAL COMPETENCE

4.7   In many European countries local authorities have the power to do anything for the benefit of their areas which is not expressly prohibited or otherwise provided for in statute. This power is called a power of general competence. Although the incidental rule relaxes the ultra vires rule it is still restrictive. The Wheatley Commission[1] recommended in 1969 that local authorities should possess a general competence which would enable them to act outside their specific statutory powers when the circumstances seemed appropriate[2]. This was rejected by the government of the day and local authorities continued to be restricted in the exercise of their discretion. Local authorities continued to argue for such a power, particularly after the Council of Europe drew up the European Charter of Local Self-Government in 1986. This Charter aims to protect and strengthen local autonomy in Europe. Article 4(2) of the Charter enshrines the principle of a power of general competence, stating that:

> '… local authorities shall within the limits of the law, have full discretion to exercise their initiative with regard to any matter which is not excluded from their competence nor assigned to other authorities'.

The UK government of the day refused to sign the Charter on the basis that councils would abuse the power. However, a month after the general election of May 1997, the new Labour government signed the Charter and ratified it a few months later. This, however, was purely symbolic and did not bring local government any wider powers.

1 *Report of the Royal Commission on Local Government in Scotland* (the Wheatley Report) (Cmnd 4150) (1969), and see ch 1 above.
2 Wheatley Commission Report, para 640.

A POWER OF GENERAL COMPETENCE AND THE SCOTTISH PARLIAMENT

4.8   The issue of a power of general competence came to the fore again in the context of devolution to Scotland. The Scottish Constitutional Convention which was established in 1989 by the Campaign for a Scottish Assembly produced a number of reports intended to be blueprints for a Scottish Parliament. Its final report *Scotland's Parliament: Scotland's Right* recommended that a Scottish Parliament should endorse the principles of the European Charter of Local Self-Government, in particular article 4.

When the Scotland Bill was making its way through the UK Parliament in 1997–98, the then Secretary of State for Scotland, Donald Dewar, appointed a Commission on Local Government and the Scottish Parliament, chaired by

Neil McIntosh who had been Chief Executive of Strathclyde Regional Council prior to its abolition in 1996. In its Report, published in 1999, the Commission recognised that a power of general competence would provide significant benefits and recommended that such a statutory power should be introduced.

The response of the Scottish Executive to the McIntosh Report[1] was generally positive and a consultation paper published in 1999 invited views on a number of proposals emanating from the Report, including a power of general competence. A further consultation paper was issued in November 2000 and a White Paper in December 2001. By this stage the power had been renamed the 'power of community initiative'. Most of the respondents to the consultations and the White Paper were in favour of such a power in some form or other and legislation followed.

The Local Government in Scotland Act 2003 provides for a new power to advance well-being (this now being the term for a power akin to one of general competence). The power to advance well-being is very similar to article 4(2) of the European Charter of Local Self-Government. It does not, however, abolish the ultra vires rule which still lurks in the background, although now further limited in scope.

1 For the McIntosh Report, see ch 8.

THE POWER TO ADVANCE WELL-BEING

4.9   A local authority now has the power to do anything which it considers is likely to promote or improve the well-being of its area and persons within it[1]. This includes power to incur expenditure; give financial assistance; enter into agreements; co-operate with, facilitate or co-ordinate the activities of any person; exercise on behalf of any person any functions of that person and provide staff, goods, materials, facilities, services or property to any person[2]. The power may also be exercised outwith the area of the local authority if it is considered that to do so would advance the well-being of the authority's own area or inhabitants[3]. Thus an urban council could use this power to provide an adventure training school in the area of a rural council. The Scottish Ministers have the power to extend the meaning of 'well-being'. Before exercising the power to advance well-being, local authorities must have regard to guidance provided by the Scottish Ministers[4] and such guidance was produced in 2004.

1 Local Government in Scotland Act 2003, s 20(1).
2 LGSA 2003, s 20(2).
3 LGSA 2003, s 20(4).
4 LGSA 2003, s 21.

4.10   The power to advance well-being has limits set by statute. Where there is a limiting provision in an Act of either Parliament or in a statutory instrument which prohibits or prevents a local authority from doing anything or somehow limits its powers, a council cannot use the power of well-being to override that provision[1]. There is some case law on the equivalent provision in English law[2]. A Pakistani national claimed assistance from Oxfordshire

County Council after the breakdown of her marriage following domestic violence. She argued that the National Assistance Act 1948 and the power to promote well-being authorised the benefits she needed. The council argued that the 1948 Act acted as a limiting provision. The Court of Appeal decided in favour of the council although it agreed that generally a wide interpretation should be given to the well-being provisions and a narrow interpretation to the limiting provisions[3].

Nor may a local authority unreasonably duplicate anything which may or must be done by someone else, without that person's consent[4]. Thus a council cannot use the power to establish its own prisons or hospitals. The power does not enable a local authority to raise money by imposing a tax or charge, apart from imposing reasonable charges for defraying costs incurred in supplying goods or services[5]. Where a local authority decides to impose a charge, it must publish the reason for doing so and an explanation as to how it arrived at the amount. The provision which enables a local authority to impose charges is limited by section 22(9) of the Local Government in Scotland Act 2003 which prevents the imposition of charges in relation to the provision of school education, public libraries, fire fighting and the registration and conduct of elections, all of which have traditionally or statutorily been provided free of charge. If a local authority wishes to use the new power to promote the economic development of its area outside the United Kingdom, it must obtain the prior consent of the Scottish Ministers.

Enforcement powers lie with the Scottish Ministers. If it appears to them that a local authority has significantly exceeded its power to advance well-being and that enforcement is justified, the Scottish Ministers may serve 'a preliminary notice' on the authority[6]. This is a written notice which requires the authority to submit to the Scottish Ministers, within a time limit, a written response which states either that it has not significantly exceeded its power, with a justification of that statement, or that it has exceeded its power but giving reasons why the Scottish Ministers should not issue an enforcement direction[7].

If an enforcement direction is issued, it requires the council concerned to take certain specified action the purpose of which is to remedy or prevent a recurrence of its significant excess of power. The local authority is under a duty to comply with an enforcement direction[8].

1 Local Government in Scotland Act 2003, s 22(1).
2 Local Government Act 2000, ss 2, 3.
3 *Oxfordshire County Council v R* (on the application of Khan) [2004] EWCA Civ 309.
4 LGSA 2003, s 22(4),(5).
5 LGSA 2003, s 22(7), (8).
6 LGSA 2003, s 26(1).
7 LGSA 2003, s 26(2).
8 LGSA 2003, s 27.

4.11   A local authority is defined so as to include joint fire and police boards and an early example of the use of the power to advance well-being was the decision by Strathclyde Joint Police Board in 2004 to allocate the sum of £500 to community police officers within part of the Strathclyde area to be used as seed funding for local projects promoting community cohesion and safety.

4.12   Although the 'incidental power' remains on the statute book, it is likely that local authorities will now use this new power to authorise innovative activities. Scottish Ministers see it as a power of first resort, not a reserve power. This means that the use of this power is to be viewed generously. Control of an excess of the power lies mainly with the Scottish Ministers, largely removed from the courts and transferred from judicial to political control. The advantage of this for someone who wishes to challenge a local authority's use of the power is that there is no need to use the expensive route of seeking judicial review in the Court of Session. However, the ultra vires rule is still there and could be used by an aggrieved person who considers that a local authority has exceeded its powers under a different statute or has exceeded its power to advance well-being but in a manner which the Scottish Ministers have judged not to be significant. In addition, a local authority which considered an enforcement direction unreasonable could still have recourse to judicial review.

THE DUTY TO SECURE BEST VALUE

4.13   The origin of the duty to secure best value has to be seen in the context of the compulsory competitive tendering (CCT) regime which was introduced by the Conservative government in 1980. The aims of CCT were to reduce the amount of work of certain types carried out in-house by councils' own workforces and to increase the amount of work carried out by the private sector. Initially, CCT applied to contracts for construction and maintenance work which had traditionally been carried out in many local authorities by the councils' own Building Departments. In 1988, CCT was extended to refuse collection, street cleaning, catering, vehicle maintenance and repair, ground maintenance and a number of other activities[1]. The Local Government Act 1992 enabled the process of CCT to be extended to architectural, engineering, legal and financial services.

Compulsory Competitive Tendering was extremely unpopular in councils which were not Conservative-controlled as it threatened the jobs of many council workers. In addition, the drive to privatise the provision of local government services threatened to undermine the traditional local government role of providers of local services by turning councils into little more than 'enablers'.

1 Local Government Act 1988.

4.14   However, the impending reorganisation of Scottish local government in 1995–96 brought about a moratorium on CCT to enable the new local authorities to settle down. Best value was initially an audit requirement and, to retain exemption from CCT, local authorities had to satisfy the Accounts Commission that they were demonstrating best value in their expenditure.

The Labour Party proposed to abolish CCT and the concept of best value appeared in their 1997 manifesto as an alternative. When Labour won the 1997 general election, it continued the moratorium on CCT but made it conditional on continuing demonstration of best value. However, the concept was extended to apply to all functions of local government, not just to those which had been subjected to CCT, and the government made it clear that this would become a statutory duty embodied in legislation.

4.15 The duty of best value is contained in Part 1 of the Local Government in Scotland Act 2003. Section 1(1) states simply that it is the duty of a local authority to make arrangements which secure best value, which is defined in section 1(2) as 'continuous improvement in the performance of the authority's functions'. This requires an appropriate balance to be struck among the quality of performance of functions, the cost to the local authority and the cost to any consumers who are charged for a service. In maintaining that balance, local authorities must take account of efficiency, effectiveness, economy and the need to meet equal opportunities requirements and must discharge their duties in a way that contributes to sustainable development[1].

1 Local Government in Scotland Act 2003, s 1(3), (4), (5).

4.16 This relatively brief section is fleshed out in considerable detail in guidance on best value, published by the Scottish Executive in 2004, which reveals how wide-ranging Scottish Ministers expect best value to be.

An authority which secures best value will be able to demonstrate the following:

- a commitment to delivering better public services year on year through acceptance of the key principles of accountability, ownership, continuous improvement and transparency;
- that councillors and senior managers have developed a vision of how best value will contribute to the corporate goals of the authority, which informs the direction of services and is communicated effectively to staff;
- a commitment to high standards of probity and propriety;
- responsiveness to the needs of communities, citizens, customers, employees and others, so that plans, priorities and actions are informed by an understanding of those needs;
- an ongoing dialogue with public sector partners and the local business, voluntary and community sectors;
- consultation arrangements which are open, fair and inclusive;
- a framework for planning and budgeting which includes detailed and realistic plans linked to available resources to achieve the authority's goals at service delivery level;
- effective performance management systems, which include the use of external comparison through which performance issues can be identified, monitored and addressed;
- making the best use of public resources, including employees, contractual agreements, ICT, land and property and financial resources – keeping a considered and appropriate balance between cost, quality and price;
- an approach to review which is rigorous and robust and achieves quantifiable benefits with no areas of work protected from consideration for review;

- that services remain competitive and provide consistently good quality; in considering opportunities for improvement a fair and open approach will be taken in evaluating alternative forms of service delivery from whatever sector;
- it is conscious of being publicly funded and is aware of the need to conduct its business in a manner which demonstrates appropriate competitive practice;
- that account is taken of the potential economic impact of the authority's activities on the local business community and others;
- a culture which encourages joint working and service provision where this will contribute to better services and customer-focused outcomes;
- the use of public performance reporting so that stakeholders are told what quality of service is being delivered and what they can expect in the future.

In relation to sustainable development and equal opportunities arrangements, a local authority should demonstrate:

- consideration of the social, economic and environmental impacts of its activities both short and long term;
- a culture which encourages equal opportunities and the observance of the equal opportunities requirements;
- that measures are in place to meet the UK-wide equal opportunities legislation such as the Equal Pay, Sex Discrimination, Race Relations and Disability Discrimination Acts;
- adoption of the meaning of 'equal opportunities' as is set out in the Scotland Act 1998[1], namely

'... the prevention, elimination or regulation of discrimination between persons on the grounds of sex or marital status, on racial grounds or on grounds of disability, age, sexual orientation, language or social origin or of other personal attributes, including beliefs or opinions, such as religious beliefs or political beliefs'.

1 Scotland Act 1998, Sch 5, L2.

The role of the Accounts Commission

4.17   The Local Government in Scotland Act 2003 extends the roles of the Audit Scotland and the Accounts Commission for Scotland into the field of best value[1]. The Accounts Commission is also enabled to conduct studies into securing best value[2].

1 LGSA 2003, ss 3–5. For Audit Scotland and the Accounts Commission for Scotland, see further chapter 6.
2 LGSA 2003, s 6.

THE DUTY OF COMMUNITY PLANNING

4.18   Community planning is a rather nebulous concept which was embraced enthusiastically by the Scottish Ministers early on in the life of the

Scottish Parliament and which has now become a statutory duty on various public bodies under Part 2 of the Local Government in Scotland Act 2003. It is seen as interrelated with the duty to secure best value and the power to advance well-being.

The Scottish Executive defined the essence of community planning as recognition that the needs of individuals and communities must be addressed collectively. Community planning is seen as involving communities in the agreeing of priorities and how these should be delivered. 'Community planning is also about bodies, groups and partnerships working together more effectively to improve services such as health, education, jobs, homes, transportation and the environment'[1].

1 Scottish Executive Policy Memorandum accompanying the Local Government in Scotland Bill when first introduced into the Scottish Parliament.

4.19   Section 15 of the Local Government in Scotland Act 2003 makes it the duty of local authorities to initiate, maintain and facilitate the process by which the public services in their areas are planned and provided after consultation among all public bodies responsible for the provision of these services and with appropriate community and other bodies. The local authorities must invite and encourage all public bodies operating within their areas and appropriate community bodies to participate in the community planning process. It is possible for two or more local authorities to perform these duties jointly. This enables small local authorities like Clackmannanshire Council to join with their neighbouring authorities to engage in the community planning process. 'Community bodies' are defined as bodies or other groupings, not necessarily formally constituted, established for purposes which include promoting or improving the interests of any communities in the area of the local authority. This includes community councils, residents' associations, local amenity societies and a wide range of ad hoc groups.

The LGSA 2003 then lays on various bodies and office-holders the duty to participate in the community planning process and assist local authorities in carrying out their community planning duties[1]. These include Health Boards, joint police and fire boards, chief constables, Scottish Enterprise, Highlands and Islands Enterprise and Strathclyde Passenger Transport Authority (now the Strathclyde Partnership for Transport). The Scottish Ministers can add bodies to or delete them from the list but the Scottish Executive/Government is not included in this list and neither are community councils. The Scottish Ministers, however, must promote and encourage community planning.

1 Local Government in Scotland Act 2003, s 16.

4.20   Local authorities must publish reports from time to time on what has been done by way of community planning in their area. Each local authority can determine the form, content and frequency of such reports, to whom they are to be given and how they are to be published. The statutory planning partners listed above must supply to the local authorities such information as might reasonably be required of them.

The Scottish Executive provided statutory guidance and all the bodies participating in the process must take account of this. Advice notes have also been provided.

All local authorities in Scotland have now formed Community Planning Partnerships. In some cases, there is a single Community Planning Partnership covering the whole of the council's area. In others, more localised partnerships have been formed. In Glasgow, for example, five local Community Planning Partnerships have been established. Ideally, the other partners should be re-aligning their service delivery area boundaries to those of the local authority and in the case of Glasgow, Strathclyde Police have re-aligned the boundaries of their divisions within the city to those of the five community planning areas.

An example of a partnership formed at regional level is the Clyde Valley Community Planning Partnership. This consists of leading councillors from Glasgow City Council and seven other local authorities surrounding the city: the Chief Constable of Strathclyde Police, the Firemaster of Strathclyde and the Conveners of the Joint Police and Fire Boards; representatives of Glasgow Chamber of Commerce, Scottish Enterprise, Strathclyde Partnership for Transport; the Greater Glasgow Health Board; and the Director and Convener of the Clyde Valley Joint Structure Plan Committee.

Issues which this partnership has discussed include: the future of air transport in the West of Scotland; the provision of national and regional sports facilities; the bid for the 2014 Commonwealth Games; and the problems of the provision of water and sewerage infrastructure for new developments in the west of Scotland. All of these concern more than one local authority and the community planning partnership provides a good forum for their discussion and for the promotion of joint initiatives.

Community planning is still in its infancy and is still bedding in. A review by the Audit Scotland in 2006 found that their complex remit made it difficult for them to achieve their aims. In addition, different geographic boundaries and accountabilities can make it hard for organizations to work well together[1].

1 Community Planning: An Initial Review, June 2006, Audit Scotland.

THE POWER TO MAKE BYELAWS

4.21   A byelaw is a form of subordinate legislation made by an authority or body which is of lower status than Parliament on a matter which Parliament has entrusted to it. It has the force of law but is applicable only to a particular area and not to the whole of the country. Local authorities have wide powers to make byelaws and these powers are contained in many different Acts of Parliament relating to particular functions of local government. For example, the Public Health (Scotland) Act 1897 gives local authorities the power to regulate offensive businesses, pigsties and lodging houses. The Children and Young Persons (Scotland) Acts enable education authorities to regulate the employment of children under school-leaving age and the Countryside (Scotland) Act 1967 empowers local authorities to make byelaws for the preservation of order and the prevention of damage to land belonging to them which is situated in the countryside. The Civic Government (Scotland) Act 1982 enables local authorities to make byelaws for the cleaning of common stairs and passages, backgreens and basements and the regulation of activities on the seashore, adjacent waters and inland waters.

There is also a general power to make byelaws for 'good rule and government' which is contained in the Local Government (Scotland) Act 1973[1] and it is this general power which we shall examine in more detail.

The LG(S)A 1973 states that a local authority may make byelaws for the good rule and government of the whole or any part of its area, and for the prevention and suppression of nuisances therein. Probably the best-known byelaw made under this section is the byelaw which is to be found in most of the local government areas of Scotland which makes it an offence to consume alcohol in designated public places. The consumption of alcohol in public was seen as a nuisance which had to be suppressed in the public interest.

1 Local Government (Scotland) Act 1973, ss 201–204.

4.22   Byelaws have to be confirmed by the Scottish Ministers and, at least one month before applying a for confirmation of a byelaw, a local authority must put an advertisement into a local paper giving notice of the intention to do so. The advertisement should also contain the location of the offices where copies of the byelaw may be inspected and indicate that members of the public should send any objections they may have to the Scottish Ministers in writing. Members of the public are entitled to be supplied by the local authority with a copy of the byelaw and can be charged the sum of 10 pence per 100 words. (The charge does not seem to have been updated since 1973.)

The Scottish Ministers have to take into account any objections and may, if they consider it necessary or desirable, arrange for a public inquiry to be held, normally by the sheriff. The Scottish Ministers have the power either to confirm the byelaw, with or without modification, or to refuse to confirm it. An example of a modification was to the byelaw made by South Ayrshire Council prohibiting dogs, horses, ponies, mules and donkeys from entering Troon (South) Beach. The Secretary of State for Scotland, who was the confirming authority at the time, thoughtfully exempted dogs assisting the police, navy, army and customs and excise officers in carrying out their duties. The Scottish Ministers can also fix the date on which the byelaw is to come into operation. If no date is fixed, it will come into effect one month after the date of confirmation.

As soon as possible after confirmation, the local authority has to place another advertisement in a local paper, giving notice of the date on which the byelaw will come into operation and the location of the offices where the confirmed byelaw can be inspected. A copy of the byelaw is open to inspection by the public free of charge at all reasonable hours and copies can be bought for 20 pence each.

4.23   Byelaws may create offences and a person who contravenes a byelaw may be liable on summary conviction to a fine not exceeding level 2 on the standard scale (£500). If the offence is a continuing one, a person can be fined up to the sum of £5 per day.

4.24   Local authorities have to review their byelaws, ten years from their coming into force and every ten years thereafter, the purpose of this being to ensure that they are still relevant. A byelaw which is no longer relevant may be revoked by the local authority which made it. As with making a byelaw, a proposal to revoke one must be advertised in a local paper and an opportunity given for objections to be made which must be taken into account. A local authority, however, may not revoke or amend a byelaw or part of one which has been inserted into a set of byelaws as a modification by the Scottish Ministers. Nor can a local authority revoke a byelaw or part of one if the effect of revocation is to widen the scope of another byelaw or the remaining part of a byelaw.

Each local authority also has to maintain a register of byelaws open to public inspection at all reasonable times and members of the public can take a copy free of charge. The register should contain a description of their byelaws and any offences or penalties created by them, any amendments to them, the dates of confirmation and of coming into effect and the dates on which they were last reviewed.

4.25   Since a byelaw is a piece of subordinate legislation, its validity can be challenged in court. The courts have held that byelaws must not be ultra vires or repugnant to the general law of the land. They must also be certain, reasonable and must have been made in accordance with the procedure prescribed.

THE POWER TO MAKE MANAGEMENT RULES

4.26   Management rules bear some similarity to byelaws but they are simpler to make and a breach of a rule does not carry a criminal sanction. The power to make management rules was introduced by the Civic Government (Scotland) Act 1982[1]. When that Act was passed, the Secretary of State for Scotland made it clear that he expected local authorities to make use of management rules, where possible, rather than byelaws. Byelaws should be reserved for situations where the possibility of disruption makes an immediate criminal sanction necessary.

Unlike byelaws which can apply to the whole of a council area, management rules regulate the use of and conduct of people in or on land or premises which is owned, occupied, managed or otherwise under the control of the local authority and to which the public have access. Therefore they are suitable for parks, libraries, leisure centres and so on. Examples of management rules which have been made include Glasgow City Council's rules for the management of its parks. They cover virtually every conceivable exigency from climbing trees and wading in ponds to using a park as an airfield (except in cases of emergency), recruiting, drilling or practising military manoeuvres – and beating carpets. Clackmannanshire Council uses management rules for the regulation of public libraries, museums and art galleries and bans spitting, smoking and the inhalation of stupefying gas or solvent vapour along with the expected prohibitions on defacing books and damaging exhibits.

1 Civic Government (Scotland) Act 1982, ss 112–118.

4.27 When a local authority decides to make management rules, it must advertise its intention in a local paper. The advertisement should contain the general purpose of the proposed rules, the place where a copy may be inspected, the fact that objections can be made and the time within which they should be made and the address to which they should be sent. Copies of the proposed management rules should be made available at the council offices and, so far as is practicable, at the land or premises to which they are to apply. Before making the management rules the local authority must take any objections into account and give objectors an opportunity to be heard. Management rules come into force on the day they are executed, that is when the council has made the decision to make them and they have been sealed with the council's seal and signed by the proper officer of the council. They do not, unlike byelaws, have to be confirmed by any external authority. Once made, the rules remain in effect for ten years, unless the council decides to revoke them.

Management rules should be displayed at the entrance to the land or premises to which they apply or elsewhere so that they can be seen by members of the public. There should also be a notice stating where copies of the rules may be inspected, free of charge.

4.28 Where an authorised officer of a local authority, for example a park-keeper or a librarian, has reasonable grounds for believing that someone has contravened, is contravening or is about to contravene a management rule, the sanction available is to expel or exclude that person from the land or premises in question. However, the officer is not authorised to use force. Failure to comply is an offence and, on summary conviction, a fine not exceeding level 1 on the standard scale (£200) may be imposed.

Persistent contravention of a management rule may result in the local authority making an exclusion order against the offender and any attempt by him or her to enter the land or premises while the exclusion order is in force is an offence which carries the penalty of a similar fine. If a local authority decides to make an exclusion order, it must give notice of its intention to do so to the person concerned along with reasons and a statement of his or her right to make written or oral representations against the decision. The local authority must consider any representations made and then decide whether to confirm its decision to make an exclusion order, or to revoke it or amend it. An exclusion order will come into effect not less than 14 days after the decision is made and may remain in force for up to one year.

As shall be seen, many decisions to be made by a local authority can be delegated to an officer of the council[1]. In the case of making an exclusion order, however, this is specifically precluded by the Civic Government

(Scotland) Act: it is for the elected members of the local authority alone to make such a decision[2].

1 Local Government (Scotland) Act 1973, s 56. See ch 5.
2 Civic Government (Scotland) Act 1982, s 117(6).

PRIVATE LEGISLATION

4.29   There may be occasions when a local authority wishes to acquire powers additional to those it possesses under statute. This can be done by the promotion of a private Act of Parliament. Extensive use of the power to promote private legislation was made in the nineteenth century by Glasgow Corporation to provide, for example, safe drinking water, trams, electricity and gas supplies, fever hospitals and so on[1]. Glasgow's example was followed by a number of other councils such as Dundee and Edinburgh Corporations. However, the need to promote private legislation declined as the UK Parliament began to provide for public services by means of Public General Acts.

However, local authorities still occasionally resort to the promotion of private legislation where they need to acquire powers to undertake or control large-scale developments in their areas. The Zetland (Shetland) and Orkney County Council Acts of 1974, for example, were necessary to give these local authorities controls over the onshore oil industry. Highland Regional Council and the Western Isles Council promoted Harbour Confirmation Acts to create new harbours in Lochinver and Berneray respectively. Western Isles Council also resorted to private legislation for the construction of a causeway linking the islands of Vatersay and Barra. Lothian Regional Council used the same power to construct the Edinburgh Western Relief Road. More unusual examples are the Scottish Borders Council (Jim Clark Memorial Rally) Order Confirmation Act 1996 which gives the council powers of extensive road closure and the attempt by Glasgow District Council in 1992 to acquire powers to lend artefacts from the Burrell Collection to museums overseas which the council was specifically prohibited from doing by the will of Sir William Burrell who had donated the collection to the people of Glasgow.

1 See ch 1.

4.30   The current legislation which gives local authorities the power to promote private legislation in the UK Parliament is the Local Government (Scotland) Act 1973[1]. The LG(S)A 1973 was amended by an order made under the Scotland Act 1998 to enable local authorities to promote private legislation in the Scottish Parliament as well as in the UK Parliament, as most of the additional powers likely to be required will relate to matters which are devolved to the Scottish Parliament. The procedures for promoting private legislation in both Parliaments are rather complex and only a brief outline is given here.

Where a local authority is satisfied that the promotion of private legislation is the best course of action it must pass a resolution to do so at a meeting of the council. Notice of its intention to pass such a resolution must be advertised in a local newspaper at least ten clear days before the meeting. The resolution must be passed by a majority of the whole number of councillors, not just by a majority of those present. Then, after an interval of at least 14 days, the local authority must hold a further council meeting, convened in the same way as the first, to confirm the resolution.

The next step depends on whether the powers sought relate to matters reserved to the UK Parliament or devolved to the Scottish Parliament. In the case of reserved matters, the local authority must submit what is called a 'draft provisional order' to the Secretary of State under the provisions of the Private Legislation Procedure (Scotland) Act 1936[2]. If the powers sought relate to devolved matters, a Bill must be introduced in the Scottish Parliament.

1 Local Government (Scotland) Act 1973, s 82.
2 The Private Legislation Procedure (Scotland) Act 1936 provides an accelerated procedure for promoting Scottish private legislation which allows the promoters and any objectors to put forward their respective cases in Scotland, obviating the need for time-consuming and expensive travel to Westminster.

4.31   Often the promotion of private legislation by a local authority is contentious and provisions are made for the proposal to be advertised and for objectors to be heard, by four commissioners appointed for the purpose by the UK Parliament where the power sought relates to reserved matters, or by a Private Bill Committee of the Scottish Parliament, where it relates to devolved matters. If the commissioners or the Committee report that the proposal should proceed, with or without modification, the appropriate Parliament will proceed to pass the Bill[1].

An express limitation on local authorities' power to promote private legislation is found in section 22 of the Local Government (Scotland) Act 1973 to the effect that a local authority cannot promote private legislation to form, abolish or alter any local government area nor to alter its status or electoral arrangements. These are the provinces of the Local Government Boundary Commission for Scotland[2].

The first private Bills promoted by Scottish local authorities in the Scottish Parliament, introduced in 2003–04 were: Stirling, Kincardine and Alloa Railway Bill, promoted by Clackmannanshire Council; Edinburgh Tram (Line 1) and (Line 2) Bills, promoted by the City of Edinburgh Council; and the Waverley Railway (Scotland) Bill promoted by the Scottish Borders Council, all of which relate to major public transport schemes in and around the councils' areas.

1 For the procedures in the UK Parliament, see C Himsworth, *Local Government Law in Scotland* (T & T Clark, 1995 pp 29–34), and for procedures in the Scottish Parliament, see McFadden and Lazarowicz *The Scottish Parliament: an Introduction* (Tottel publishing 3rd edn, 2003 pp 63–4).
2 For the Local Government Boundary Commission for Scotland, see ch 2.

PUBLICITY POWERS

4.32   There is a fairly anodyne provision in section 88 of the Local Government (Scotland) Act 1973 which enables a local authority to make (or assist in the making of) arrangements for members of the public to obtain information about services provided within the local authority area by the council itself, by other public authorities, by government departments or by charities and other voluntary organisations. 'Information' is not further defined. As originally enacted, section 88 also permitted local authorities to arrange for the publication within their area of information 'relating to local government'. They were also permitted to arrange lectures, film shows and exhibitions relating to local government.

During the initial years of the Conservative government under Mrs Thatcher, many local authorities which were not Conservative-controlled, both north and south of the border, made use of the powers under section 88 and its equivalent in English law to produce newspapers, pamphlets and other publicity materials which were highly critical of central government's increasing controls over local government and which promoted the political measures which the councils had taken in attempting to combat these controls. An example was the *Lothian Clarion* which was produced by the Labour-controlled Lothian Regional Council in the 1980s. The leader of the Conservative group on the council, Councillor Brian Meek, took the Regional Council to court, arguing that the contents of the *Lothian Clarion* went beyond the powers contained in section 88. However, the court held that 'information', which was not defined in the LG(S)A 1973, could include explanations of and justifications for decisions taken by councils[1]. In another case, however, the court decided that the production of materials, such as leaflets, badges, balloons and T-shirts, carrying the slogan '*Edinburgh District Council – Improving Services – Creating Jobs*' was unlawful as the slogan did not convey information[2].

The government became convinced that councils were abusing their powers to publish information, using them to indulge in anti-government political propaganda rather than publishing information. It therefore asked the Committee of Inquiry into the Conduct of Local Authority Business which it had established in 1985, under the chairmanship of David Widdicombe QC, to submit an early interim report on the use made by some local authorities of the their publicity powers 'to engage in overtly political campaigning at public expense'[3]. The Interim Report, *Local Authority Publicity,* was published later in 1985[4]. Its main recommendation was that there should be an express statutory prohibition on publicity of a party political nature. The government adopted this recommendation and introduced legislation on publicity which became Part 2 of the Local Government Act 1986. The provisions of this Act were subsequently amended and strengthened by the Local Government Act 1988.

1 *Meek v Lothian Regional Council* 1983 SLT 494.
2 *Commission for Local Authority Accounts in Scotland v City of Edinburgh District Council* 1988 SLT 767.
3 The Secretary of State for the Environment announcing the terms of reference of the Wisdicombe Committee in the House of Commons on 6 February 1985.
4 HMSO 1985.

4.33 The position now is that section 88 of the Local Government (Scotland) Act 1973 has been amended and narrowed so that a local authority may arrange for the publication within its area of information relating to local government *functions*. In addition, there is now a specific prohibition on political publicity. A local authority must not publish any material which either in whole or in part appears to be designed to affect public support for a political party[1]. In deciding whether material is so designed, account has to be taken of the content and style of the material, the time (for example, close to an election) and the likely effect on those to whom the material is directed. In particular, regard has to be had as to whether the material refers to a political party or to people identified with a political party; whether it promotes or opposes a point of view on a question of political controversy which is identifiable as the view of one political party and not of another, and, if the material is part of a campaign, the effect which the campaign appears to be designed to achieve. A local authority cannot get round the prohibition on political publicity by giving financial or other assistance to some other person or body to do so. The effect of this is to prevent local authorities from making a grant for campaigning purposes to voluntary organisations or charities such as Age Concern which might campaign against policies of central government.

'Publicity', 'publish' and 'publication' are given a very wide meaning. They refer to any communication, in whatever form, addressed to the public at large or to a section of the public. So not only are the written and spoken word affected: cartoons, photographs, pictures, music and websites are all covered; even the flying of a flag from the top of the town hall is covered by this definition.

1 Local Government Act 1986, s 2.

4.34   A code of recommended practice covering contents, style, distribution and costs and related matters was issued in 1988 and local authorities must have regard to the code in coming to any decision about publicity. Local authorities also have to keep a separate account of expenditure on publicity, open to inspection by members of the public at all reasonable times, free of charge.

4.35   The restrictions on local authority publicity were very controversial at the time and local authority lawyers pored over the pages of councils' newspapers and other publicity materials to ensure that they were free from party political contamination and unlikely to be challenged in court. That did not prevent a challenge to Grampian Regional Council by the Commission for Local Authority Accounts in Scotland (the financial watchdog of Scottish local authorities)[1]. Grampian Regional Council made three annual grants of £500 between 1988 and 1990 to the Campaign for a Scottish Assembly and a grant of £1,000 in 1990 to the Scottish Constitutional Convention, a body which was also campaigning for a Scottish Parliament. They stipulated that the money was to be used for research and administration and not for publicity. Nevertheless, the Commission for Local Authority Accounts in Scotland which had examined the Region's accounts found that the payments were contrary to law. The council invoked the jurisdiction of the Court of Session which directed the Commission to state a case. One of the Commission's arguments was that campaigning for a Scottish Parliament was a matter of political controversy and that the use to which the grants had been put was bound to have an effect on people's voting intentions and was thus contrary to section 2 of the Local Government Act 1986. However, the court decided that the Commission had not demonstrated, despite holding an inquiry, that the money paid to these campaigning organisations had been spent on publicity. This made it impossible to judge whether the expenditure was indeed unlawful[2].

1 For the Commission for Local Authority Accounts in Scotland (now known as the Accounts Commission), see ch 6.
2 *CLAAS v Grampian Regional Council* 1994 SLT 1120.

PROHIBITION ON THE PROMOTION OF HOMOSEXUALITY BY LOCAL AUTHORITIES

4.36   Section 28 of the Local Government Act 1988 contained an amendment to the Local Government Act 1986 which became section 2A of the latter Act. This was the notorious 'Clause 28' or 'Section 28' which stated that

'... a local authority shall not intentionally promote homosexuality or publish material with the intention of promoting homosexuality nor shall a local authority promote the teaching in any (local authority) school of the acceptability of homosexuality as a pretended family relationship'.

These extraordinary provisions remained on the statute book until the advent of the Scottish Parliament. No case reached the Scottish courts to enable judicial interpretation of the provisions of section 2A as a result of self-regulation by local authorities, although shortly before the section was repealed in 2000, Glasgow City Council suspended payment of a grant to a gay health group in the face of an impending interim interdict by a Glasgow resident.

The Scottish Executive decided to use the vehicle of the Ethical Standards in Public Life Bill to repeal section 2A of the LGA 1986. This produced as much of a furore in Scotland as the original enactment of the provision had in the United Kingdom in 1988 and a private individual was so incensed by the proposal to repeal the provision that he financed a private national referendum on the issue. Nevertheless, the Scottish Executive and Scottish Parliament were not deflected from their intention and the section was repealed by section 34 of the Ethical Standards in Public Life etc (Scotland) Act 2000. However, as a sop to those dismayed at the idea of repeal, section 35 of the ESPL(S)A lays upon councils, in the performance of their functions which relate principally to children, the duty to have regard to the value of stable family life in a child's development and to ensure that the content of instruction is appropriate to each child's age, understanding and stage of development.

Section 2A remained in force in England, as a result of opposition from the House of Lords, until it was finally repealed by the Local Government Act 2003.

THE POWER TO CONDUCT RESEARCH AND COLLECT INFORMATION

4.37 Section 87 of the Local Government (Scotland) Act 1973 enables local authorities to conduct or assist in the conducting of investigations into and the collection of information relating to matters concerning their areas. They may also make arrangements by which any such information and the results of such investigations are made available to government departments or to the public. Ministers can also require councils to provide them with information which is in their possession.

This section has occasionally been used in an unexpected manner by councils, to gauge local public opinion on matters of political controversy emanating from central government. The biggest such exercise was carried out in 1993–94 by Strathclyde Regional Council, which was opposed to government proposals to remove water and sewerage functions from local authority control. They decided to use the power to conduct research and collect information to carry out a region-wide referendum. Postal ballot papers were issued to almost two million residents in Strathclyde. The question asked was 'Do you agree with the government's proposals for the future of water and sewerage services?' There was a return of 71.5 per cent, much higher than the average turnout at a local government election. Of these, 97.2 per cent (1,194,000) voted against the government's proposals. The government eventually decided against any form of privatisation of the water and sewerage functions and transferred them instead to three Water Authorities whose members would be appointed by the Secretary of State for Scotland, thus keeping the services under a form of public control[1].

Use was also made of section 87 of the Local Government (Scotland) Act 1973 to test public opinion on the government's proposals for the boundaries of some of the new single-tier local authorities to be formed under the Local Government etc (Scotland) Act 1994.

1 Local Government etc (Scotland) Act 1994, Pt 2.

THE POWER TO ACQUIRE AND DISPOSE OF LAND

4.38 Local authorities have statutory duties to provide council housing, schools, libraries, roads, offices and other facilities so they need to be able to acquire land to carry out these duties. The 'incidental power' discussed above includes the acquisition of property and there is also a general power to acquire land by agreement, whether situated inside or outside their areas[1]. The land may be acquired for any authorised purpose and it does not matter if the land is not immediately required.

In many cases, however, it may not be possible to secure the agreement of the landowner and local authorities are given further powers to acquire land compulsorily[2]. A compulsory purchase order has to be approved by the Scottish Ministers and landowners who lose their land in this way are entitled to compensation.

Land acquired for one purpose may be appropriated by a local authority for another purpose[3] but land which is held for use as allotments is protected from appropriation.

Local authorities may also dispose of land held by them in any manner they wish, normally for not less than its full value. Previously, if a local authority wished to dispose of land at less than full value, the consent of Scottish Ministers was required. The Scottish Parliament has recently reduced the inflexibility of this rule and now in certain circumstances land may be disposed of for a lower price[4]. Independent valuers determine the value of the land.

Where the land forms part of the common good and a question arises as to the local authority's right to dispose of the land, an application may be made to the Court of Session or to the sheriff for authorisation to dispose of it[5].

1 Local Government (Scotland) Act 1973, s 70.
2 LG(S)A 1973, s 71.
3 LG(S)A 1973, s 73.
4 Local Government in Scotland Act 2003, s 11.
5 LG(S)A 1973, s 75. See *West Dunbartonshire Council v Harvie* 1997 SLT 979.

THE POWER TO MAKE CONTRACTS

4.39   Local authorities have to make all sorts of contracts, week in week out. To give some mundane examples, books have to be bought for schools and libraries, brushes and bins have to be provided for the street-sweepers, toilet rolls provided for the public toilets. Large items of machinery have to be provided for the disposal of refuse and the maintenance of roads and parks. Stationery, computers and all sorts of office equipment have to be provided for administrative staff. Large contracts for the construction of council buildings have to be made.

The general power to contract is found in section 69 of the Local Government (Scotland) Act 1973 (the incidental power). The LG(S)A 1973 also provides that local authorities *may* make standing orders to regulate the making of contracts by them or on their behalf and, in practice, all local authorities do this[1]. However, they *must* make standing orders to regulate the supply of goods or materials or the execution of works, for example, construction contracts. These standing orders must contain provisions for ensuring competitive tendering although they may exempt small contracts, below a certain amount, from the requirements of competitive tendering. The standing orders should also regulate the manner in which tenders are to be invited, that is how they are to be advertised. Membership of the European Union has imposed further obligations in relation to contracts above a certain financial threshold.

In the 1980s, the Conservative government became concerned that local authorities were using their not inconsiderable purchasing powers to influence matters which were extraneous to local government, such as the campaign against apartheid in South Africa, the conduct of employers in industrial disputes and the wages and conditions of service offered by contractors to their employees. The government introduced legislation to outlaw local authorities' taking into account what they termed 'non-contractual considerations'[2]. Some of these restrictions, relating to employment issues, were relaxed by the Local Government in Scotland Act 2003[3].

The Local Government (Goods and Services) Act 1970 which restricted the parties with whom councils could trade has also been amended to enable councils to trade more widely. So, subject to certain restrictions, local authority Parks and Catering Departments, for example, can compete with the private sector in the lucrative wedding market[4].

1 Local Government (Scotland) Act 1973, s 81.
2 Local Government Act 1988 ss 17–19.
3 Local Government in Scotland Act 2003, s 7.
4 LGSA 2003, s 8.

Chapter 5

How councils work

5.1   Councils take literally thousands of decisions every year. Some of them will be quite mundane such as to employ an additional squad of street cleaners, to buy new books for a local library or to purchase enough toilet rolls to supply all the schools in the area. Others will be of more significance, such as a decision to grant planning permission for a major new housing or commercial development or to build a new leisure centre. Some may involve major policy issues such as a decision to enter into a partnership with the private sector for the refurbishment of public buildings.

5.2   In law, a council is a corporate body and all of its decisions are taken by or on behalf of the full council. The council itself is the only source of executive authority. In this respect the organisation of local authority business is very different from the central government model, both in Holyrood and Westminster, where executive decisions can be taken by ministers and ministers are accountable to the Parliament from which they are drawn but do not act on behalf of the Parliament.

The running of council business is subject to various Acts of the UK and the Scottish Parliaments. Some of the Acts relate only to local government such as the Local Government (Scotland) Act 1973 and the Local Government (Access to Information) Act 1985. Other Acts, such as the Freedom of Information (Scotland) Act 2002 and the Data Protection Act 1998 relate to public bodies generally. The former are dealt with more fully than the latter in this chapter.

THE FIRST MEETING OF THE COUNCIL

5.3   The first business of a local authority after an ordinary election is to receive the report of the Returning Officer as to the results of the elections in each of the council's wards. The council must then elect the councillor who is to be the chairman or chairwoman of the council, generally referred to as the 'convener'[1]. The council may also decide to appoint a depute convener from among the councillors.

1 For roles of convener and depute convener, see paras 3.19–3.21 at p 37 above.

5.4   Councillors will then be appointed to the various committees, boards, joint committees and joint boards and any outside bodies on which the council has representatives. Various procedural documents will have to be approved at this meeting. These include the following:

- the standing orders of the council and its committees, which set out how business is to be conducted, quorums, methods of voting etc;

- the terms of reference of each committee, which set out in broad terms the areas of council work that each committee will deal with;
- the scheme of delegated functions, which sets out the powers of the council that have been delegated to committees, sub-committees and officers of the council;
- a list of officers by whom delegated powers are exercisable;
- standing orders relating to contracts, including the submission, opening and acceptance of tenders; and
- financial regulations which will cover such things as banking arrangements, risk management, security, insurance and audit.

THE FULL COUNCIL

5.5   The full council, that is the total number of elected members meeting together, is the body in which the constitutional status of the council resides and from which any committee or sub-committee receives its status and powers, as described above. However, it would be impossible to involve all the councillors, at meetings of the full council, in every single decision which has to be made. Any attempt to do so would bring the work of the council to a grinding halt, even if the full council were to meet every single day, rather than on the four or six-weekly cycle which is common among local authorities. Some system must be adopted which will allow for the efficient conduct of business combined with the democratic accountability expected from an elected body. The most important of the council's decisions on policy issues and on finance should be taken at meetings of the full council (and, in addition, the council meetings can be used to enable members to debate matters of local (and perhaps national and international concern) in public). Some matters are specifically reserved to the full council by various Acts of Parliament and cannot lawfully be dealt with by committees, sub-committees or officers. These include the annual setting of the council tax for the local authority area and the borrowing of money[1]. Formal reports by the council's head of paid service (the Chief Executive) or by the monitoring officer[2] must also be considered by the full council [3] as must certain reports from the Scottish Public Services Ombudsman[4], the Standards Commission[5] and the Accounts Commission[6].

There are several different models of local government decision-making found in other parts of the world and, more recently, in England which are dealt with later in this chapter[7]. In Scotland, however, for over a century, councils have adopted the 'traditional' model of decision-making which is based on the committee system, although, of late there has been some experimentation with variations on the traditional model. The committee system remains the most common at present and will thus be dealt with more fully. Some councils use the term 'Board' rather than committee but both are essentially the same.

1 Local Government (Scotland) Act 1973, s 56(6).
2 The monitoring officer is a senior officer of the council whose duty is to report to the council if it appears that a proposal or decision has given rise to or is likely to give rise to an unlawful act or to maladministration or injustice.
3 Local Government and Housing Act 1989, ss 4, 5.

4 For the Scottish Public Services Ombudsman, see ch 7.
5 For the Standards Commission, see ch 7.
6 For the Accounts Commission, see ch 6.
7 For alternative forms of decision-taking, see. paras 5.18–5.23.

THE COMMITTEE SYSTEM

5.6   The committee system is provided for by the Local Government (Scotland) Act 1973[1] and in other Acts which deal with specific functions of local authorities.

Section 56 of the LG(S)A 1973 enables local authorities to arrange for the discharge of their functions (subject to the exceptions mentioned above) by a committee, a sub-committee or an officer of the authority or by any other local authority in Scotland. This is known as delegation of decision-making. The discharge of functions also includes doing anything which is calculated to facilitate or is conducive or incidental to the discharge of any of these functions.

1 The main provisions are contained in the Local Government (Scotland) Act 1973, ss 56–63.

5.7   What is not permitted is the delegation of decision-making to an individual councillor as there cannot be a committee or sub-committee consisting of only one member[1]. This prohibition hinders the establishment of a 'cabinet system' in local government whereby an individual councillor is given executive powers in relation to a specific function of the local authority, such as education, analogous to the executive powers conferred on a Secretary of State or a Scottish Minister.

The prohibition on delegation to a single councillor can cause difficulties in cases of urgency or when the council is in recess over holiday periods and in such cases power should be delegated to an officer to take decisions, subject to consultation with a member, provided that the final decision is that of the officer and not the member. An English case which illustrates this distinction is *R v Port Talbot Borough Council, ex p Jones*[2]. In this case a decision to allocate a councillor a house not in accordance with the local authority's housing policy was held to be unauthorised and unlawful because the housing officer who made the decision had been heavily influenced by the chairman of the authority's housing tenancy committee.

1 *R v Secretary of State for the Environment, ex p Hillingdon Borough Council* [1986] 1 WLR 807, CA.
2 [1988] 2 All ER 207.

5.8   Committees may further delegate decision-making to sub-committees or to officers, and sub-committees may delegate to officers. If powers are delegated to an officer, that officer should be duly designated and empowered either in the council minutes or in a separate scheme of delegation. The designated officer should not further sub-delegate decision-making to another officer (other than a designated depute) without the express authority of the council, especially if the delegated function requires the exercise of judgement or discretion and is not a purely administrative act.

Any arrangement for the delegation of decision-making made by a local authority or by a committee can be withdrawn by the local authority or by the committee at any time but it has been decided in the English courts that a council is not entitled to withdraw a committee's delegated powers retrospectively with the effect of making invalid the acts or decisions of the committee in the exercise of its powers[1].

1 *Battelly v Finsbury Borough Council* (1958) 56 LGR 165.

5.9   The Local Government (Scotland) Act 1973 also allows two or more local authorities to arrange for the joint discharge of any of their functions by setting up a joint committee, and the joint committee can delegate some of its powers to sub-committees and to officers of the constituent authorities. The constituent local authorities jointly contribute to defraying the expenses incurred by the joint committee. An example of a joint committee is the West of Scotland Joint Archaeological Committee which consists of members appointed by the twelve councils which lie within the boundaries of the former Strathclyde Regional Council and oversees the work of the West of Scotland Archaeological Service.

5.10   Much of the local government legislation passed prior to the introduction of the two-tier system by the Local Government (Scotland) Act 1973 required local authorities to appoint specific committees to deal with specific statutory functions. Examples of these were an education committee and a finance committee. This rather rigid structure tended to encourage narrow departmentalism and discourage the tackling of issues on a corporate basis, sometimes leading to less than effective overall management of the local authority. When the two-tier structure was established in 1974–75, the opportunity was taken to enable councils to adopt a more flexible committee system and the LG(S)A 1973 reduced the number of statutory committees. However, the regional and islands councils were required to establish social work and education committees. The Local Government etc (Scotland) Act 1994, which abolished the two-tier system, removed these requirements and councils now have almost total freedom as to which committee structure to adopt[1]. A council may have various 'service' committees which have responsibility for various statutory functions, such as education and social work, and 'resource' committees which deal with finance and personnel. However, the freedom as to committee structure allows for a 'cross-cutting' approach. Thus a council might decide to establish a Children's Services Committee which combines responsibility for various education and social work functions and a Culture and Leisure Committee with responsibility for libraries, museums, parks and leisure centres. Many councils will set up a Policy or Executive Committee with an overall policy co-ordination role.

1 There remain some minor statutory requirements in relation to children's panel advisory committees and committees dealing with the superannuation of local government employees.

5.11   Local authorities are also empowered to set up advisory committees and joint advisory committees which can consist of such persons as the local authorities may decide to appoint[1]. There is no requirement for any of the members of an advisory committee to be councillors.

The councils' standing orders will set out procedures for committees and sub-committees governing meeting arrangements, quorum, method of voting and so on.

1 Local Government (Scotland) Act 1973, s 57(4).

Membership of committees

5.12   There are no statutory rules in force in Scotland as to which councillors should be appointed to which committee. In England and Wales, in contrast, councils are under a duty to allocate seats on committees and sub-committees in such a way as to reflect political proportionality, as far as possible, if the members of the authority are divided into different political groups[1]. This duty could be imposed on Scottish councils if the Scottish Ministers so decided. However, the position at present is that councils have a free hand to decide the membership of their committees and sub-committees. There is nothing in law to prevent a council from appointing one-party committees but in practice councils appoint councillors on a basis that reflects roughly the political make-up of the council as a whole. The council leadership may try to take members' preferences into account in allocating seats.

1 Local Government and Housing Act 1989, s 15.

5.13   Subject to a couple of restrictions, councils are also free to appoint to their committees and sub-committees people who are not elected members[1]. These appointed members are usually known as 'co-opted' members. However, in the case of committees (not sub-committees), at least two-thirds of the members must be councillors. In addition, it is not lawful to appoint co-opted members to a committee dealing with finance, which is considered to be a function of elected members alone. Co-opted members must not, with one exception, be disqualified from membership of the council[2]. The exception is a committee which deals with the council's functions as an education authority. Councils have the power to co-opt to such a committee teachers who work in their own schools and who would otherwise be disqualified by reason of being local government employees. There is a further provision relating to such committees which restricts a local authority's freedom to appoint whomsoever it chooses to membership. Three representatives of churches and denominational bodies (not disqualified from membership of the local authority) must be appointed. One of these must be a representative of the Church of Scotland and, other than in the islands councils, one must be a representative of the Roman Catholic Church. The third – or in the case of the islands councils, the second and third – comes from other churches or denominational bodies and, in their selection, councils must have regard to the comparative strength within the local authority area of such churches and bodies. Subject to this restriction, councils may co-opt up to one-half of the membership of a committee dealing with educational matters[3].

The power to co-opt is a useful one which enables a local authority to bring into membership people with special expertise or knowledge. Thus a local authority may decide to appoint to a committee dealing with economic development representatives of such bodies as the local Chamber of Commerce or economic development agency. In the case of area committees, representatives of community councils or residents' associations may be appointed to enable local views to be expressed. Subject to some exceptions, co-opted members have the same voting rights as the elected members.

1 Local Government (Scotland) Act 1973, s 57.
2 For the various disqualifications, see ch 3.
3 Local Government etc (Scotland) Act 1994, s 31.

THE EXECUTIVE AND SCRUTINY COMMITTEE SYSTEM

5.14   The Executive and Scrutiny Committee system is a variant on the traditional committee system and the rules described above generally apply. It is partly based on a recommendation made by the McIntosh Commission[1].

There is an Executive Committee which consists of the Leader of the Council and a number of senior councillors each one of whom has political responsibility for a particular service area, such as Education, Social Work and so on. The Executive Committee will have considerable delegated powers. However, although its members may be described as Executive Members, these members do not have individual executive powers because it is not legally possible to delegate decision-making to a single member[2]. They are, however, the spokespersons, for their service areas.

There are several Scrutiny Committees, mirroring the service areas of the Executive members. These will be chaired by senior councillors. The remit of the Scrutiny Committees is to scrutinise the decisions of the Executive Committee and to hold the Executive members to account. In addition they may have roles in policy review and development and best value and performance management. Normally, Executive members should not be members of Scrutiny Committees.

Ideally, the officers who service the Scrutiny Committees should not be the same as those who service the Executive Committee, but this does not always seem to be the case in practice.

In addition, there will be a procedure for a number of councillors to "call-in" decisions of the Executive Committee within a set number of working days after the decision in question has bee taken. A minimum number of councillors' signatures will be required for a valid call-in. The call-in will be dealt with by the appropriate Scrutiny Committee. If the Scrutiny Committee agrees on a majority vote with the decision of the Executive, it can be implemented without further delay. If the Scrutiny Committee on a majority vote does not agree with the decision of the Executive, it will be referred back to the Executive Committee with recommendations for alternative action.

Alongside the Executive and Scrutiny Committees, there will be several of the traditional committees, particularly the quasi-judicial committees, which deal with planning and licensing applications, and an Audit Committee.

1 See para 5.17 below.
2 Local Government (Scotland) Act 1973, s 56.

THE ROLE OF POLITICAL GROUPS IN DECISION-MAKING

5.15   As has already been seen, the vast majority of councillors are elected on a party political basis. These councillors then form themselves into party groups, assuming there are at least two members of each party. The formation of party groups is now recognised in law for some purposes, such as the allocation of seats on committees. If more than half of the members of a council are in the same party group, that group will be the majority or controlling group and will form the administration. If there is no majority group, two or more groups may form a coalition administration or the largest group may form a minority administration.

The controlling group will probably have a smaller group, consisting of the leader and conveners of key committees, often known as 'the executive'. This should not be confused with the Executive Committee described above which is a properly constituted committee of the council. The party group executive has no legal status. The executive will meet in private to discuss policy issues and decide what recommendations to put before their party group.

Party groups will hold group meetings prior to council meetings and sometimes before committee meetings to debate their executive's recommendations and decide, after a vote if necessary, what the party line is to be on various issues. However, in the case of quasi-judicial decisions such as the granting of various licences and planning permissions, party political decisions are not generally taken and the new code of conduct now precludes this. Officers of the council such as directors of departments may be invited to advise the group members on issues but they cannot be forced to attend, as the group meeting is not a statutorily recognised council or committee meeting. The officers should leave the group meeting before the councillors take their decisions.

Once the party line on an issue is decided upon, this then becomes a 'group decision' and is considered to be binding on all the members of the group. An office-bearer of the group will be appointed as whip and it is his or her task to make sure that all group members know what the group decisions are and that they vote in accordance with them. A group member who fails to vote in accordance with group decisions will face some form of censure. In the case of a very important decision, an errant group member might even face expulsion from the group.

5.16   There are some obvious problems with this system. First, group decisions are taken in advance of the council or committee meeting and, if new information is made available to the councillors at the meeting, whipped members of a group might find themselves in something of a dilemma. If they vote against the group decision, they might find themselves in hot water with the whip; if they adhere to the group decision, in the face of the new information, they may well feel that the group decision is no longer the correct decision to take. The sensible way out of this dilemma, which maintains the unity of the party group, is to ask for the item of business to be continued, that is deferred, to a future meeting. This allows the group to review their decision in the light of the new information.

A second problem with the party group system is the lack of transparency of decision-making. Groups meet in private. Non-members of the group, except for invited officers who leave the group meeting before group decisions are taken, are generally not allowed to be present. The minutes of the group meeting are not made available to members of the public. All of this flies in the face of the various statutes which deal with the public's rights of access to information[1].

If we take the two problems together, we can see that a member of the public who attends a council or a committee meeting at which group decisions come into play may well feel that the meeting is a charade with the councillors not bothering to discuss issues of public concern and the meeting, despite a fairly lengthy agenda, being over perhaps in a matter of minutes.

1 For the public's rights of access to information, see below.

5.17   The McIntosh Commission[1] examined the role of party groups in local government and concluded that party group meetings held in private are not objectionable in themselves but that the party groups should somehow be held to account for the decisions they reach by the council as a whole. The Commission's recommendation was that the leadership group or executive should be put on a formal, open and accountable footing so that policy proposals and matters for decision by the council should be subject to open debate and the actions of the leadership group scrutinised by the council[2]. The Scottish Executive's response was to announce that all councils were to undertake a review of their organisational structures assisted by a Leadership Advisory Panel[3].

The McIntosh Commission also considered the use of the party whip. It was recognised that whipping was almost inevitable on issues of policy which had been contained in a party's manifesto but it was believed that the use of the whip had become more aggressive and unselective in recent years. Arguably this undermined accountability and reduced council and committee meetings to little more than a rubber stamp for decisions taken elsewhere in private. The Commission recognised that it would be impossible to legislate whipping out of existence. It was rather a matter for self-regulation and it was recommended that the political parties should review their practices at local level. The Commission further recommended that councils should consider adopting a rule that, where whipping was applied in council business, it should be declared at the commencement of the relevant discussion and minuted for public information and record[4].

In discussions following the publication of the McIntosh Report, many councillors felt that the Commission had overestimated the actual use of the whip and that the vast majority of council decisions were uncontentious and not dealt with in a partisan way.

1 The Report of the Commission on Local Government and the Scottish Parliament (the McIntosh Committee). See further ch 8.
2 Report of the McIntosh Commission (1999) para 103 .
3 For further discussion see ch 8.
4 McIntosh Report paras 123 and 124.

ALTERNATIVE MODELS OF DECISION-MAKING

5.18   Throughout the world, local government business is organised in a variety of ways. There are three broad models: the directly elected provost or strong mayor; the council manager; and the cabinet model[1].

1 For more information on alternative models, see The Internal Management of Local Authorities in Scotland (HMSO) (1993); Local Government Political Management Arrangements – An International Perspective (Scottish Office) (1998).

The directly-elected provost or strong mayor

5.19   Under this system there are two separate elections – one for the councillors and one for the provost or mayor. The elected provost or mayor is given substantial executive powers compared to those of the council. He or she is in effect the directly elected chief executive of the council and as a result has a high public profile. The provost's powers might include the preparation of the budget, the control of the administration of the council and the appointment of chief officers. There might also be a power to veto measures passed by the council. The council, on the other hand, would be responsible for the development of policy, the authorisation of the budget and review of the provost's performance. The council would also retain executive responsibility in certain areas.

This model is found in certain cities in the United States. New York is a good example. Mayor Guliani had an extremely high profile during his term of office, particularly in the aftermath of the terrorist attack on the Twin Towers in September 2001. Directly elected mayors are now to be found in England, the first being Ken Livingstone who was directly elected as the Mayor of the Greater London Authority in 2000 and re-elected in 2004. He was defeated by Boris Johnson in 2008.

Unfortunately this system of direct election of provost or mayor can have some unforeseen results: in Hartlepool, an English local authority, a person who campaigned dressed in a monkey suit, promising free bananas to the voters, was elected as mayor in 2002.

The council manager

5.20   Under this system an officer entitled 'council manager' is appointed by the council. The discharge of functions is not delegated to the council manager as in the traditional system. He or she has a statutorily defined executive role which is completely separate from the role of the council. Decisions taken by or on behalf of the council manager cannot be overruled by the council. The council retains overall policy responsibility but has little involvement in day-to-day decision-making. That is left to the council manager.

There are several variants of this model. In one form or another it is found in Ireland, New Zealand and the United States.

The cabinet model

5.21   Under this system a cabinet is established within a local authority comprised of around ten of the leading elected members of the controlling group or groups. Each member holds an individual portfolio, such as education, social work, finance or economic development, or possibly cross-cutting each cabinet.

Overview or scrutiny committees draft their own work programmes which can include holding the cabinet to account through call-in procedures, policy development and review, and examining areas of wider concern.

Under this model, the role of the council is to consider the council's budget and policy framework. It can also allocate time for cabinet members to report and take questions, receive public petitions and have a public question time.

5.22   To establish these in Scotland would require new legislation in the case of the first two, while the cabinet model would require amendments to existing legislation because, as seen above, it is not possible to delegate decision-making to a single councillor.

Recent developments

5.23   In England and Wales, central government has been quite prescriptive as to how councils should organise their business[1]. All but the smallest must opt for either:

- an elected mayor and cabinet executive;
- a leader and cabinet executive; or
- a mayor and council manager.

The Scottish Executive, in contrast, has not been prescriptive as to how Scottish councils should organise their business. After the review required by the Scottish Executive, most councils continued to operate under the committee system. More recently a number have chosen to move to a formalised executive structure and separate scrutiny function as recommended by McIntosh[2]. That, however, is no more than a variant of the committee system.

Experience in England shows that there are some problems with the formalised executive and scrutiny committee model and these are beginning to manifest themselves in Scotland. Decision-making is centralised in the hands of the small group of councillors who form the executive. Councillors perceive themselves as divided into two classes: the executive who are 'information-rich' and the backbenchers who are 'information-poor'. Backbenchers may feel that they do not have as a useful role as they enjoyed under the traditional committee system. In addition, party political ties may make some members of the scrutiny body reluctant to criticise their colleagues in public, whereas they would have had no compunction about doing so at a private group meeting.

In addition, the role of officers may be changed: in those councils where, instead of all officers serving the council as a whole, there is a corps of officers who serve the executive and another corps who serve the scrutiny body.

For the time being, however, the Scottish Government seems to be content to leave councils to choose their own organisational model.

1 Local Government Act 2000 Pt II.
2 See above para 5.14.

ALTERNATIVE FORMS OF SERVICE DELIVERY

Arms Length External Organisations (ALEOs)

5.24   Councils may decide, for various reasons, to use external bodies rather than the traditional council committees and departments to deliver certain services.

This is not a new concept and has existed in some form or another for a long time. Some departments, such as Social Work and Housing have provided grants to voluntary organisations to enable them to provide services for many years. Other departments fund economic development bodies, cultural and leisure organisations, environmental services and so on.

These local authority funded organisations are generally known as Arms Length External Organisations (ALEOs).

In 2005 Audit Scotland reported on a review of ALEOs in Scotland[1].

The review found that councils provided £220 million to 14,000 ALEOS in Scotland. However, over three-quarters of the grants were for less than £10,000 and, provided that there are proper financial controls, these are not normally problematic.

1 Following the Public Pound: A Follow-up Report, 2005. See also Code of Guidance on Funding External Bodies and Following the Public Pound, Cosla and the Accounts Commission, 1996.

5.25   More than half of the ALEOs are voluntary or community organisations. However, as councils explore alternative ways of delivering services, the types of ALEOs have become increasingly diverse, and new forms of ALEOs have sprung up such as companies, limited liability partnerships, joint ventures and trusts with charitable status. These ALEOs differ from the traditional model in that, although they are legal entities in their own right, with their own constitutions and aims, they are often wholly owned subsidiaries of the council with the majority of board members being councillors. Others may be owned with other public bodies or with the private sector and elected members may not be in the majority on the Board. Some are subject to company law and/or charity law and members thus may have conflicting responsibilities. These ALEOs often receive large amounts of public money and provide extensive services. This can raise issues of accountability and governance.

Examples include the Archaeolink Trust established by Aberdeenshire Council to run an outdoor "pre-historic" park with councillors as trustees; Edinburgh Leisure, a non-profit-distributing company which manages sport and leisure facilities for Edinburgh City Council; City Building (Glasgow), a Limited

Liability Partnership which not only carries out work previously done by Glasgow's Building Department, but bids for work from other bodies. An example of an ALEO with two partners is Glasgow Community Safety Services, a company limited by guarantee with charitable status whose membership consists of Glasgow City Council and Strathclyde Police. Probably the largest ALEO in Scotland is Culture and Sport Glasgow Ltd which receives an annual service payment from Glasgow City Council in the region of £70m.

In the case of ALEOs which are wholly owned by councils or on which a council has majority control it can be argued that the ALEO itself is a procuring authority under the European Procurement Rules and subject to much of the same regulatory legislation as the various councils themselves such as Freedom of Information (FOI). This also means that the ALEO is able (though not bound) to utilise council support services (such as human resources and payroll) and that the council can contract with the ALEO for the services that it provides without having to procure those services on the open market.

Regardless of representation on Boards, councils should ensure that the ALEOs they fund, are subject to regular and proper scrutiny, performance and financial monitoring and that proper governance arrangements in place. Examples of this would be Standing Orders in relation to contracts and decision making, a FOI publication scheme, and a procurement manual to ensure compliance with relevant legislation. As an independent entity it may also be the case that the ALEO will have to submit accounts and annual returns to Companies House or to the Office of the Scottish Charities Regulator (OSCR). It should also be noted that these ALEOs are also accountable to their members or shareholders. For example, where a council is the controlling member of an ALEO it is important that councillors who are not members of the ALEO Board are kept as fully informed of its activities through the agreed governance reporting framework. The Code of Guidance for ALEOs is discussed in Chapter 6[1].

1 See para 6.44.

Community Health and Care Partnerships

5.26   Community Health and Care Partnerships (CHCPs) are a relatively new service delivery model and consist of joint organisations run by the National Health Service in Scotland and local authorities to deliver health and social services more effectively at a local level. The NHS can set up CHCPs under the National Health Service Reform (Scotland) Act 2004.

CHCPs require the NHS to work in partnership with the local authorities to ensure that health and social work services are delivered at a community level. .An integrated approach between the various agencies involved is designed to improve health and social care in the various CHCP areas.

The process for the set up CHCPs, their membership and scheme of establishment are contained in The Community Health Partnership (Scotland) Regulations 2004. These regulations contain guidance on the formation of a

CHCP, which must be approved by the Scottish Government. The scheme must set out the following:

- The geographic area and population;
- The services which the CHCP will coordinate;
- The functions of the CHCP;
- The membership of the CHCP;
- How the CHCP will relate to the public, local authorities voluntary organisations and the NHS Board.

Each CHCP has a Director who is responsible for the delivery of the statutory functions of the NHS primary care for the CHCP area. Each Director will be responsible for the management of the CHCP, including its devolved budget. The Director will be accountable to the NHS Board through the CHCP Committee, a formal sub-committee of the Board. The CHCP will also be monitored by its local authority partner through its committee structure.

In addition to this each CHCP will be required to have its own governance framework and procedures.

Community Justice Authorities

5.27   Community Justice Authorities (CJAs) were established under the Management of Offenders etc (Scotland) Act 2005 to prepare strategic area plans to reduce re-offending; monitor the performance of local authorities and their statutory partners who co-ordinate offender services; promote best practice and allocate resources to local authority criminal justice social work services. There are 8 CJAs in Scotland. They report to the Scottish Ministers. The CJA members are appointed by the local authorities within its area and the Chief Officer, whilst appointed by the CJA, is accountable to the Scottish Ministers.

INVOLVING THE PUBLIC

5.28   The raison d'etre of local government is to provide, directly or indirectly, a wide range of services to the local population and to act as the voice of the people. The councillors are elected by local people and are their representatives.

However, councils will want to involve local people in the work of the authority in a variety of ways and, in some cases, may be required to do so by statute. For example, if a local authority proposes to make a byelaw or a set of management rules, the proposal must be advertised in a local newspaper. Proposals to make traffic regulation and other types of orders must also be advertised. Community councils must be consulted about planning applications and have the right to object to applications to the Licensing Board to sell alcohol. Proposals involving school closures and other issues relating to school catchment areas must be the subject of consultation.

Most councils will go beyond their statutory duties to involve the public. Councils may carry out council-wide consultations in an attempt to gauge public opinion on controversial issues, such as the consultation carried out by Glasgow City Council in 2004 on public processions (mainly Orange Walks) and demonstrations. Consultation may also be carried out on proposals contained in a council's proposed annual budget. Occasionally, councils will carry out referendums such as the referendum carried out by the former Strathclyde Regional Council on the government's proposals in the 1990s to remove the provision of water and sewerage services from local government control.

Some councils make use of Citizens' Panels or Juries which involve a representative group of members of the public, as large as one thousand, providing feedback on a range of issues such as the level of satisfaction with various council services, perceptions of the role of councillors, satisfaction with neighbourhoods and key priorities for the local authority area. Organisations such as MORI may be asked to carry out opinion polls on similar issues. Council newspapers and other publications will be used to keep citizens informed of current developments. Increasing use is made of information technology and all Scottish councils have their own websites with interactive facilities.

Most councillors hold regular surgeries in their wards. There is no legal requirement to do so, although the political parties may make the holding of surgeries a condition of re-selection as a candidate. Surgeries can be useful in gauging opinion at a very local level on an issue such as the re-routing of buses or accident hotspots.

Members of the public may also be co-opted onto certain committees, including area committees set up under the statutory decentralisation schemes which councils must make[1].

1 See ch 2.

ACCESS TO MEETINGS AND INFORMATION

5.29   The press have had access to local authority meetings since 1908[1], but it was not until 1960 that access was widened to include the public more generally when Margaret Thatcher introduced a Private Member's Bill which became the Public Bodies (Admission to Meetings) Act 1960. This Act initially applied only to full council meetings and to education committees and was extended by the Local Government (Scotland) Act 1973 to apply to all committee meetings of a local authority, but not to sub-committees. These provisions for access to meetings were not, however, particularly generous to the public.

In 1985, another MP, this time a Liberal, Robin Squire, brought forward a Private Member's Bill which became the Local Government (Access to Information) Act) 1985. This Act amended the LG(S)A 1973 by adding new sections 50A–50K and a new Schedule 7A[2].

1 Local Authorities (Admission of the Press to Meetings) Act 1908.
2 See further ch 3, para 3.33.

5.30   The first general principle is that notice must be given to the public of the time and place of all meetings of a local authority (including committees and sub-committees) by being posted at the offices of the council normally at least three clear days beforehand. The second general principle is that all meetings of the council, including committee and sub-committee meetings, must be open to the public, except in specific circumstances. When the meeting is being held in public, members of the public must not be excluded except to prevent disorderly conduct or other misbehaviour. In addition, accredited representatives of the press (newspapers, news agencies, radio and television) must, so far as is practicable, be given reasonable facilities for compiling reports and for making telephone calls back to their offices at their own expense. There is nothing in the legislation which requires the council to allow photographs to be taken or to permit the recording or live broadcasting of the proceedings of meetings. However, councillors rarely object to being photographed, filmed or recorded and permission is usually given. Some councils make use of modern technology to webcast meetings.

5.31   The council may resolve to exclude members of the public (including the press) from a meeting during items of business when it is likely, in view of the business to be transacted or the nature of the proceedings, that, if the public were present, there would be disclosure to them of what is called 'exempt information'. The various categories of 'exempt information' are to be found in Schedule 7A of the Local Government (Scotland) Act 1973 and include information relating to individual employees, tenants, clients; information relating to local authority contracts; the prevention or investigation of crime; information relating to the care, adoption, fostering or education of any individual child; information which would reveal that a local authority is proposing to issue a statutory notice. If a local authority resolves to exclude the public from a council or committee meeting, the resolution must identify the proceedings, or the part of the proceedings, to which it applies and the description of the exempt information giving rise to the exclusion. When there are items on an agenda which involve exempt information, the business is usually ordered so that these items are grouped at the end of the agenda to avoid the inconvenience to the public of excluding them and then bringing them back into the meeting.

5.32   There is no appeal against a local authority's decision to exclude the public. The only way to challenge such a decision is by way of judicial review in the Court of Session[1].

The exclusion of the public described above is at the discretion of the local authority. However, there are circumstances where the local authority *must* exclude the public from meetings. These are when there are items on the agenda where it is likely that if the public were present confidential information would be disclosed to them in breach of an obligation of confidence. 'Confidential information' is defined[2] as information furnished to the local authority by a government department on terms forbidding its disclosure to the public, and information the disclosure of which to the public is prohibited by or under any enactment or by a court order.

1 For judicial review of local authority decisions, see ch 7.
2 Local Government (Scotland) Act 1973, s 50A.

5.33 Admission to meetings of a local authority and its committees and sub-committees is not particularly useful to members of the public if they do not have information to enable them to understand what is actually going on. The Local Government (Access to Information) Act 1985 improved the public's rights to information by setting out in detail the documents which must be made available to them before, during and after meetings.

Papers which members of the public are entitled to have access to prior to a meeting are agendas, reports for the meeting and background papers for reports. An agenda is not defined in the legislation but is generally understood to be a numbered list of the items of business to be considered at a meeting. Neither is a report defined but it is taken to mean a paper written by an officer which explains the background to an item of business and may contain recommendations to the members. Background papers for a report are defined as documents relating to the subject matter of a report which disclose facts or matters on which, in the opinion of the proper officer, a report or an important part of it is based and have been relied on to a material extent in preparing the report but do not contain any published works.

Agendas and reports must be made available for inspection at least three clear days before the meeting, unless the meeting has been convened at short notice in which case they must be open to inspection from the time the meeting is convened. It is lawful to exclude any reports or parts of reports which, in the opinion of the proper officer are likely to be considered when the public has been excluded from the meeting. No item of business can be considered at a meeting unless the agenda including the item has been open to inspection by the public for at least three days (or shorter period if the meeting was convened at short notice). However, if the convener of the meeting is of the opinion that an item should be considered as a matter of urgency, he or she may so rule and the reason for the special circumstances should be specified in the minutes of the meeting.

The local authority must also make available for inspection copies of a list of the background papers for the report and at least one copy of each of the documents. All of the documents which the public have the right to inspect prior to a meeting must be available at the offices of the authority, at all reasonable hours, free of charge except that a reasonable fee may be charged for inspection of background papers. Members of the public can make copies of the documents or request photocopies on payment of a reasonable fee. Members of the press have enhanced rights of access. They can request that copies of agendas, reports and various other documents be supplied to them on payment of the postage or any other necessary charge for transmission.

It is a criminal offence to obstruct a person exercising the right to inspect or copy documents and to refuse to make photocopies available.

5.34 Members of the public may wish to attend meetings of a local authority or its committees or sub-committees and, of course, have the right to do so, subject to the exceptions mentioned above. To make the business more comprehensible, a reasonable number of agendas and reports must be made available in the meeting room for members of the public.

A problem for members of the public is that committee and sub-committee meetings tend to be held with members and officers sitting round a large table while the seats for the public are ranged along the walls, thus making it difficult to hear what is going on or to see any plans or models which may be set out on the table. Councils are making increasing use of microphones, overhead projectors, PowerPoint and other electronic devices to aid public understanding of proceedings.

5.35   The public also have rights to inspect various documents after meetings are over. For a period of six years from the date of each meeting, there must be kept available for inspection a copy of the minutes of the meeting, the agenda and any reports supplied to the councillors.

FREEDOM OF INFORMATION (SCOTLAND) ACT 2002

5.36   The Freedom of Information (Scotland) Act 2002, which came into full force in 2005, vastly increased the public's right to information. The Act gives a general statutory right of access to all types of recorded information held by Scottish public authorities, and Scottish local authorities are covered by the Act. Subject to certain conditions and exemptions, anyone who makes a request for information in a form which can be referred to subsequently for reference, such as by letter or by email, will be entitled to receive it. The FOI(S)A 2002 is retrospective, applying to information of any age. An independent Scottish Information Commissioner has been appointed to promote and enforce the Act.

5.37   Each public authority is required to adopt and maintain a publication scheme, which must be approved by the Commissioner. The scheme should set out:

- the classes of information the authority publishes;
- the manner in which the information is published; and
- details of any charges.

The FIO(S)A 2002 requires an authority to have regard to the public interest in allowing access to the information it holds about the following:

- the provision, cost and standard of service provision;
- factual information or analysis informing decision-making; and
- the reasons for its decisions.

5.38   A request must satisfy certain conditions. It must be in a form capable of being used for subsequent reference and must include sufficient information to enable the authority to identify the information requested. Authorities will not have to comply with vexatious or repeated requests. They do, however, have to explain to the applicant why they consider the request to be vexatious or repeated[1].

Authorities must respond to requests within 20 working days and a fee may be charged.

Some types of information may be regarded as exempt. Exemptions fall into two classes: 'absolute exemptions' where the authority has an absolute right not to release the information; and 'discretionary exemptions' where the authority has to carry out a balancing exercise, weighing up the public interest in disclosing the information against the public interest in not disclosing it. For certain exemptions, an authority must also consider whether the release of information would prejudice substantially the purpose to which the exemption relates. So, in relation to law enforcement, the question to be considered is whether the release of information would prejudice substantially the prevention or detection of crime. This is known as the 'harm test'.

1 It must be the request which is repeated or vexatious, not the requestor!

5.39   A request from an individual for information about himself or herself is exempt under the Freedom of Information (Scotland) Act 2002 and is handled under the Data Protection Act 1998 (see below).

5.40   A person who is dissatisfied with the way an authority has dealt with a request for information may seek an internal review and thereafter may apply to the Scottish Information Commissioner for a decision. The Commissioner has the power to serve an enforcement notice on an authority if he is satisfied that the authority has failed to comply with the FI(S)A 2002.

Both applicants and public authorities can appeal, on a point of law only, to the Court of Session against certain decisions of the Commissioner[1].

1 The Commissioner's website is to be found at www.itspublicknowledge.info

THE DATA PROTECTION ACT 1998

5.41   The Data Protection Act 1998 (and regulations made under it) create a complex but self-contained set of rules covering all aspects of the use of personal information by organisations and confer a number of rights on the individuals whose information is being processed.

Some of the aspects of the Act which relate to local government, are dealt with here very briefly.

The DPA 1998 gives individuals an enforceable right, with very few exceptions, to see information which a council holds on them. Each council is a data controller in terms of the Act and must abide by the data protection principles in processing personal data. Processing must be fair and lawful and most data processing by councils will be covered by the condition that the process is necessary for the exercise of its statutory and public functions. In the handling of sensitive personal data, a council will generally be covered by the condition that the processing is necessary for the exercise of its statutory functions. It could be argued, however, that much of the processing carried out by councils is to improve service delivery and is not technically 'necessary'. In such cases, the consent of the individual should be obtained. Any processing, ie acquisition, use, storage, disclosure etc, of personal data must comply with the data protection principles or else fall into one of the small number of areas where processing is exempt from all or some of the requirements.

5.42   Councillors are legally distinct from the council except when at meetings of the council, its committees and its sub-committees. Disclosure of personal data to councillors, other than at meetings, counts as disclosure to a third party and has to be justified in relation to the principles and conditions set out under the Data Protection Act 1998. However, if a council receives a communication from a councillor or other elected member following a query from a constituent on whom data is held (a data subject), disclosure of personal data will generally be justified to the extent that it is necessary to respond to the inquiry. If the councillor is following up an inquiry from someone other than the data subject, disclosure is justified only where the data subject cannot give consent; where the council could not reasonably be expected to seek consent; where seeking consent would prejudice the action the elected member wishes to take; or where disclosure is necessary in the interests of someone else and consent has been unreasonably withheld.

5.43   Everyone has the right to see the information held which relates to him or her. A response to a request must be made within 40 days of receiving proof of a person's identity and a maximum fee of £10 may be levied. There is a very limited number of grounds on which a council can refuse to provide personal data in response to such a request.

If an individual's personal data contain references to a third party, these should not be disclosed without the consent of the third party.

5.44   Data protection is a reserved matter and responsibility for enforcement lies with the UK Information Commissioner[1].

1 The Commissioner's website can be found at www.ico.gov.uk

THE HUMAN RIGHTS ACT 1998

5.45   The Human Rights Act 1998, which came into force in the United Kingdom in 2000, places all public authorities, including councils, under a duty to avoid acting in a way which is incompatible with Convention rights. Anyone who alleges that a public authority has violated his or her Convention rights may raise an action against the authority in the domestic courts. All legislation, past and future, must be read so far as it is possible to do so in a way which is compatible with Convention rights. This can mean that what was previously regarded as settled law, except for Acts of the UK Parliament[1], may be susceptible to fresh challenges.

The main Convention rights which impact on local government are as follows:

- **Article 6: the right to a fair trial**. In the determination of civil rights and obligations or of any criminal charge, everyone is entitled to a fair and public hearing within a reasonable time by an independent and impartial tribunal established by law. The reference to civil rights means that article 6 applies for example, to the procedures of Licensing Boards and committees dealing with planning applications, and Education Appeals Committees.

- **Article 8: the right to respect for private and family life, home and correspondence**. A wide range of local government activities can impinge on this right from the fostering and adoption of children to the eviction of tenants of council property. There may also be a breach of human rights if a local authority fails to take enforcement action against a third party whose anti-social behaviour is interfering with a neighbour's privacy. Covert surveillance carried out by benefit fraud teams and trading standards officers has its own set of rules under the Regulation of Investigatory Powers Acts 2000 to ensure that Article 8 infringements are lawful.

- **Article 11: the right to freedom of peaceful assembly and association**. This right covers the right to march or demonstrate in the streets and to form and join trade unions. The Loyal Orange Order invoked this right when Aberdeen City Council sought to ban an Orange march in the city[2].

- **Article 14: the prohibition of discrimination in the enjoyment of the rights and freedoms contained in the Convention**. It is not discrimination per se which is prohibited, but discrimination in relation to another right under the Convention. Thus discrimination against travelling people by preventing them from having a site where they can park their caravans would involve article 8 as well as article 14.

- **First protocol, article 1: right to the peaceful enjoyment of possessions**. This article includes, but is wider than, the protection of property. It impinges upon council activities which involve compulsory purchase, charging orders and debt collection and covers such things as the impact of a bad neighbour development on people in the surrounding area. Protected property includes liquor and other licences and planning permissions.

Prior to the Human Rights Act 1998 coming into force, Scottish local authorities conducted audits of all council activities to identify areas where they might be vulnerable to challenge and to improve procedures to make them compliant with Convention rights. Best practice in this area was shared across Scotland and beyond. Possibly as a result, there have been few successful cases against Scottish local authorities.

1 In the UK constitution, Acts of the UK Parliament are supreme and cannot be struck down by the courts.
2 *Aberdeen Bon-Accord Loyal Orange Lodge 701 v Aberdeen City Council* 2002 SLT (Sh Ct) 52. See also *Wishart Arch Defenders Loyal Orange Lodge 404 v Angus Council* 2002 SLT (Sh Ct) 43 for a successful challenge under article 6.

LOCAL GOVERNMENT STAFF

5.46   Almost a quarter of a million people work in local government in Scotland and the council is in many cases the major employer in the area. The

Local Government (Scotland) Act 1973 enables local authorities to appoint such officers as they think necessary for the proper discharge of their functions on such reasonable terms and conditions as the authority thinks fit[1]. All appointments must be made on merit. Chief officer appointments must be approved by the full council. Ex-councillors cannot be appointed as officers of their council until three months have elapsed since they ceased to be councillors[2].

In the past, councils had to appoint certain named chief officers such as a town or county clerk, a director of education and a director of social work. Most of these requirements have been removed over the years and local authorities now have considerable freedom in the appointment of chief officers. Those who must still be appointed are electoral registration officers and assessors (a combined post), public analysts and chief social work officers, registrars of births, marriages and deaths, chief constables and firemasters. There must also be an officer designated as head of paid service (usually called 'the Chief Executive'), a monitoring officer[3] and an officer responsible for the proper administration of financial affairs.

Powers are delegated to officers by the council and the scheme of delegation should be approved by the council at the first meeting following the election. Local authorities must maintain a list, open to public inspection, of the powers which are being exercised by officers, including the title of the relevant officer and the period for which the powers are exercisable.

1 Local Government (Scotland) Act 1973, s 64. The staff of local authorities are usually referred to as 'officers'.
2 This period has been reduced from 12 months, except in the case of ex-councillors who were either involved in appointments to politically restricted posts or who apply to be appointed to such posts: Local Governance (Scotland) Act 2004, s 10.
3 It is the duty of the monitoring officer to prepare a report for the council if it appears to him or her that the council, a committee, sub-committee or an officer is likely to contravene the law or give rise to maladministration or injustice.

5.47   There are rules regarding conflicts of interests. If it comes to the notice of an officer that he or she has a financial interest, direct or indirect, in a contract which has been or is about to be entered into by the local authority, that interest should be declared in writing as soon as possible. An officer must not, under colour of his or her office or employment, accept any fee or reward other than the proper remuneration. Although breach of these rules is a criminal offence, the rules relating to conduct of officers are considerably weaker than the rules which apply to councillors under the Ethical Standards in Public Life etc (Scotland) Act 2000[1].

1 See chs 3 and 7.

5.48   Officers serve the council as a whole and the task of senior officers is to give advice to councillors, the council and its committees. Traditionally, they are expected to be politically neutral, serving whichever party may be in political control. In the 1980s, however, the Conservative government became concerned that local government officers were losing their neutrality, becoming overtly party political and expressing views which were in direct opposition to government policies. They were also concerned about 'twin-tracking', the practice (relatively uncommon in Scotland) whereby the holder of a senior post in one local authority was a senior elected member of another local authority. The government established the Committee of Inquiry into the Conduct of Local Authority Business, chaired by David Widdicombe QC. Its report led to the Local Government and Housing Act 1989 and the introduction of politically restricted posts and restrictions on party political activity by officers.

5.49   The Local Government and Housing Act 1989 disqualifies certain people from becoming or remaining a councillor in any local authority in Great Britain[1]. This restriction includes chief officers and deputes and officers whose posts are listed on statutorily required lists including officers to whom statutory powers have been specifically delegated and (until recently) officers who hold posts which attract a salary of £31,536 or more per annum[2].

This last category caught a very large number of employees as the salary threshold is quite low in local government terms. As political restriction applies to election to any local authority in Great Britain, it means that employees who live in one local authority area and work in another are unable to be councillors in their own local communities. Not only that, a holder of a politically restricted post is banned from engaging in various forms of political activity such as holding office in a political party, canvassing at election and even writing to newspapers in such a way as to affect support for a political party.

A case was brought before the European Court of Human Rights, in which the restriction of senior employees was challenged as a breach of their human rights under article 10 of the European Convention on Human Rights and Fundamental Freedoms which guarantees freedom of expression[3]. However, the Court found that the restrictions were not in breach of the European Convention on Human Rights. Rather, the restrictions pursued the legitimate aim of protecting the rights of others (council members and the electorate) to effective political democracy at local level.

The local government trade unions continued to lobby on the issue of politically restricted posts and the Scottish Executive consulted on this issue. There was general support for removing the disqualification based on a salary threshold and the Local Governance (Scotland) Act 2004[4] removed such posts from the politically restricted category, thus allowing such post holders to take part in political activities and those with an appropriate local connection to stand for election.

1 Local Government and Housing Act 1989, ss 1–3. See also ch 3, para 3.11. These officers are also disqualified from membership of the House of Commons, the Scottish Parliament and the European Parliament.
2 £31,536 was the figure in 2003. It is based on spinal column point 44 in the local government salary scale and the amount rises automatically when a salary increase is applied.
3 *Ahmed v United Kingdom* [1998] HRCD 823, ECtHR.
4 Local Governance (Scotland) Act 2004, s 9.

CORPORATE GOVERNANCE

5.50   The term corporate governance came into common use in the UK in a company context following the publication of the Cadbury Report in 1992[1].

Cadbury defined corporate governance as 'the system by which organisations are directed and controlled'; it was restricted to the control and reporting functions of PLC boards.

Early work on corporate governance in public services took Cadbury as a starting point. Work on conduct in public life was taken forward by the Nolan Committee on Standards in Public Life[2].

The Chartered Institute of Public Finance and Accountancy (CIPFA) and the Society of Local Authority Chief Executives and Senior Managers (SOLACE) have developed the work of Cadbury and Nolan and drawn up a single framework of corporate governance for use in local authorities[3].

The principles which they identified as underpinning good governance are as follows.

- **Openness and inclusivity**. Openness is required to ensure that stakeholders[4] can have confidence in the decision-making and management processes of local authorities and of the individuals within them. Openness involves genuine consultation and access to full, accurate and clear information. Openness requires inclusivity, seeking to ensure all stakeholders have the opportunity to engage effectively with the decision-making processes and actions of local authorities.
- **Integrity**. This is defined as straightforwardness and completeness, based on high standards of propriety and probity in the stewardship of public funds and management of a local authority's affairs. It is dependent on an effective control framework and the personal standards and professionalism of the elected members and staff.
- **Accountability**. This is defined as the process whereby local authorities are responsible for their decisions and actions and submit themselves to appropriate external scrutiny.

The principle of **leadership** is said to overarch these principles, exercised through the local authority providing vision for its community and leading by example in all its processes and actions.

This Framework was revised in 2007[5]. It is intended to be followed as best practice for developing and maintaining a local code of governance and making adopted practices open and explicit. In addition CIPFA have issued a Code of Practice for local authorities[6] requiring annual assurance statements on internal financial control and governance arrangements. This statement will encompass not only Council departments but also any Arms Length External Organisations (ALEOs) which sit within the group accounts of local authorities. The statement should include:

- a description of the role of internal audit;
- the details of the reviews undertaken to inform the assessment of the effectiveness and operation of financial control; and
- an explanation of identified weaknesses and planned remedial actions.

Although there is no statutory requirement to do so, it is expected that local authorities will approve and adopt a code of corporate governance consistent with these principles and make it available for public inspection.

1 Report of the Committee on the Financial Aspects of Corporate Governance (1992).
2 See ch 7.
3 CIPFA and SOLACE Guidance Note for Scottish Authorities Corporate Governance in Local Government: A Keystone for Community Governance (2001).
4 Stakeholders are defined as the local electorate; local businesses; service users; other public bodies; resource providers; employees; voluntary organisations and the wider community.
5 CIPFA and SOLACE Delivering Good Governance in Local Government 2007.
6 CIPFA Code of Practice on Local Authority Accounting in the United Kingdom 2008: A Statement of Recommended Practice.

Chapter 6

Financial matters[1]

INTRODUCTION

6.1   Local government expenditure is a major element of public spending, accounting for approximately one-third of the total in Scotland. Scottish Executive Government funding accounts for around 80 per cent of local government's net revenue funding and only about 20 per cent is contributed by the council tax-payer.

The rules relating to local government finance are rather complex and what is offered here is a very brief and somewhat simplified account. Readers who wish more detail on any aspect are referred to the publications of the Chartered Institute of Public Finance and Accountancy[2].

The financial management of local authorities is recognised in the Local Government (Scotland) Act 1973. Section 95 specifies that every local authority must make arrangements for the proper administration of its financial affairs and secure that the proper officer has responsibility for the administration of those affairs. The 'proper officer' usually has the title of Director of Finance[3] and each local authority will have a committee of elected members to which the chief finance officer reports, which may be known as the Finance Committee or perhaps the Policy and Resources Committee or Executive Committee. The Director of Finance is a key officer in a local authority and will usually be a senior member of the authority's management team.

1 The author acknowledges the assistance of the Chartered Institute of Public Finance and Accountancy (CIPFA) and of Lynn Brown, Executive Director of Finance in Glasgow City Council and her Depute, Morag Johnston in compiling this chapter.
2 For example, the Guide to Local Government Finance in Scotland. Further information can be obtained from www.cipfascotland.org.uk.
3 The title of Treasurer for the chief financial officer is common in joint boards whereas in some councils the title of Treasurer is given to the councillor who chairs the committee which deals with finance.

LOCAL GOVERNMENT FINANCE – A BRIEF GUIDE

Revenue and capital expenditure

6.2   Local government expenditure can be divided into revenue expenditure and capital expenditure. Revenue expenditure tends to be recurring expenditure, its benefits consumed over a short period. Broadly it covers the annual costs of delivering local government services. Typical examples of revenue expenditure are employee wages and salaries, telephone, postal and heating bills and office supplies. Scottish local authorities incur revenue expenditure of around £11,000 million per annum, which works out at about £2,150 per head of population. Education is the largest area of revenue expenditure at about £4,400m per annum, made up of teachers' and other salaries and various school supplies such as textbooks and jotters. Local authorities incur a further £1,000m expenditure per annum on council housing which is raised from rents[1].

1 The figures given relate to 2007–8.

6.3   Capital expenditure creates a new asset or increases the value of an existing asset, the useful economic life of which is greater than one year. Examples of capital expenditure are the construction of a new school or the refurbishment of a museum. Scottish local authorities incur capital expenditure of around £2,200m per annum. Key areas of capital expenditure are housing, education, roads and transport. Until recently, local authorities could not incur capital expenditure without the consent of the Scottish Ministers. This control was generally known as 'section 94 consent' as ministerial powers of control were contained in section 94 of the Local Government (Scotland) Act 1973 and regulations issued under that section. Section 94 was, however, repealed by the Local Government in Scotland Act 2003 (LGSA 2003) and replaced by a duty on a local authority to determine and keep under review the maximum amount which it can afford to allocate to capital expenditure[1]. However, local authorities do not have total freedom over capital expenditure and have to comply with various regulations made by the Scottish Ministers. In particular they have to comply with what is known as the Prudential Code for Capital Finance in Local Authorities, devised by the Chartered Institute of Public Finance and Accountancy[2].

Local authorities can increase their capital expenditure by using capital receipts from the sale of assets such as land owned by the authority and by making contributions to the capital account from the revenue account. They are also able to use private money to finance major capital projects, using what is known as a Public Private Partnership (PPP).

Local authorities must keep separate revenue and capital expenditure accounts but there is a clear relationship between the two. So if a local authority decides to build a new library (which will be classified as capital expenditure), it must provide the revenue expenditure to pay the salaries of the librarians and other staff, to pay the bills for heating and lighting the building and to buy the books and other equipment. In addition the costs of repaying the money borrowed to finance the construction of the library (plus interest) are charged as revenue expenditure.

1 Local Government in Scotland Act 2003, s 35.
2 Local Government Capital Expenditure Limits (Scotland) Regulations 2004, SSI 2004/29.

Where the money comes from – revenue

6.4   To meet their revenue expenditure, local authorities must have income and all income and expenditure (with the exception of income and expenditure on council housing) accounted for through an account called the General Fund.

The main sources of income are:

- Revenue Support Grant from the Scottish Government;
- Ring-Fenced Grants also from the Scottish Government;
- Non-domestic rates;

(The three entries above are collectively referred to as Aggregate External Finance or AEF)

- Fees and charges;
- Council tax.

Each year in December, the First Minister announces the level of Government Supported Expenditure (GSE) and the level of Aggregate External Finance.

Government Supported Expenditure

6.5 Government Supported Expenditure is the level of resources which the Scottish Executive considers that local authorities require in order to incur expenditure on delivering services and paying back loan and leasing charges. The amount for paying back loan and leasing charges is 'top-sliced' from the level of GSE. What is left is known as Grant Aided Expenditure (GAE) and Grant Aided Expenditure figures are used as the basis for deciding Aggregate External Finance. Grant Aided Expenditure figures are then further refined into GAEs for each local authority service (for example, education) and for sub-services (for example, secondary school teachers). The GAE for each local authority is then worked out. This is the amount that the Scottish Executive considers each local authority requires to spend on the provision of services. This does not necessarily reflect a local authority's real need to spend nor is it the budget for a local authority. Rather it is the Scottish Executive's assessment of a local authority's relative need to spend compared with the other local authorities in Scotland, such that the level of council tax would be the same throughout Scotland.

Aggregate External Finance

6.6 As mentioned above, Aggregate External Finance is made up of Revenue Support Grant (the largest element), Ring-Fenced Grant and Non–Domestic Rates Income. Revenue Support Grant is calculated after account has been taken of Ring-Fenced Grant and Non-Domestic Rates Income and so will be dealt with last.

Ring-Fenced Grant, as the name suggests, is made up of grants which are for a specific named purpose or which are intended to achieve a specific policy objective and are normally linked directly to actual expenditure. Examples of these are the Fairer Scotland Fund to fund social regeneration projects in the most deprived areas and funding to promote the Gaelic language. The total annual amount of Ring-Fenced Grants is around £760m which is about 8 per cent of the total AEF. The largest single grant is that for policing in Scotland (around £580m per annum) which finances 51 per cent of expenditure on policing (this position has changed due to how the funding of Police Pensions was treated in 2008–09 but it has not moved greatly).

Ring-Fenced Grants are called 'ring-fenced' because local authorities do not have total discretion as to how the grant is to be spent. They have to spend the money on the Scottish Executive's Government's policy objectives, regardless of whether or not they are the policy objectives of the individual local authorities.

6.7 Non-Domestic Rates are also known as Business Rates. The non-domestic rate is a tax on the property of each commercial or industrial business in Scotland. Each property is given a valuation which is called its annual rateable value. These annual rateable values are used as the basis for calculating the rate to be levied, which is expressed as a 'rate poundage'. Thus if a property has an annual rateable value of £10,000 and the rate poundage is set at 40 pence in the pound, the proprietor is required to pay £4,000 in that year.

The level of the non-domestic rate used to be set by the individual local authorities, just as the level of the council tax is set by them at present, and the income was collected and retained by them. However, the Conservative governments of the 1980s and 1990s believed that many local authorities were setting the business rates at higher levels than were necessary in order to increase their income and therefore their expenditure. Many businesses complained at the differentials between the non-domestic rates in different local authority areas and demanded a 'level playing-field'. As a result, since 1989 the rate has been set nationally by the Secretary of State for Scotland (now the Scottish Ministers)[1]. A further change was made by the Local Government Finance Act 1992 (LGFA 1992) as a result of which the income from all the business rates in Scotland is pooled and redistributed back to local authorities on a population basis as Non-Domestic Rates Income. The actual collection of Non-Domestic Rates Income, however, remains the responsibility of the individual local authorities. Local authorities which collect more than their share of the national pool have to pay the surplus into the pool while those who collect less have their Non-Domestic Rates Income topped up from the pool[2]. Before the start of each financial year, the Scottish Government decides what the national Non-Domestic Rate should be and this affects decisions as to the total of Non-Domestic Rates Income for that year. It works out at about £2,000m per annum or 20 per cent of the total Aggregate External Finance.

1 Once central government took control of the determination of the level of the non-domestic rate, it gradually reduced the rate poundage until, in 1995, a common rate poundage with that of England was achieved.
2 The fact that a local authority does not receive from the national pool all the income it raises from non-domestic rates is a source of irritation to some local authorities. Glasgow City Council, for example, raised £287m in 2007–08 but received only £211m, a net loss of £76m.

6.8 Revenue Support Grant is the largest element of AEF – around £7,300m or 72 per cent of the total. It is calculated by the deduction of Ring-Fenced Grant and Non-Domestic Rates Income from the total AEF figure.

To enable local authorities to plan ahead, the then Scottish Executive announced provisional RSG figures for the three years to 2007–08 and the Scottish Government again from 2008–09 to 2010–11.

Fees and charges

6.9 Local authorities are empowered to charge the users for the provision of certain services. The fees or charges may be discretionary or mandatory. Discretionary charges are charges for services which could be provided for nothing but for which the local authority has decided to impose a charge. Examples of services where charges are typically imposed are leisure services, such as the use of football pitches, tennis courts or swimming pools. Some charges are also imposed for some educational services such as the let of school halls or school trips. Parking fees also provide a source of income.

A mandatory charge is a charge which a local authority must impose such as the fee for a planning application, a taxi licence and a firearms certificate. In some cases the level of the mandatory fee may be set by the Scottish Executive. The amount raised by local authorities by way of fees and charges forms a very small percentage of each council's annual budget.

THE COUNCIL TAX AND ITS PREDECESSORS

6.10 One of the features of local government which entitles it to be called 'government' rather than local administration is the power which each local authority has to levy a local tax. A local tax gives councils a level of autonomy and independence from central government and makes them more accountable to the people who elect them. The larger the percentage raised by the local tax, the greater the autonomy.

For many years, the local tax was a property tax known as the rate or rates. The rate paid by residents, as opposed to industrial or commercial businesses, was known as the domestic rate. As has been described above in relation to non-domestic ratepayers, each dwelling was given an annual rateable value and each local authority decided the annual rate poundage which determined how much had to be paid by the resident or residents of each dwelling in each financial year.

Taxes are never popular and the rates were very unpopular. The system was perceived to be very unfair as it failed to take account of ability to pay. The oft-quoted example was that of the elderly widow living alone in a four-bedroomed house after her children had flown the nest, who paid the same amount in rates as her next-door neighbours who had five adults in the family, all earning good salaries. There were, of course, some measures which were designed to protect less well-off ratepayers, such as a system of rates rebates, but the rates system increasingly became the focus of political criticism.

6.11 The Labour Government elected in 1974 set up a Committee of Inquiry into Local Government Finance under the chairmanship of Frank

Layfield QC. The Layfield Committee reported in 1976[1]. The Committee considered various different types of taxation which might be used as alternatives (or supplements) to the system of rates. These included sales taxes, a corporate profits tax, a payroll tax and a local income tax. They considered that a local income tax had possibilities as an alternative, despite its drawbacks. However, the Labour government took no action on the report. The Conservative government elected in 1979, with Mrs Thatcher as Prime Minister, issued a consultation paper in 1982, *Alternatives to Domestic Rates*[2], which included various options, ranging from a local income tax, a local sales tax to a reformed domestic rates system. A per capita tax (a poll tax) was mentioned but it was not suggested that such a tax should be used as the sole alternative to rates.

1 *Local Government Finance* (HMSO) (Cmnd 6435) (1976).
2 *Alternatives to Domestic Rates* (Cmnd 8449) (1982).

6.12 A statutory revaluation of properties for rating purposes due in Scotland in 1985–86 raised the spectre of huge rates increases and the prospect of consequent unpopularity galvanised the government into action. They picked up the idea of a poll tax, which had been developed by the Adam Smith Institute, and promoted it in another consultation paper, *Paying for Local Government*[1], as their preferred scheme of local taxation. The new tax was officially called the 'community charge' but it was almost universally known as the 'poll tax'.

The government decided, out of political expediency which proved to be misplaced, to introduce the community charge into Scotland a year ahead of England and the Abolition of Domestic Rates etc (Scotland) Act was passed in 1987. As the Act was short-lived, being repealed by the Local Government Finance Act 1992, the details of the 1987 Act need not be considered in detail here. Broadly, it abolished the system of domestic rates and replaced it with a personal community charge which was levied at a flat rate on every adult over 18, resident in each local government area in Scotland. There were some exemptions and a rebate system for less well-off taxpayers.

The poll tax was hugely unpopular. It was widely perceived as an unfair tax, with the laird in his castle paying the same rate as the tenants on his estate. It was an administrative nightmare and could potentially be avoided more easily than the property-based rates system. Thousands of people disappeared from the electoral roll in the mistaken belief that the poll tax was somehow connected with the right to vote and that if they were not on the electoral register they might avoid liability for the poll tax. Various left-wing groups advocated non-payment and huge arrears were built up, causing financial problems for local authorities, as they were not achieving the income they had budgeted for. At one point almost one-third of adults in Scotland were in arrears to some extent. As late as 2004, 12 years after the poll tax was abolished, it was estimated that nearly £500m was still outstanding with local authorities still trying to collect the money.

The poll tax was one factor which led to the downfall of Mrs Thatcher as Prime Minister in 1990 and her successor, John Major, immediately established another review of local government finance. The government settled on a new tax which was partly a property tax and partly a personal tax, known as the 'council tax' and this was brought into effect by the Local Government Finance Act 1992. The poll tax was abolished as from 31 March 1993 and from 1 April 1993 each local authority had to impose a council tax on each chargeable dwelling in its area[2].

Since 1999, under Schedule 5 of the Scotland Act 1998, local taxation has been devolved to the Scottish Parliament. In 2007, following the Scottish Parliament elections, a minority SNP Government was formed. It announced that its intention was to replace the council tax with a local income tax and, at the time of writing in 2008, had produced a consultation document on the issue[3].

1 *Paying for Local Government* (Cmnd 9714) (1986).
2 Local Government Finance Act 1992, s 70.
3 See further para 6.24.

Council tax

6.13   The council tax is a compulsory levy, based on the assumption that there are at least two adults over the age of 18 in each dwelling. The total charge is 50 per cent property-based and 50 per cent personal. Certain groups are considered to be jointly and severally liable for council tax, for example joint owners, joint tenants and couples living together as husband and wife, whether married or not[1].

A discount of 25 per cent is made when there is only one adult in the dwelling. Certain adults, such as students, student nurses, apprentices, people who are mentally impaired, long-term hospital patients and people in residential care and certain care workers are not counted for discount purposes. So a single mother with two children who are both students and a parent in an old persons' home qualifies for a 25 per cent discount. If there are no permanent residents in the dwelling a further discount is available. The discount for second homes, originally set at 50%, may be further reduced, at the discretion of individual councils, to a minimum of 10%[2].

In certain circumstances, complete exemption from council tax may be granted. These include dwellings occupied only by students or persons under the age of 18, and dwellings which are unoccupied and unfurnished or undergoing structural repair.

People who are on a low income with savings below a certain level or who are in receipt of state benefits may be entitled to council tax benefit or rebate of up to 100 per cent. The benefit applies only to council tax and not to the charges for water and waste water which are imposed by Scottish Water but are collected on its behalf by local authorities along with the council tax. There is a right of appeal against the assessment of council tax benefit.

1 Local Government Finance Act 1992, s 77.
2 S 51 2005/51.

6.14   For council tax purposes, dwellings are grouped into eight bands according to capital values as at 1 April 1991. The decision to allocate a dwelling to a particular band is taken by the local assessor who is a local authority employee.

The eight valuation bands are:

Band A: Value not exceeding	£27,000
Band B: Value not exceeding	£35,000
Band C: Value not exceeding	£45,000
Band D: Value not exceeding	£58,000
Band E: Value not exceeding	£80,000
Band F: Value not exceeding	£106,000
Band G: Value not exceeding	£212,000
Band H: Values exceeding	£212,000

A household which includes a disabled person, adult or child, may be awarded a reduction in council banding if medical evidence confirms that the disability is substantial and permanent[1].

1 A recent change has been the inclusion of an additional band called Band A (Subject to Disabled Reduction which provides a Council tax equivalent to 5/9 of Band D) where the house has been adapted for a disabled resident.

6.15   After the council has decided on the total amount of money to be raised by way of the council tax (see below), the tax levels for individuals are calculated by reference to Band D. Each band is allocated a statutorily prescribed proportion as follows:

Dwellings in Band A	6/9
Dwellings in Band B	7/9
Dwellings in Band C	8/9
Dwellings in Band D	9/9
Dwellings in Band E	11/9
Dwellings in Band F	13/9
Dwellings in Band G	15/9
Dwellings in Band H	18/9

Band D is the taken to represent 100 per cent and each council sets the level of the council tax for each financial year at Band D, say at £1,000. So residents in dwellings in Band A pay £666.70 in that year, Band B, £777.80 and so on up to Band H where residents pay £2,000.

6.16   The valuations are based on 1991 capital values as there has been no revaluation since then. A dwelling which was valued at £80,000 in 1991and placed in Band E may now be worth £200,000, yet the residents still pay the Band E figure. A dwelling valued at £220,000 in 1991 may now be worth over £500,000 but the residents still pay only three times as much in council tax as the residents of a dwelling in Band A. The Local Government Committee of the Scottish Parliament has recommended that the Scottish Executive should set in train a revaluation of domestic properties in Scotland. It also recommended a review of the banding, with the addition of new bands at both the upper and lower ends of the existing scale. So far, however, there has been no decision to implement either of these recommendations.

Provision is made for new dwellings to be allocated to a band. The local assessor can also move an existing dwelling into a higher band on the grounds that its value has materially increased as a result of some improvement work[1]. Similarly a dwelling can be moved into a lower band as a result of reduction in its value caused by partial demolition or by a change in its physical locality. An adaptation to make the dwelling suitable for a physically disabled person may also result in a move to a lower band.

A council taxpayer may have the right of appeal to the local assessor against the banding allocated where there has been a change of circumstances such as the partial destruction of the dwelling or a re-banding by the assessor as a result of improvements to the property prior to its sale. There is also a right of appeal against the determination of a person as a liable council taxpayer. There is a further appeal from the decision of the local assessor to the local Valuation Appeal Committee.

1 Such a movement to a higher band can only take place when the improved dwelling is sold.

Setting the council tax

6.17   The local government financial year runs from 1 April each year to 31 March the following year and each local authority must set its budget and decide the level of the council tax for the forthcoming financial year by 11 March. The budget is the financial expression of a local authority's policies and is a key strategic planning and implementation tool.

The total of council tax to be raised in each financial year is decided at the end of each local authority's budgeting process. The annual budgeting process is very time-consuming and preparations for the following financial year may start almost as soon as one annual budget is finalised. Some policy initiatives involving major capital expenditure, such as the refurbishment of a local authority's schools, will have to be planned over several financial years. To assist financial planning, the Scottish Executive now issues draft figures for revenue grant settlements for three-year periods, allowing councils to plan ahead.

For the revenue budget, the previous year's budget (the base budget) may serve as the starting point for the following year. Councillors should not, however, consider the base budget as set in stone. They should be constantly re-examining the policies which led to the base budget to ensure that they are still relevant.

6.18   Early in each new financial year, all council departments will be asked by the Director of Finance or Chief Finance Officer to examine their individual budgets and to identify growth and savings against detailed guidelines drawn up to take account of the council's policies. A target of x per cent savings may be set for the coming financial year.

Existing commitments should then be added to the base budget and known savings or reductions should be deducted. Annual pay awards for staff should be estimated and annual salary increments accounted for. Changes in prices or charges to the council should also be estimated and added to the base budget. Account must also be taken of the revenue consequences of capital expenditure, for example the payment of staff and the purchase of new equipment required for a new library.

The Director of Finance will aggregate the departmental estimates and ensure that the council's policies have been taken into account. The figures will then be presented to the elected members. The involvement of the elected members varies from one local authority to another. In some councils it may be the members of the departmental committees (Education, Social Work etc) who scrutinise the detailed figures and question the departmental directors; in others it may be the members of the Policy and Resources Committee or the Finance Committee. In yet others, the figures may be scrutinised by a group of senior councillors meeting in private as a Budget Working Group who carry out the initial detailed scrutiny behind closed doors[1].

1   A Working Group is, unlike committees and sub-committees, not subject to the provisions relating to access to information (see ch 5) and can thus meet in private.

6.19   In December or January each local authority will be given provisional notification by the Scottish Executive of its Grant Aided Expenditure Assessment (GAE) and Aggregate External Finance (AEF). At this stage, the local authority will be able to make a fairly accurate estimate as to the impact on the council tax of their budget process. If there is a shortfall between AEF and the council's estimated expenditure for the following year, the shortfall will have to be met by the council tax, reductions in expenditure, from the council's reserve funds or from a combination of all three. It is unlawful to budget for a shortfall, so each council must balance the books. This is referred to as a 'balanced budget'.

A summarised example of the calculation made to arrive at the level of the council tax is as follows[1]:

Service expenditure	£2,397,506,600
Service income	£ 852,362,400
Total net expenditure	£1,538,144,200
Central Govt. Grant	£1,295,745,000
Changes in Balances	£ 5,000,000
Balance to be met from council tax	£ 247,399,200
Number of Band D equivalents dwellings	£ 214,689
Band D Council Tax	£ 1,213

1   The example given is the budget for Glasgow City Council for 2008–9.

6.20   The setting of the council tax is a decision which cannot be delegated to an officer or to a committee or sub-committee of the council. It is a decision which must be taken by the full council[1]. Any councillor who has arrears of council tax (or water charge) of two months or more and who is present at the meeting must declare this debt as soon as practicable after the start of the meeting. While the councillor is able to take part in debate on the budget, he or she must not take part in any vote[2]. The latest date by which the decision has to be taken is 11 March but in practice most councils set their council tax levels in February. This enables the bills to be sent out before the beginning of the new financial year so that payments can start as soon as possible.

Once the new financial year has begun, the Director of Finance and the members of the council should closely monitor the income and expenditure of each department on a regular basis so that if expenditure in any area appears to be exceeding that which is budgeted for or income falling short, corrective action can be taken. This monitoring may be carried out by a Financial Monitoring Committee or sub-committee and should also be carried out by the departmental committees.

1 Local Government (Scotland) Act 1973, s 56(6).
2 Local Government Finance Act 1992, s 112.

Council tax capping

6.21   Scottish Ministers have inherited from the Secretary of State the power to cap the level of council tax set by a local authority. The Secretary of State has had powers over the level of the local tax since 1929 but they were not well known until the 1980s when they were strengthened and used to reduce the rates set by several Scottish councils, including Glasgow District Council. These powers are now contained in the Local Government Finance Act 1992[1].

If the Scottish Ministers are satisfied that the total estimated expenses of a local authority in any financial year are excessive or that there has been an excessive increase over the previous year's expenses, they may lay before the Scottish Parliament a report proposing a reduction in that local authority's council tax. The local authority is given the opportunity to make representations against the proposed reduction. If the report is approved by the Scottish Parliament, the local authority must set a new lower council tax. This will involve the repayment of some money to council taxpayers who have already paid the full amount.

These powers have not been used since the Scottish Parliament came into existence in 1999.

1 Local Government Finance Act 1992, s 94 and Sch 7.

Collecting the council tax

6.22   The council tax is generally collected by the council in instalments over ten months from April to January. Local authorities encourage taxpayers to pay by direct debit and it is now possible to make payments using the Internet. Cash and credit card payments are also acceptable. Failure to pay an instalment on time results in a reminder to pay within seven days. If payment continues to be outstanding, the right to pay by instalments is withdrawn and the full outstanding balance becomes payable. A final reminder is issued giving a further 14 days in which to pay. If payment is still not made, the council applies to the sheriff court for a summary warrant and a statutory surcharge of 10 per cent is added to the amount outstanding. If the debt is not settled, the council can pass the task of enforcement to sheriff officers or collection agents who can apply any form of diligence authorised by the warrant. These include arrestment of earnings and bank accounts. The sheriff officers' or collection agents' fees are recoverable from the debtor. Failure by the taxpayer to supply details of his or her employer and bank or building society details can result in a penalty of £50 and a further £200 for each subsequent failure[1]. There is joint and several liability between joint owners, joint tenants and couples living together as man and wife, so local authorities can pursue the debtor either jointly or on an individual basis.

If the taxpayer in arrears is in receipt of income support and a summary warrant has been granted by the sheriff, the local authority can apply to the Department of Work and Pensions for flat-rate weekly deductions to be made from the benefit to pay off the outstanding arrears.

The collection of the council tax regularly receives a great deal of attention from the media and the amount of council tax money collected during the year it is due is considered to be an important indicator of a council's overall performance. The average in-year collection rate[2] in Scotland is around 94 per cent with fluctuations between councils ranging from 88 to 98 per cent. Factors which can influence the collection rate include the levels of poverty, deprivation and unemployment in a local authority area and a history of non-payment of the poll tax[3].

1 Although these powers exist local authorities do not use them as experience shows it is highly unlikely that the penalty will be collected.
2 In-year collection means the amount of council tax payable in any one financial year which is actually collected in that year. It does not include the collection of arrears from previous financial years.
3 Accounts Commission for Scotland *Report on Council Tax Collection* (1998).

Some problems

6.23   When councils could decide the level of the non-domestic rate, local government raised about 50 per cent of its revenue income from domestic and non-domestic rates combined. Now, with the nationalisation of the non-domestic rate and other changes in the local government finance system, local authorities raise less than 20 per cent by way of local taxes. This, along with Ministers' reserve powers to cap the council tax, has reduced the autonomy of councils to determine the levels of service to their citizens and has seriously undermined local government. The complexity of the system means that many members of the public assume that the council tax pays for local government services in their entirety and cannot comprehend how service levels may remain the same despite increases in the council tax. Worse, if a council wishes to spend 2 per cent above that assumed in the Scottish Government's/ Executive's calculation, the 'gearing effect' comes into play, forcing the council to raise the council tax by around 10 per cent. The electorate in general, cannot understand this.

The McIntosh Commission[1] recommended, in 1999, that the Scottish Executive should institute an inquiry into local government finance. The Scottish Executive refused to do so, and the Local Government Committee of the Scottish Parliament undertook such an inquiry, recommending in 2002 that the central–local funding balance should be restored to 50:50. The Scottish Executive rejected this at the time but as part of the coalition agreement with the Liberal Democrats, following the election of 2003, announced that a review of local government finance would take place sometime in the near future.

1 For the McIntosh Commission, see ch 7.

6.24   Meantime, resentment about the council tax continues to increase. Council tax makes up 18 per cent of the annual cost of running a house in Scotland, compared with 15 per cent in the United Kingdom. Many councils impose annual increases of more than the rate of inflation which hits people on small fixed incomes particularly hard. Council tax bills have increased by almost 50 per cent since 1996. A further difficulty is that charges for water and waste water services, which are set by Scottish Water, are collected by the local authorities along with the council tax in a single bill, making the increases in the council tax seem greater than they actually are. Another problem is that there has been no revision of the council tax bands since they were first established in 1991. With the rapid rise in house prices over that period, fewer and fewer houses are valued at less than £106,000, the second highest band, yet they remain in the bands into which they were originally placed. The creation of more high-price bands would ensure that the better off make a larger contribution to the local tax.

The Scottish Executive announced an independent review of local government finance in June 2004. The Review Committee was chaired by Sir Peter Burt, a businessman and former banker. The review examined different forms of local taxation, including a local income tax, property taxes and possible reform to the council tax. Associated issues considered were non-domestic rates, the impact of changes on the GAE/RSG system, the mechanism for distributing grant between local authorities and the relationship with domestic water and sewerage charges.

The main recommendations of the Burt Report[1] were that:

- A local income tax should not be introduced;
- The council tax should not be retained in its current form;
- A new local property tax should be introduced, assessed as a proportion of the capital value of homes in Scotland.

The Labour/Liberal Democrat Scottish Executive took no action on the Burt Report prior to the Scottish Parliamentary elections in 2007.

Following the elections in 2007, a minority SNP Scottish Government was formed and announced its intention to replace the council tax with a local income tax. However, although it is called a local income tax, what is proposed is a tax, set *nationally* at 3 pence in the pound. There are several problems associated with this proposal not the least of which is that if the level of the tax is set nationally, the local discretion which is so essential to the concept of *local* government is lost. In addition, the yield of a 3p tax on the incomes of residents in some local authority areas may not be equivalent to the yield of the current council tax, raising the possibility of cuts in local services.

1 A Fairer Way: Report of the Local Government Finance Review Committee (The Burt Report) 2006.

THE CAPITAL BUDGET

6.25   As has been explained earlier, capital expenditure is defined as expenditure on assets which will result in a flow of benefits over a number of years, such as the building of a new school or road or the refurbishment of a museum or a library. Large capital projects may take several years from planning to completion. Thus local authorities prepare their spending plans for capital expenditure over a period of years, normally three or four. Detailed capital budgets, generally referred to as capital programmes, are prepared on an annual basis. They will include the expenditure predicted for the forthcoming financial year on projects already approved and underway as well as estimated expenditure over the next two or three years for new projects.

The need for new projects will be identified by the individual departments and committees and will be submitted to the Finance Department. The departmental Directors may be asked to rank them in priority order as they are better equipped to determine their urgency than the officers in the Finance Department, but priorities should take account of the council's policies. Departmental Directors should also provide an estimate of the revenue consequences of new projects, such as staff salaries and wages, equipment and general running costs.

The Finance Department co-ordinates the capital budget process and examines the proposed expenditure against known resources. There will be consultation with elected members who provide the political input and the capital budget will be put before the full council in February or March of each year, normally at the annual meeting which determines the level of the council tax.

Where the money comes from – capital

6.26   Up to 2003–04, the Scottish Ministers set a limit on capital expenditure for each local authority. This was generally known as the 'section 94 capital allocation' as the Scottish Ministers' power to set the limits was contained in section 94 of the Local Government (Scotland) Act 1973. However, the Finance Committee of the Scottish Parliament was very critical of that system of capital control and recommended that the Scottish Executive should devise a new system of capital finance which enhanced local decision-making but was based on prudential rules. The Scottish Ministers accepted this recommendation and section 94 of the LG(S)A 1973 was repealed by the Local Government in Scotland Act 2003. This was welcomed by Scottish local authorities as it gives them much more flexibility to plan and execute their capital programmes.

It should be noted that the capital allocation previously issued by the Scottish Ministers was not a grant of money. It was simply permission to the local authority to borrow money to pay for capital projects and borrowing is still the main source of money. The general power to borrow money is contained in the Local Government (Scotland) Act 1973 and any borrowing must be done in accordance with any relevant enactments[1]. An important example of these is the Local Government Capital Expenditure Limits (Scotland) Regulations 2004[2] which requires councils to have regard to the Prudential Code for Capital Finance for Local Authorities developed by the Chartered Institute of Public Finance and Accountancy.

In relation to borrowing, the Prudential Code provides a framework for local authority capital finance to enable individual councils to demonstrate that all external borrowing and other long term liabilities are within prudent and sustainable levels and that capital expenditure plans are affordable. The Code requires a range of indicators to be set to demonstrate, for example, that, over the medium term, external borrowing is used only for capital purposes. Authorised limits for external debt must be set, that is the amount beyond which a local authority has decided not to borrow. In making decisions on capital investment, a local authority must have regard to option appraisal, asset management planning and strategic planning, but the Code is not prescriptive as to how a council should have regard to these factors. Scottish Ministers retain some reserve powers to intervene where they believe that councils have acted contrary to the Code but they have stated that these reserve powers will not be used in a heavy-handed manner and will be subject to the scrutiny of the Scottish Parliament.

1 Local Government (Scotland) Act 1973, s 69(1), (2).
2 Local Government Capital Expenditure Limits (Scotland) Regulations 2004, SSI 2004/29.

6.27   The sources from which local authorities may raise money include the Public Works Loans Board (which charges reduced interest rates), banks and other financial institutions. Capital expenditure can also be met by using capital receipts, that is money acquired from the sale or lease of council-owned land or property. If a council has built up reserves in its revenue account, these may also be used to finance capital schemes. Councils may also apply to the National Lottery, to Local Enterprise Companies and to the European Regional Development and Social Funds for grants towards approved capital projects. The Scottish Executive may also provide capital grants towards approved capital projects.

Local authorities can augment their capital programmes by working with private companies and the Scottish Executive is keen to encourage local authorities to explore ways of attracting private finance by way of Public Private Partnerships (PPPs) when these can be shown to be economical, cost-effective and represent value for money. Public Private Partnerships can take a number of forms such as joint ventures, outsourcing and partnership companies.

A Private Finance Initiative (PFI) is another form of financing which involves private investment. It is an arrangement whereby a local authority purchases a service, usually capital intensive, from a private sector provider under a long-term contract. It normally involves building new facilities or refurbishing existing property. The contractor is responsible for investing in the capital assets, financing the investment and managing the facilities to provide the level of service which the local authority has specified in the agreement. The local authority makes payments for the service as and when received and payments depend on the contractor's performance reaching an agreed standard. The business risk lies with the private sector.

Private Finance Initiatives have been used to finance the modernisation of schools in a number of local authority areas. The term PPP is now common for all public/private sector schemes.

6.28   The Scottish Government formed after the elections of 2007 announced in December of that year a consultation on the Scottish Futures Trust (SFT) which is intended to provide an alternative to current arrangements for the funding of public infrastructure projects. They believe that it would be more effective than the traditional PFI. The Scottish Government's response to the consultation exercise was published in May 2008. It recommended that a Scottish Futures Trust should be established and tasked with commencing business planning and "early win activities"[1]. Local authorities will be encouraged to work together and issue bonds to fund projects. At the time of writing, the timescale for this is not clear.

1 See www.scotland.gov.uk/Publications/2008/05/19155435/0.

6.29   Expenditure on the capital budget has to be as carefully monitored as expenditure on the revenue budget. As most capital projects will normally be spread over more than one financial year, both annual expenditure and total cost should be monitored by both officers and councillors to ensure that any overspend is identified as soon as possible and action taken either to bring expenditure into line or to authorise additional expenditure to cover unforeseen contingencies.

HOUSING FINANCE[1]

6.30   Most local authorities provide council housing although housing stocks have diminished over the last 20 years, partly as a result of the tenants' right to buy their council houses at discounted prices[2] and more recently by the transfer of some stock to housing associations[3].

The income from and expenditure on such council housing as remains in local authority ownership must be accounted for in a separate account known as the Housing Revenue Account, the expenditure of which covers such items as the repair, maintenance, management and capital financing costs of the council housing stock and a provision for bad debts (mainly rent arrears). The expenditure is funded mainly by income from tenants' rents and charges such as those for heating. A very small number of local authorities receive Housing

Support Grant from the Scottish Executive, and from 2008–9 to 2010–11 only Shetland Islands Council will receive Housing Support Grant.

Housing capital expenditure is funded by borrowing and by receipts from the sale of council houses and other land or property contained in the Housing Revenue Account and the costs of borrowing are charged to the Housing Revenue Account.

1 As housing is a specific local authority function and thus outwith the scope of this book, only the briefest of outlines of housing finance is given here.
2 The tenants' right to buy is contained in the Tenants' Rights etc (Scotland) Act 1980.
3 Stock transfer is provided for in the Housing (Scotland) Act 2001.

PUBLIC ACCOUNTABILITY

6.31   Local authorities are under a duty to observe proper accounting practices and the framework of public accountability has been extended over recent years. Some of the measures which have been developed are discussed below.

Internal audit

6.32   There is no statutory requirement for a local authority to carry out internal audit, although central government strongly recommends it[1]. In practice, all Scottish local authorities provide an internal audit service. The role of internal audit is to contribute to management's responsibility to have robust internal controls of the local authorities' systems and the work of internal audit may lead to the strengthening of these internal controls.

The tasks of the internal audit team include evaluating the integrity of systems, such as computer systems, to identify unsatisfactory controls and recommend improvements in procedures and practices; identifying uneconomical or less than satisfactory results coming about from decisions or established policies and practices; and recommending action to remedy identified weaknesses and risks. Internal audit will also carry out investigations into allegations of fraud and other irregularities and undertake value for money auditing.

Internal audit is primarily a management tool but the elected members should be involved in receiving reports and monitoring the effectiveness of any remedial action taken. Most councils will have a separate Audit Committee or sub-committee to maintain a measure of independence with this aspect of work, which will be open to the press and public.

1 See eg Scottish Office Circular 5/85.

External audit

6.33   The Accounts Commission for Scotland is the body responsible for securing the audit of all Scottish local authorities and joint boards. It was established by the Local Government (Scotland) Act 1973[1]. The Commission is an NDPB[2] (or quango) and consists of between 11 and 15 members appointed by the Scottish Ministers. Reports are made to the members by an officer appointed by them called the Controller of Audit. The reason for giving the task of external audit to a quango was to ensure a measure of independence from ministerial control.

In addition to its main function of auditing local authority accounts, the other main responsibilities of the Accounts Commission include the following:

- ensuring the satisfactory resolution of concerns identified by the audit process;
- reviewing the local authorities' management arrangements for the achievement of value for money;
- carrying out studies for the securing of best value by local authorities;
- carrying out value for money studies to improve economy, efficiency and effectiveness in local government in Scotland; and
- ensuring the annual publication of performance indicators.

1 Local Government (Scotland) Act 1973, s 97.
2 Non-Departmental Public Body.

6.34   Services are provided to the Accounts Commission by Audit Scotland which was established in 2000[1]. Audit Scotland appoints auditors to carry out the external audits who may be their own employees or private firms of auditors.

The auditors are required, under a code of audit practice, to plan their work from a wide perspective including examination of local authorities' accounts on an annual basis. They must satisfy themselves that the accounts have been prepared in accordance with the Code of Practice of Local Authority Accounting in the United Kingdom and that proper accounting practices have been observed. They must also satisfy themselves that the local authority has made proper arrangements for securing economy, efficiency and effectiveness in its use of resources. They review the local authorities' internal control mechanisms, and audit their progress in achieving best value[2]. The auditors have the right of access to all necessary documentation.

Once the examination of accounts is finished, the auditors place a certificate on an abstract of the accounts to the effect that the accounts have been audited in accordance with the statutory provisions and are 'presented fairly'. Copies are sent to the local authority concerned and to the Accounts Commission[3].

The local authority must lay the certified abstract of accounts and any report it has received from the Controller of Audit before a meeting of the council within three months of receiving them[4]. It must also make copies available for inspection by and sale to members of the public.

The Accounts Commission may require the Controller of Audit to make a report to it in relation to the audited accounts of any local authority. The Controller himself can decide to make a report to the Commission on any matter arising from the accounts which he thinks should be brought to the attention of a local authority or the public. Such reports must be considered (as opposed to being laid before the council) by a full meeting of the council held within a period of four months at which the members must decide what action, if any, should be taken in response. The Controller must be informed of any decision made and a summary of the decisions must be published in a newspaper circulating locally[5].

1 Public Finance and Accountability (Scotland) Act 2000.
2 The general duties of auditors are to be found in the Local Government (Scotland) Act 1973, s 99.
3 LG(S)A 1973, s 101(4).
4 Local Authority Accounts (Scotland) Regulations 1985, SI 1985/267.
5 Local Government Act 1992, ss 5, 6.

Special reports by the Controller of Audit

6.35   The 'special report' is the most powerful tool in the Controller's armoury but, due to changes made to the law by the Ethical Standards in Public Life etc (Scotland) Act 2000, it is not quite the big stick it used to be.

The Controller may make a special report to the Commission, if, having considered any matter arising from the audit of a local authority's accounts and having made any further inquiries he considers necessary, he is of the opinion that:

- any item of account is contrary to law; or
- there has been a failure by anyone to bring into account any sum which ought to have been brought in; or
- any loss has been incurred or deficiency caused by the negligence or misconduct of anyone or by the failure of a local authority to carry out a statutory duty; or
- any sum has been credited or debited to the wrong account and he is not satisfied that the local authority is taking or has taken the necessary steps to remedy the matter[1].

He must give copies of his proposed report to the local authority concerned and any person named in it and give them an opportunity to make representations to him. After that, copies of his finalised report to the Commission must be sent to the local authority concerned, to any officer of the council who may be involved, to any member of the public who might have flagged the matter up to the Controller[2] and to any other person he thinks may be affected.

Where a special report has been made to the Commission by the Controller, the Commission may decide to take no action on it or may direct the Controller to carry out further investigations. The Commission may decide to hold a hearing and must do so if requested to do so in writing by the local authority concerned or by anyone blamed in the report or by anyone else who has been sent a copy of the report by the Commission. The Commission may also state a case on any question of law arising from the special report for the opinion of the Court of Session and must do so if directed to do so by the Court[3].

The members of the Commission who have conducted a hearing must state their findings in writing and send a copy of their findings to the local authority concerned, to any officer or member blamed in the report and to any other person the Commission deems appropriate. Members of the public may also purchase copies of the report[4].

1 Local Government (Scotland) Act 1973, s 102(3).
2 Interested persons have the right to inspect a local authority's accounts and to lodge objections with the auditors and the authority. LG(S)A 1973, s 101.
3 LG(S)A 1973, s 103B. For examples of cases stated, see *Commission for Local Authority Accounts in Scotland v Stirling District Council* 1984 SLT 442; *Commission for Local Authority Accounts in Scotland v City of Edinburgh District Council* 1988 SLT 767; *Commission for Local Authority Accounts in Scotland v Grampian Regional Council* 1994 SLT 1120.
4 LG(S)A 1973, s 103D.

6.36   The local authority concerned must consider the Commission's findings at a full meeting of the council held within three months of receiving them and the council must decide whether to accept any or all of the recommendations made and what, if any, action they are to take in response. Notice of the council meeting must be advertised at least seven days in advance in a newspaper circulating locally and the notice must describe the Commission's findings and recommendations, if any. After the council meeting has been held, the local authority must notify the Commission of any decisions reached in relation to the Commission's findings and publish an approved summary of its decisions in a local newspaper[1].

If the members of the Commission who conducted the hearing find that any item of account is contrary to law or wrongly accounted for or finds that there has been failure to account for any sum or that a loss or deficiency has been caused by the negligence or misconduct of any person or by a failure of the local authority, they may impose a sanction.

1 Local Government (Scotland) Act 1973, s 103E.

6.37   It is in the area of sanctions that the most significant changes to the law have been made. Before the Ethical Standards in Public Life etc (Scotland) Act 2000 came into effect, the ultimate sanction was the personal surcharge of a councillor or an officer, possibly running into many thousands or even millions of pounds which could result in the councillor or officer being bankrupted[1]. Bankruptcy of a councillor results in the disqualification of the councillor as a member of the local authority[2]. Briefly, if the Commission found one of the contraventions listed above, it could recommend to the Secretary of State for Scotland that an order be made requiring the person responsible to pay an amount of money up to the sum unlawfully incurred or the loss unlawfully made. The Secretary of State had a certain amount of discretion as to whether to make such an order and as to what amount of surcharge to specify, having regard to the means of the person or persons concerned and their ability to pay. If more than one person was surcharged, liability was joint and several.

The penalty of surcharge was not imposed very often but there have been some high-profile cases in England, though fewer in Scotland. For example in the 1920s, councillors in Poplar Borough Council were surcharged for their decision to pay their employees a weekly wage which was above the national average and for deciding to pay their female employees the same rate as their male employees[3]. Many of the councillors were bankrupted and took the surcharge to their graves. In 1972 councillors of Clay Cross Council refused to raise council house rents to the level required by statute and were surcharged the amount of the loss of rental income incurred. In Scotland, at around the same time, a number of councillors were surcharged for a similar refusal. The surcharge was lifted only following a change of government in 1974. It might be thought that surcharge would apply only to councillors determined to take a political stand on some issue of principle, but officers too have been surcharged. In the 1980s, the Director of Social Work in Strathclyde Regional Council faced a surcharge of several million pounds for making payments to the families of strikers during the miners' strike of 1984–85. In the 1990s, the Commission recommended that the Depute Director of Finance of the Western Isles Island Council should be surcharged following the loss to the Council of £24m after the collapse of the Bank of Commerce and Credit International. Thankfully for the officers concerned and their families, neither of these was pursued to the point of payment.

As a generality, officers who have faced surcharge found themselves in that situation as a result of a misunderstanding of the law or of inadequate legal advice rather than a deliberate act. Councillors, on the other hand, are not involved in accounting or signing cheques and, in the few cases where councillors have been surcharged, it has usually been as an act of defiance against government policies which they considered to be unfair. The example has been given above of Housing Finance Acts which forced councillors to raise council house rents to a level which they considered to be unacceptable.

1 The law relating to surcharge was contained in the Local Government (Scotland) Act 1973, ss 103 (part) and 104 as originally enacted.
2 See ch 3.
3 See *Roberts v Hopwood* [1925] AC 578.

6.38   If councillors were about to consider taking an illegal action, they were well warned by the councils' lawyers that what they were about to do might result in surcharge and possible bankruptcy. This was usually sufficient to cause them to draw back. When the poll tax was introduced in Scotland, several councillors in various district councils in Scotland toyed with defying the law which forced them to supply information about poll tax payers to the Community Charge Registration Officers but the threat of surcharge was enough to prevent a majority vote in favour of illegal action.

Local authority officers and elected members made representations to central government over many years that surcharge was not only a draconian penalty but was patently unfair as it applied only to local government and not to members of Parliament or to members of quangos. The Ethical Standards in Public Life etc (Scotland) Bill did not contain any provision for abolishing surcharge but a number of representations were made to that effect during the Bill's consultation stage and these were accepted by the Scottish Ministers who proposed amendments to the Bill. The Parliament accepted the amendments and section 33 of the ESPL(S)A 2000 amends considerably the provisions in sections 102–104 of the Local Government (Scotland) Act 1973.

The position now is that a financial penalty can no longer be imposed on an officer or a member as a result of an adverse finding by the Accounts Commission. The sanctions which can now be imposed are almost exactly the same as the sanctions which the Standards Commission can impose on a councillor found guilty of a breach of the Code of Conduct[1]. They are[2] as follows:

- censure of an officer or a councillor;
- suspending, for up to one year, a councillor's entitlement to attend all meetings of the council; all meetings of one or more committees or sub-committees of the council; all meetings of any other body to which the councillor has been as a nominee or representative of the council[3];
- suspending, for up to one year, a councillor's entitlement to attend all of the above;
- disqualifying a councillor, for a period of up to five years, from being a councillor, from being nominated for election or from being elected as a member of the council.

Members and officers alike are no doubt relieved that there is no longer the threat of a huge financial penalty hanging over them for failure, negligence or even misconduct. It would appear from the list of sanctions above that an officer would get off more lightly than a councillor However, it should be remembered that it would be open to the local authority which employs the officer to take further disciplinary action, possibly to the extent of dismissal.

1 For the Standards Commission and the Code of Conduct, see ch 7.
2 Local Government (Scotland) Act 1973, s 103F(2)
3 The councillor may be suspended from one or more of these types of meetings but not from all of them.

6.39   Censure or suspension from attendance at all or some meetings does not otherwise affect the councillor's status as a councillor. He or she continues to be an elected representative and can continue to take up constituents' complaints, receive documents and attend informal meetings. If a period of suspension is imposed which would continue beyond the date of the next council election, the suspension ends on the beginning of the day of the election, thus allowing the councillor to stand for election again with a clean sheet.

Disqualification is, however, a very severe penalty. It has the effect of removing the councillor from office as a member of the council and from any other body to which he or she has been appointed by the council. He or she cannot stand for election again until the period of disqualification has expired. No doubt disqualification would be reserved for the most serious financial misconduct, falling short of criminality, on the part of councillors. Many councillors feel that the disqualification of an elected member by a quango is undemocratic and that a final decision on the fate of a councillor who has not been guilty of a criminal act should be taken by the electorate, while criminal acts should be dealt with by the courts.

The amendments made to the pre-existing law also allow the Accounts Commission to suspend a councillor if, having received an interim report from the Controller, it believes either that the further conduct of the investigated would be prejudiced without suspension or that otherwise suspension would be in the public interest[1]. There is no requirement for the Commission to give the councillor a hearing but he or she must be afforded an opportunity to make representations on the allegation contained in the Controller's interim report. The suspension continues until the final findings of the Commission are issued and the member is either cleared of the allegations or has a sanction imposed on him under section 103F of the Local Government (Scotland) Act 1973 as described above.

There is a right of appeal by an officer against the imposition of a censure. In the case of a councillor, there is a right of appeal against censure, suspension and interim suspension. Curiously, there is no appeal against the most severe penalty of disqualification. This may simply be as a result of an error in drafting the law. The appeal is to the local sheriff principal who may confirm the finding of the Commission, quash it entirely or quash it and remit it back to the Commission for reconsideration. There is a further appeal to the Court of Session[2].

In the case of a loss or deficiency caused by a failure of a local authority to carry out a statutory duty, rather than an individual officer or councillor, the Commission can make such recommendations to the Scottish Ministers as it thinks fit, including a recommendation that they should make an order directing the authority to rectify its accounts[3].

1 Local Government (Scotland) Act 1973, s 103G(1), (2).
2 The right of appeal is conferred by LG(S)A 1973, s 103J.
3 LG(S)A 1973, s 103F(3).

Best value

6.40   Best value has been mentioned as one of the duties laid upon local authorities[1]. Best value is defined as continuous improvement in the performance of a local authority's functions and in securing best value a local authority has to maintain an appropriate balance between the quality of its performance and the cost to the authority and its customers of that performance[2]. Thus it is partly a duty relating to finance and audit but it goes much wider than that. In maintaining the balance between quality and cost the local authority has to consider not only economy, efficiency and effectiveness but also equal opportunities and sustainable development.

Best value was introduced on a non-statutory basis by the Labour government elected in 1997 as a replacement for compulsory competitive tendering and a framework for its development on a statutory basis was devised by a partnership of local and central government with input from the Accounts Commission. Best value has been embraced enthusiastically by local authorities. Both councillors and officers have found that departmental reviews of activities have resulted in sensible, and in many cases cost-saving, improvements to services.

The statutory duty to secure best value is dealt with in two fairly short sections of the Local Government in Scotland Act 2003[3] but the duty is fleshed out in considerable detail in guidance issued by the Scottish Ministers to which local authorities must have regard. Local authorities must also account for the cost of services in accordance with the Best Value Accounting Code of Practice published by CIPFA. Adherence to the Code will generally be considered by auditors as part of the examination of accounts.

1 See ch 4.
2 Local Government in Scotland Act 2003, s 1(2), (3).
3 LGSA 2003, ss 1 and 2.

6.41   The Accounts Commission has a role in monitoring and enforcing the duty of local authorities to secure best value. On behalf of the Commission, Audit Scotland carries out a rolling programme of audit of best value and each Scottish local authority is audited every three years. If, on a report from the Controller of Audit, the Commission finds that a local authority is failing or has failed to comply with its duty to secure best value, it can:

- direct the Contoller of Audit to carry out further investigations; or
- hold a hearing; or
- state its findings[1].

The findings of the Accounts Commission are reported to the local authority concerned and any other interested party and progress is subsequently monitored.

Local authorities which have been the subject of critical reports include[2]:

- Inverclyde Council (2005), where the Commission found extensive and fundamental weaknesses in leadership and direction by elected members and senior management which were preventing the Council from improving.
- West Dunbartonshire Council (2006), where, after holding a public hearing, the Commission found decision-making was not as open and transparent as it should be; inadequate scrutiny; serious problems of staff morale; lack of effective leadership from senior members and officers; and poor relationships between members and officers.
- Aberdeen City Council (2008), where, after holding a public hearing, the Commission found a lack of effective leadership and direction in education and social work services; weak governance arrangements and lack of effective scrutiny; a fundamental problem of low morale amongst staff; and a very serious financial position, with expenditure significantly in excess of budget over the previous three years[3].

1 LGSA 2003, s 3.
2 Full reports can be found at www.audit-scotland.gov.uk
3 The financial situation of Aberdeen City Council in 2008 is probably the most serious ever encountered in modern Scottish local government.

6.42   If necessary, the Accounts Commission may recommend to the Scottish Ministers that enforcement action should be taken[1]. Even without a recommendation from the Accounts Commission, the Scottish Ministers can decide to take enforcement action against a local authority if they believe that enforcement is justified to protect the public from substantial harm[2]. The first stage of enforcement is the service on the local authority concerned of a preliminary notice which informs the authority, in writing, of its apparent failure to comply with its duty to secure best value and requires the authority to submit a written response, within a specified time, stating either that it has not failed in its duty (and justifying that statement) or that it has failed in its duty and giving reasons as to why further action should not be taken against it.

The second stage is the service of an enforcement direction which requires the local authority concerned to take specified action to remedy the situation.[3] An enforcement direction will be served on a local authority if its response to a preliminary notice fails to convince the Scottish Ministers that the authority is now complying with its duty. The enforcement direction may include action to rectify the local authority's accounts. The local authority must comply with the enforcement direction. The Scottish Ministers also have the power to make recommendations to local authorities, either along with or instead of an enforcement direction. Recommendations do not have the force of an enforcement direction in that they are not binding.

1 Local Government in Scotland Act 2003, s 23(1).
2 LGSA 2003, s 23(2).
3 LGSA 2003, s 24.

6.43   The Scottish Ministers must lay a report before the Scottish Parliament if they exercise the power to give an enforcement direction to a local authority (or to vary or revoke such a direction).

The Local Government Committee of the Scottish Parliament was concerned that the issuing of a binding direction by the Scottish Ministers, no doubt on the advice of civil servants, to a democratically elected council as to what it should or should not do in the performance of its functions was a very serious matter. It recommended that the Scottish Parliament, as opposed to the Scottish Ministers, should have the power to scrutinise and nullify an enforcement direction, but the Scottish Executive refused to accept this check on its power to intervene in local government affairs. To date, it has not exercised the power and it is to be hoped that it would be used only in the most extreme circumstances.

ARMS LENGTH EXTERNAL ORGANISATIONS

6.44   The use of Arms Length External Organisations by local authorities was discussed briefly in ch. 4. Audit Scotland and the Accounts Commission are involved directly in the auditing of the ALEOs' accounts. The external auditors appointed to audit the councils' annual accounts are required to audit the arrangements which councils have made for substantial funding agreements. In addition, they are required to measure councils' compliance with the Code of Guidance produced by Cosla and the Accounts Commission in 1996[1].

The Guidance is intended to ensure proper accountability for public funds and that the principles of regularity and probity are not circumvented. The Code consists of six principles which councils should be clear about:

- Purpose – the reasons for council involvement in any arms-length funding arrangement;
- Financial regime – the extent of the financial commitment and the nature of the relationship;
- Monitoring – financial and performance monitoring and reporting arrangements;
- Representation –how their interests are represented in arms-length bodies;
- Limitations – limitations in any funding relationship and an exit strategy;
- Accountability – how the council and its external auditors may access the ALEOs' records.

These principles are further developed in the Accounts Commission's follow-up report of 2005[2].

1 Code of Guidance on Funding External Bodies and Following the Public Pound, Cosla and Accounts Commission 1996.
2 Following the Public Pound: A Follow-up Report, Audit Scotland, 2005.

SIGNIFICANT TRADING OPERATIONS

6.45 The Local Government in Scotland Act 2003 ended the system of compulsory competitive tendering which had existed since 1980 and replaced it with a framework for reporting and monitoring on the financial performance of 'significant trading operations', requiring that they should break even over a three-year rolling period[1].

In response to these requirements, the Scottish CIPFA Directors of Finance and the Local Authorities Scotland Accounts Advisory Committee have produced Guidance for Practitioners on the use of Trading Accounts in Scottish local government. This guidance, amongst other things, considers what is meant by 'trading operation'.

The guidance suggests that the test of what constitutes a trading operation is likely to be based on whether a service meets **both** the following criteria:

(a) the service is provided in a 'competitive environment' – i.e. the user has discretion to use alternative service providers; and
(b) the service is provided on a basis other than straightforward recharge of cost – i.e. users take the service on the basis of quoted lump sums, fixed periodical charges, or rates, or a combination of these.

Trading operations may therefore include;

- services to the public or client groups which are subject to charging; or
- work for other council services where a council has decided to subject it to a test of competition as part of a Best Value review; or
- services where users are free to buy from outside the council.

There is no compulsion to maintain trading accounts where a council believes Best Value can be demonstrated without market trading or tendering, and where users are not allowed to buy services externally. A council would, however, have to be able to clearly demonstrate that Best Value is being achieved in the absence of any form of competition for services which have external markets.

1 LGSA 2003, s 10.

Test of Significance

6.46 The test of significance is important as it determines which trading operations require to maintain a statutory trading account, must comply with the statutory requirement to break even over a rolling three year period, and must disclose trading performance in the public performance report. Each local authority should set its own parameters for significance. The guidance sets out some suggested criteria as to what constitutes 'significant', and these include;

Financial Criteria	Non Financial Criteria
The size of the turnover of the trading operation, relative to the size of the Council's net revenue budget.	The importance of a trading account to demonstrating service improvement and achievement of targets.
The risk of financial loss to the authority is exposed in carrying out the operation.	The authority is exposed to the risk of service reputational loss in carrying out the operation.
	The service areas likely to be of interest to its key stakeholders and their needs.

PUBLICATION OF INFORMATION ABOUT FINANCE AND PERFORMANCE

6.47 Local authorities have been under a statutory obligation to pursue value for money and to publish information about the standards of their performance (performance indicators) for some time. The Local Government Act 1988 amended the Local Government (Scotland) Act 1973 to give the Accounts Commission the duty to undertake or promote comparative studies designed to enable it to make recommendations for improving economy, efficiency and effectiveness (or value for money) in the provision of council services and for improving councils' financial or other management[1]. The Commission has the power to demand relevant information from local authority officers and members. The statutory duty to make arrangements for securing economy, efficiency and effectiveness in the use of resources was incorporated into the Local Government (Scotland) Act 1973 at the time of the reorganisation of local government under the Local Government etc (Scotland) Act 1994[2]. Recent reports published by the Commission include *Bye now, pay later*, a review of the management of early retirement and *Moving to mainstream*, dealing with the inclusion of pupils with special educational needs in mainstream schools.

The Local Government Act 1992 gave the Accounts Commission the added duty of giving directions to local authorities requiring them to publish information relating to their activities in any financial year which would enable the Commission to carry out comparative studies. The criteria for these comparative studies are economy, efficiency and effectiveness and comparisons can be made between different local authorities in the same financial year or in different financial years[3]. These are generally referred to by the media as league tables. Local authorities must make arrangements for ensuring that information to be made available for publication is accurate and complete.

1 Local Government (Scotland) Act 1973, s 97A (added by the Local Government Act 1988, s 35).
2 LG(S)A 1973, s 122A (added by LG(S)A 1994, s 170).
3 Local Government Act 1992, s 1.

6.48   The Local Government in Scotland Act 2003 lays on local authorities the duty of reporting to the public the outcome of the performance of their functions[1]. This duty is intended to cover all of an authority's functions. It is generally left to the local authorities' discretion to decide on the form, content and frequency of reports, to whom they are to be given and the means by which they are published or made available to the public[2], although the Scottish Ministers retain the power to make regulations governing any of these matters. Despite the statement of local authorities' discretion, the LGSA 2003 then lists a number of matters which may be included in such reports under Scottish Executive regulations. These include:

1   provision for a summary of the local authority's assets and their value, its sources of income and the amounts derived from them and its expenditure;

2   provision for the local authority's trading accounts (or summaries of them);

3   provision for a summary of the local authority's expenditure on various works contracts;

4   provision for the publication of information about standards of performance required by the Local Government Act 1992[3].

In relation specifically to best value, the regulations may include provision for the following:

a   a statement setting out the arrangements made in the previous financial year for performance of its functions, what it did and to what effect, including an account of how what it did contributed to the achievement of sustainable development;

b   a statement specifying how and when the local authority proposes to carry out its duties for the remainder of the year in which the statement is made; and

c   a statement specifying any unimplemented recommendations made to the local authority about the performance of its functions by anyone who has either a power or a duty to make such recommendations.

1 Local Government in Scotland Act 2003, s 13.
2 LGSA 2003, s 13(2).
3 These are performance indicator reports which local authorities have previously been required to make under the Local Government Act 1992, s 1.

6.49 In addition to its role in monitoring best value the Accounts Commission also has a role in monitoring the duty of local authorities to report on their performance generally[1]. If the Commission finds that a local authority has failed to comply with its duty, it can recommend to the Scottish Ministers that enforcement action should be taken. The procedure for enforcement is the same as that described above for enforcing the duty to secure best value.

It is clear that the role of the Accounts Commission has changed over the years from being purely that of financial watchdog of local authorities to a much broader role encompassing monitoring economy, efficiency, effectiveness, best value and the performance of councils generally. Its role in enforcement action against councils has widened too. This can be seen as part of a centralising tendency on the part of central government[2].

1 Local Government Act in Scotland Act 2003, ss 3,4.
2 See further ch 8.

The Crerar Report[1]

6.50 The Scottish Executive in 2006 commissioned an independent review of regulation, audit, inspection and complaints handling of public services in Scotland. It was chaired by Professor Lorne Crerar and reported in 2007.

The Report considers how Scotland's systems of regulation, audit, inspection and complaints handling (referred to as "external scrutiny") could be improved.

Crerar concludes that the unique role of external scrutiny is to provide independent assurance that services are well-managed, safe and fit for purpose and that public money is being used properly. Although the primary responsibility for improving services lies with the organisations which provide them, the Report recognizes that external scrutiny can also be a catalyst for improvement.

Local government was only one of the areas examined by Crerar, the others being health, social care and social housing.

In the case of local government, Crerar recommended that the Accounts Commission should work with other scrutiny organizations to develop a corporate performance audit which absorbs other corporate level inspections in local government and that local government should be a priority sector in which self-assessment becomes the core toll of accountability, with less reliance on external scrutiny.

1 Report of the Independent Review of Regulation, Audit, Inspection and Complaints Handling of Public Services in Scotland (the Crerar Report) 2007. See the Scottish Government website www.openscotland.gov.uk/publications/2007.

Chapter 7

The Ombudsman, the Standards Commission and the courts

7.1 In chapter 6 we examined the controls which the Accounts Commission can exercise in relation to local government. In chapter 8 we will examine the controls which the Scottish Ministers (and in some cases UK Ministers) possess in the context of central–local relations. There are two other major bodies which have considerable powers in relation to local government. These are the Scottish Public Services Ombudsman and the Standards Commission for Scotland. In certain circumstances the courts, too, can intervene in the affairs of local government.

THE SCOTTISH PUBLIC SERVICES OMBUDSMAN

7.2 When a citizen is aggrieved by some action or inaction of the council, are there ways he or she can get redress? The first port of call should be the department involved, where there should be mechanisms in place for handling complaints. If that fails, the person should contact his or her local councillor who may be able to resolve the problem. Sometimes the aggrieved citizen will still not be satisfied and may want a further investigation by an independent body. Such an independent body exists in the office of the ombudsman.

7.3 The word 'ombudsman' is Swedish and means a representative of the people. The UK government decided to introduce the ombudsman system into Britain in the 1960s. The office of parliamentary ombudsman was the first to be established in 1967; entitled the Parliamentary Commissioner for Administration. The Commissioner's role is to investigate complaints by members of the public that they have suffered injustice as a result of maladministration by departments of government[1]. Maladministration was deliberately left undefined so that it could be interpreted widely. The ombudsman system was extended in 1972–73 with the establishment of Health Service Commissioners for England, Wales and Scotland. Commissioners for Local Administration or local government ombudsmen were established for England and Wales in 1974 and for Scotland in 1975[2]. In Scotland, the Local Government Ombudsman became an established feature on the local government landscape.

1 Parliamentary Commissioner Act 1967.
2 Local Government Act 1974, Local Government (Scotland) Act 1975.

7.4 When the Scottish Parliament was established in 1999 arrangements had to be made for an ombudsman system to investigate complaints made by members of the public to MSPs alleging maladministration by members of the

Scottish Executive or any other member of the Scottish Administration, including civil servants[1]. Initial arrangements for an ombudsman for the Scottish Parliament were put in place by the Secretary of State for Scotland. These set up the office of the Scottish Parliamentary Commissioner for Administration with powers very similar to those of the UK Parliamentary Commissioner and the person appointed to the Scottish post was the person who was the UK Parliamentary Commissioner at the time.

1 Scotland Act 1998, s 91.

The Scottish Public Services Ombudsman Act 2002

7.5   The Scotland Act 1998 did not require any action to be taken by the Scottish Parliament in respect of the roles of the other public sector ombudsmen in Scotland, but the Scottish Executive decided to take the opportunity to reorganise the whole system quite radically. After two rounds of public consultation[1], a Bill was published which provided for the establishment of a 'one-stop shop', combining the roles of the Scottish Parliamentary Ombudsman, the Health Service Ombudsman and the Local Government Ombudsman. The roles of the Housing Association Ombudsman (not strictly a public sector ombudsman), the Mental Welfare Commissioner and the External Complaints Adjudicators who dealt with complaints against Scottish Enterprise, Highlands and Islands Enterprise and Local Enterprise Companies were also included in the one-stop shop.

The Scottish Public Services Ombudsman Act 2002 (SPSOA 2002) established a new office of Scottish Public Services Ombudsman who can be supported by up to three deputies, appointed by the Crown on the nomination of the Scottish Parliament[2]. The Ombudsman is Professor Alice Brown. She has three part-time deputies and her office became operational in autumn 2002[3].

1 Scottish Executive *Modernising the Complaints System* (2000); Scottish Executive *A Modern Complaints System* (2001).
2 Scottish Public Services Ombudsman Act 2002, s 1.
3 www.scottishombudsman.org.uk.

The Scottish Public Services Ombudsman and local government

7.6   Although the new office combines the roles of all the former ombudsmen, the text will concentrate here on its powers in relation to local government. Local authorities, committees, joint committees, joint boards and local government officers with delegated powers are all liable to investigation[1]. The Ombudsman may investigate actions or service failures by or on behalf of any of the above only where a member of the public claims to have sustained injustice or hardship as a result of maladministration in connection with the exercise of an administrative function[2].

1 Scottish Public Services Ombudsman Act 2002, s 2 and Sch 2.
2 SPSOA 2002, s 5.

What cannot be investigated?

7.7   The Ombudsman cannot investigate discretionary decisions but the processes leading up to such decisions will be open to investigation. The complainant should have exhausted any available complaints procedures operated by the local authority[1]. The Ombudsman cannot investigate any matter where the aggrieved person has a right of appeal to a Minister or a tribunal or a remedy in any court of law unless she considers it unreasonable to expect the person to resort to such a right or remedy. Certain matters are specifically excluded from the Ombudsman's remit. These include: actions taken in relation to contractual or commercial transactions; personnel matters; the giving of instruction, conduct, curriculum and discipline in any local authority educational establishment; and the setting of rents or service charges[2].

1 Scottish Public Services Ombudsman Act 2002, s 7.
2 SPSOA 2002, s 8 and Sch 4.

Who can complain?

7.8   When the office of Local Government Ombudsman was set up in 1975, there was put in place what was called a 'councillor filter'. This meant that any aggrieved person had to submit his or her complaint to the Ombudsman via a councillor. This requirement was removed in 1988, enabling people to lodge complaints directly with the Ombudsman[1]. There was a similar MSP filter in relation to complaints made to the Scottish Parliamentary Commissioner. All such filters have been removed by the Scottish Public Services Ombudsman Act 2002 to make the new Ombudsman as accessible as possible.

A complaint can be made by the person aggrieved or by a person authorised in writing to act as a representative. Where a complainant has died or is unable to act for some other reason, a representative can take the matter forward. The complainant should normally be resident in the United Kingdom and should make the complaint within 12 months. Complaints should be submitted in writing or electronically, although in special circumstances an oral complaint may be considered[2].

1 Local Government Act 1988, s 29.
2 Scottish Public Services Ombudsman Act 2002, ss 9 and 10.

Investigations by the Ombudsman

7.9   Once a complaint has been received, the Ombudsman has to decide whether or not to investigate. If she decides not to investigate – for example because the complaint refers to a personnel issue or to another excluded matter – she must send a statement of her reasons to the complainant (or his or her representative), to the local authority concerned and to any person who is alleged to have taken the action complained of. If she decides to investigate, the investigation is carried out in private. The local authority and any person alleged to have been involved in the action complained of must be given an opportunity to comment on the allegations made. Every attempt will be made to reach a solution acceptable to all without the necessity of a formal report. In carrying out the investigation, the Ombudsman has powers to require relevant information and documents to be produced and anyone who obstructs the Ombudsman may be dealt with by the Court of Session as if a contempt of court had been committed[1].

1 Scottish Public Services Ombudsman Act 2002, ss 11–14.

Reports on investigations

7.10   After conducting an investigation, the Ombudsman must send a copy of her report to the complainant, to the local authority concerned and to any person alleged to have taken the action complained of. Copies must also be sent to the Scottish Ministers and laid before the Scottish Parliament. Apart from identifying the local authority concerned, the report should not mention the name of anyone involved. The local authority must make and publicise arrangements for the public to inspect and obtain copies of the report[1]. In a report, the Ombudsman will detail the factual and legislative background to the complaint and will conclude whether there has or has not been maladministration and whether that has caused injustice or hardship to the complainant. The report may contain recommendations about improvements in the local authority's procedures and may also recommend that the local authority should apologise and offer financial compensation to the complainant. In the past 20 years or so local authorities have almost invariably accepted the Ombudsman' recommendations.

1 Scottish Public Services Ombudsman Act 2002, s 15.

Special reports

7.11   However, if the local authority concerned fails to carry out the Ombudsman's recommendations, the only other weapon she has is the power to make a special report on the case. Copies of this go to all those who received her original report and a copy must be laid before the Scottish Parliament. The Ombudsman can make arrangements (for which the local authority must pay) for the special report to be made available to the public[1].

The powers of the Scottish Public Services Ombudsman are actually weaker than the powers of the Local Government Ombudsman whom she replaces. He could require a local authority which had failed to remedy an injustice to publish a statement in a local newspaper giving details of the Ombudsman's recommendations and explaining why they had not been followed. In addition, where a councillor, as opposed to an officer of the council, had been involved in the action constituting maladministration and the councillor's conduct constituted a breach of the National Code of Local Government Conduct, he had the power to 'name and shame' that councillor[2].

1 Scottish Public Services Ombudsman Act 2002, s 16.
2 Local Government and Housing Act 1989, s 32.

Lack of enforcement powers

7.12   None of the Ombudsmen in Great Britain have ever had powers to enforce their recommendations. It has been argued that this is a flaw in the system. However, the Scottish Executive took the view that it should be left to the Scottish Ministers and the Scottish Parliament to take whatever enforcement action they might consider necessary. This might take the form of the relevant committee of the Parliament calling the Chief Executive or member of a local authority to account for his or her actions or the Scottish Ministers promoting legislation to correct procedures or provide for payments.

Miscellaneous

7.13   The Ombudsman must prepare and lay before the Scottish Parliament an annual report which can include recommendations which may have arisen from her work over the previous year[1].The annual reports give a summary of the year's activities and contain brief summaries of the most interesting cases[2].

Local authorities must take reasonable steps to publicise the existence of the Ombudsman's office, the public's right to complain, the time limits which apply and information as to how to contact the Ombudsman[3].

A new provision in the Scottish Public Services Ombudsman Act 2002 is the ability of a local authority to request the Ombudsman to investigate a matter[4]. This allows a local authority to have an independent investigation of aspects of its work where there has been public criticism that its performance has caused injustice or hardship but no official complaint has been made to the Ombudsman. In such a case the local authority should have taken all reasonable steps to deal with the criticism itself and the request for an investigation by the Ombudsman should be seen as a last resort.

1 Information can be accessed at www.spso.org.uk
2 Scottish Public Services Ombudsman Act 2002, s 17.
3 SPSOA 2002, s 22.
4 SPSOA 2002, s 2(2).

Local government and the Ombudsman: an evaluation

7.14   The former office of Local Government Ombudsman was in existence from 1975–76 to 2002[1]. Over that period the various holders of the office made strenuous efforts to publicise the existence of the ombudsman system as a cheap and relatively easy way of resolving complaints against local government. However, the public remained fairly ignorant of the office and what it could do. Many of those who did know of the office complained of its lack of teeth.

About one thousand complaints were made every year to the Local Government Ombudsman, against virtually all the Scottish local authorities. Complaints about council housing departments usually topped the list followed by complaints about planning and finance. The vast majority of complaints were not subject to formal investigation. Some were outside the Ombudsman's jurisdiction but most were resolved informally after discussion with the local authority concerned. Successive holders of the office tried, with considerable success, to get the local authorities on their side in an effort to reach a satisfactory solution to complaints without resorting to formal investigation. The number of formal investigations undertaken in any one year rarely exceeded a dozen.

Maladministration was not found in every case investigated. Where it was found, in the last 20 or so years, the local authority concerned adopted the Ombudsman's recommendations almost without exception[2]. The Local Government Ombudsman also had a general power to issue advice and guidance to local authorities about good administrative practice and to publish that advice and guidance for the information of the public. An example of this is the advice note on setting up a complaints system[3]. Over the years, councils and councillors gradually became more supportive of the system.

1 The office of Local Government Ombudsman (or Commissioner for Local Administration) was established by the Local Government (Scotland) Act 1975, Part II.
2 An exception was the case of the picnic-hut in Perthshire, discussed in 46 SPEL 99, 57 SPEL 101.
3 Issued in 1993.

7.15   The new office of the Scottish Public Services Ombudsman has been in existence only since the autumn of 2002. In the first year following the establishment of the office, the focus of work was on merging the offices of the former ombudsmen, harmonising the terms and conditions of members of staff and creating a new staffing structure based on a new complaints system. New premises were found and a new IT system and logo designed. During the period of transition, undetermined complaints were transferred to the new service and new complaints continued to be received. The necessity of laying reports before the Scottish Parliament appears to have had the unfortunate effect of delaying their release to the public. The emphasis remains on reaching informal resolution of complaints in as many cases as possible. The new Ombudsman also aims to enhance the public profile of her office and it is likely that, as the office is constituted as a 'one-stop shop', it will have a higher profile than its predecessors.

7.16   In its first year of operation, the Ombudsman's office received around 1,800 complaints and enquiries. Since then the number of complaints and enquiries has risen steadily, to 2,377 in 2004–5; 3,698 in 2005–6 and 4,228 in 2006–7 (the latest statistics available at the time of writing). Enquiries now outstrip complaints, reversing the trend of the first few years. The increase in workload has led to an increase in funding for the SPSO's office. It also suggests a growing awareness of the existence of the Ombudsman's office and her powers.

In 2006–7, 1,124 enquiries and 1,017 complaints were received about local government. Just under half of the complaints were closed as premature, often because the complainant had not raised the issue with the council concerned. This suggests that councils' complaints handling processes are not as well known or not as helpful as they should be. The highest numbers of local government complaints were related to housing, closely followed by complaints about planning. Social work complaints come third, followed by complaints about finance (mainly related to council tax).

An initiative was proposed by the SPSO in 2004–5, entitled "Just Say Sorry", whereby a public body would give a complainant an apology, without the apology being seen as an admission of liability or negligence (which might lead to litigation). This would require legislation comparable to s 2 of the Compensation Act 2006 which applies only to England and Wales. Unfortunately, the Scottish Government has not, so far, seen fit to promote such legislation.

THE COUNCILLORS' CODE OF CONDUCT AND THE STANDARDS COMMISSION FOR SCOTLAND

Background

7.17   Councillors are, of course, subject to the law and if found guilty of fraud, or other criminal offences, will be punished appropriately. However, they regularly take decisions on the awarding of large contracts for the provision of goods and services, large building contracts and on applications for valuable planning permissions and licences where they (and officers) might be open to outside influence. There are statutory codes which deal specifically with bribery in public authorities. These are contained in the Public Bodies Corrupt Practices Act 1889, the Prevention of Corruption Act 1906 and the Prevention of Corruption Act 1916. These Acts make it an offence corruptly to give, solicit or receive any gift, reward or other advantage as a reward for or an inducement to a member, officer or servant of a public body, including a local authority, to do or not do something concerned with the functions of the body.

In the course of their council work, councillors may find themselves in less clear situations where their private interests might conflict with their public duties without being criminal. They may also find themselves offered gifts or hospitality which are not obviously bribes or rewards and which may be acceptable for a private individual to accept but which may not be appropriate for a councillor to accept. Attempts have therefore been made to regulate other aspects of the conduct of members. The Local Government (Scotland) Act 1973 (LG(S)A 1973) contained provisions which required members to disclose direct or indirect financial interests in contracts or other relevant matters and not to take part in discussion of or vote on such matters. Failure to do so was an offence and the member, on conviction, was liable to a hefty fine. The LG(S)A 1973 also made it possible for, but did not require, a member to give a general notice in writing to the proper officer of the member's and his or her spouse's employment, business partnerships and tenancies of council property[1]. The proper officer was required to record these disclosures in a book open for inspection by any local government elector for the area. This general notice was deemed to be a sufficient disclosure of interest but there was no compulsory register of interests. There were two main criticisms of these arrangements. First, a member who had disclosed an interest at a meeting was not required to withdraw from that meeting and it was felt that his or her continued presence might influence the votes of the other members of the committee. Second, the general disclosure, recorded in a book whose existence was not generally known, relieved the councillor of the necessity of disclosing interests at meetings and this did not lead to transparency in councillors' dealings.

There was also a non-statutory national code of local government conduct, issued in 1975 by the Secretaries of State for Scotland, Wales and the Environment, which encouraged proper conduct by councillors but whose existence was not well known either among councillors or the general public. Few councils regularly brought it to their members' attention and as a result councillors were not as conscious of its provisions as they might have been.

1 Local Government (Scotland) Act 1973, ss 38–40.

7.18   The Widdicombe Committee on the Conduct of Local Authority Business examined the rules relating to disclosures of interests and the code of conduct and concluded that the rules should be tightened up, that the code of conduct should be put on a statutory basis and that newly elected councillors should undertake to be guided by the code when making the declaration of acceptance of office[1]. These recommendations were implemented in the Local Government and Housing Act 1989 (LGHA 1989) and regulations made under that Act. A register of interests was made compulsory, a new national code of local government conduct was published and an undertaking to be guided by the national code was added to the declaration of acceptance of office. The code contained guidance on conflicts between public duty and private interest, the use of confidential and private information, how to deal with gifts and hospitality, the use of council facilities and so on. Although the code was now put on a statutory footing, the guidance did not have the force of law and there was no real sanction against a councillor who breached the code[2].

1 *Report of the Committee of Inquiry into the Conduct of Local Authority Business* (Cmnd 9797) (1986) ch 6.
2 The Local Government and Housing Act 1989, s 32 empowered the Local Government Ombudsman to name a councillor involved in maladministration where his or her conduct constituted a breach of the national Code of Local Government Conduct. For ombudsmen, see paras 7.2–7.15, pp 127–132 above.

7.19   In 1994, there was a high-profile outbreak of what the media calls 'sleaze' in the House of Commons. The Prime Minister of the day, John Major, established a Committee on Standards in Public Life, chaired by Lord Nolan. The Committee published a number of reports, the third of which dealt with standards of conduct in local government[1]. The Committee made a number of recommendations about a new ethical framework for local government, including the establishment by each council of a Standards Committee.

Following the publication of the Nolan Report, a number of Scottish councils voluntarily established Standards Committees. It is debatable, however, whether these committees worked satisfactorily. In some cases, frivolous complaints were submitted by councillors who had grudges against colleagues. In others, the councillors who were members of the Standards Committee dealt with the complaints along party political lines. However, there was a general and genuine desire to deal seriously with standards of conduct in local government.

1 Third Report of the Committee of Standards in Public Life *Standards of Conduct in Local Government in Scotland, England and Wales* (the Nolan Report) (Cm 3702) (1997).

7.20   Responsibility for legislating on standards of conduct in Scottish local government passed from the UK government and Parliament to the Scottish Executive and Scottish Parliament in 1999 and, following a period of consultation, the Scottish Parliament passed the Ethical Standards in Public Life etc (Scotland) Act 2000.

ETHICAL STANDARDS IN PUBLIC LIFE ETC (SCOTLAND) ACT 2000

7.21   The Ethical Standards in Public Life etc (Scotland) Act 2000 provides for a statutory Code of Conduct which contains principles and rules governing the conduct of councillors, the registration and declaration of their financial and non-financial interests and their ineligibility to discuss or vote on council business affecting their interests[1]. It also establishes the Standards Commission for Scotland, assisted by a chief investigating officer to investigate allegations of breaches of the Code.

A duty is laid on every Scottish council to promote the observance of high standards of conduct by its councillors and to assist them in observing the Code. Councils organise training sessions for councillors on the requirements of the Code soon after each ordinary election and try to make attendance at these compulsory.

1 The Ethical Standards in Public Life etc (Scotland) Act 2000, s 1. The Act also makes provision for codes of conduct for members of devolved public bodies (quangos) in Scotland.

The Code of Conduct

7.22   The key principles of the Code of Conduct are[1]:

* duty;
* selflessness;
* integrity;
* objectivity;
* accountability and stewardship;
* openness;
* honesty;
* leadership; and
* respect.

Councillors are expected to apply the principles of the Code in informal dealings with council employees, party political groups and others as scrupulously as at formal meetings of the council and its committees.

Various principles of general conduct are set out in the Code as follows:

- a duty to follow the Protocol for relations between councillors and employees contained as an annexe to the Code;
- a duty to comply with the rules for payment of remuneration, allowances and expenses;
- detailed guidance as to the acceptance of gifts and hospitality along with a duty to ensure that all are recorded in a document available for public inspection;
- a duty to respect all present during council or committee meetings and to comply with rulings from the chair;
- a duty to observe any confidentiality requirements;
- a duty to use council facilities for council duties only;
- a duty to observe the rules of the Code of Conduct in carrying out the duties of any partner organisation to which a councillor is appointed;
- a duty not to seek preferential treatment in any dealings with the council on a personal level, such as council taxpayer, tenant, applicant for a licence etc;
- a duty to avoid indebtedness to the council.

1 The key principles are dealt with in more detail in ch 3.

Registration of interests

7.23   From 1 May 2003, each council came under a duty to establish and maintain a register of councillors' interests and make it available for public inspection[1]. Councillors are required to register their interests within a month of the declaration of acceptance of office and the Code sets out seven categories of registrable interests. These are:

1   remuneration (other than that received as a councillor);
2   related undertakings (these include directorships which are not remunerated);
3   contracts (where a councillor or a firm or undertaking in which he or she is a partner or director has a contract for the supply of goods or services which has not been fully discharged);
4   assistance towards election expense received in the previous 12 months;
5   ownership or tenancy or any other right or interest in houses, land or buildings;
6   interests in shares or securities (greater than 1 per cent of the issued share capital or greater than £25,000);
7   non-financial interests (such as membership of public bodies, companies, clubs, societies, trade unions and voluntary organisations).

(Although not included as a category of registrable interest, details of any gifts or hospitality received must be recorded and the record should be available for public inspection.)

Each council must appoint a proper officer whose duty is to maintain a record of information relating to each councillor's register of interests and the register of interests is open to public inspection at no charge. The record is to be kept for five years after the councillor ceases to be a member of a local authority. Any change to a councillor's interests must be registered within one month of the change occurring.

1 Ethical Standards in Public Life etc (Scotland) Act 2000, s 7.

Declaration of interests

7.24   Interests are to be declared at meetings of the council, committees, joint boards and committees, party group meetings and other informal meetings where the member is representing the council and where an item under consideration affects the councillor personally in some way. The responsibility for taking the decision as to whether or not to declare an interest is that of the councillor alone, taking advice, if necessary, from appropriate council officers or others such as lawyers. The advice in the Code is to err on the side of caution. The test for deciding whether to declare an interest is whether a member of the public, acting reasonably, would think that a particular interest could influence a councillor.

Interests which have to be declared may be financial or non-financial. Most will be personal interests but the councillor must take account of the interests of others such as a spouse or partner, family members or friends.

7.25   Financial interests specifically excluded from declaration by the Code are interests as council taxpayer, ratepayer or the recipient of services which are offered to the public generally, such as admission charges to leisure centres. Also excluded are councillors' remuneration and facilities provided to assist councillors in carrying out their duties.

7.26   In certain very limited circumstances, the Standards Commission may grant a dispensation from the duty to declare an interest and refrain from taking part in the decision-making process. Since 1966, councillors who were tenants of council houses were granted a general dispensation allowing them to take part in decisions about council housing in general and the levels of council house rents in particular. The Standards Commission has continued this dispensation. It does not apply, however, to a councillor who has rent arrears or when any matter relating to a councillor's individual tenancy is before the council or any of its committees. There is also a dispensation for the setting of the level of the council tax. Again this does not apply to a councillor with council tax arrears of two months or more.

The reason for these dispensations is that councillors who are tenants of council houses and councillors who live in the council area (as most of them do) have a financial interest in the level of rents and/or council tax. If they all declared an interest and took no part in the decision, there might not be a quorum to take the decision.

7.27   Non-financial interests are difficult to define but can include membership, as a councillor, of what are generally called 'outside bodies' or external organisations. These include boards and management committees of limited liability companies, public bodies, societies and other organisations. Following representations made by councillors, the Standards Commission has granted a dispensation in respect of membership of some outside public bodies, but the councillor concerned must still register and declare an interest. There are also limited dispensations for councillors who are also members of the Cairngorm National Park Authority in relation to certain planning matters.

If there appears to be a conflict of duties, the councillor should take legal advice. There will also be private and personal interests in societies and organisations which are not related to work as a councillor. Such an interest should be declared unless the councillor considers it to be irrelevant or insignificant. Again, the test is what a member of the public, acting reasonably, would think.

The same test applies to the financial and non-financial interests of other people, such as spouses, cohabitees, family and friends.

7.28   An oral declaration of interest should be made as soon as practicable at any meeting where that interest arises. If a financial interest is declared, the councillor is prohibited from participating in any discussion and from voting on the matter and the councillor should leave the meeting room until that item of business has been disposed of. Where the interest declared is non-financial, the councillor has to exercise judgement as to whether to take part in the discussion and vote, or to leave the room. The test again is whether a member of the public, knowing all the relevant facts and acting reasonably, would consider that the councillor would be influenced by the interest.

If a councillor's interests lead to frequent declarations of interest at meetings of a particular committee, the councillor should consider relinquishing membership of that committee.

7.29   These general provisions of the Code are not particularly contentious although many councillors are unsure of the breadth of the category of non-financial interests and are indeed erring on the side of caution, sometimes ludicrously so. However, the requirement to leave the room has, in many cases, been ignored mainly because of the administrative inconvenience of interrupting a meeting to bring the member back in after an absence of perhaps 30 seconds.

Lobbying

7.30   The Code also includes advice to councillors on how to deal with being lobbied by individuals or other bodies prior to decisions by the council or its committees. It is accepted in the Code that lobbying is an essential part of the democratic process. However, it is advised that particular considerations apply when councillors are dealing with planning applications or applications for certain licences. Party political group meetings must not be used to decide how councillors should vote on such applications and it is a breach of the Code for a councillor to vote in accordance with a political group decision if it differs from the councillor's own views.

Dealing with planning applications

7.31 The Code contains a special section on dealing with planning applications and it is here that members who have responsibility for dealing with such applications have been experiencing real difficulties.

Some of the rules are uncontentious. For example, councillors who have substantial property interests which would prevent them voting on a regular basis should not sit on committees dealing with planning applications. Councillors should not act as agents for applicants for planning permission other than in a professional capacity, which should have been declared in the register of interests. They should play no part in the development control process if making a planning application for their own property and they should never attempt to pressurise planning officers into making a particular recommendation on a planning issue.

7.32 The Code then moves into more contentious areas. Councillors should not organise support for or opposition against, lobby other councillors or act as an advocate to promote a particular recommendation. This rule might be fine in an ideal world where people do not speak to each other. In the hothouse atmosphere of a local council, where councillors meet regularly on both a formal and an informal basis, it is a little unrealistic to imagine that they would not discuss major planning issues such as a proposal to erect a casino or a waste incinerator. The dividing line between discussion and lobbying is a very fine one.

The Code becomes even more problematic in relation to lobbying by constituents. If a councillor has been so lobbied (and the Code elsewhere recognises that lobbying councillors is an essential part of the democratic process), and the councillor decides to respond to the lobbying by indicating support for the constituents' point of view prior to the meeting, he or she must declare an interest, take no part in consideration of the application and leave the meeting room until consideration of the matter is concluded. If, however, the councillor decides to take part in the consideration of the application, the councillor must not make public statements about the application, indicate or imply support or opposition to it or declare his or her voting intention in advance. In response to constituents' lobbying, the councillor must say that he or she has no opinion and will not formulate one until all the information is to hand and has been considered by the committee.

If 'consideration of the matter' means discussion and voting on the issue, then the constituents cannot rely on their local councillor putting their point of view to the meeting. This undermines the representative role of the councillor and can have electoral consequences. At least one councillor (in Midlothian) lost his seat at the election in 2003 by following these rules and refusing to indicate his position on a locally contentious issue. Ironically, the candidate who defeated him as a result of his public and vocal opposition to the issue found himself barred from taking part in its consideration once he was elected and bound by the rules of the Code.

7.33 No doubt the Standards Commission had article 6 of the European Convention on Human Rights and Fundamental Freedoms in mind when drawing up the rules relating to planning decisions. Article 6 guarantees, in the determination of civil rights, a fair and public hearing by an independent and impartial tribunal. However, councillors who sit on planning committees are not judges. They are acting in a quasi-judicial role, not a judicial one. Quite rightly, they should not be bound in advance of the meeting to vote in a particular way by a decision taken in private at a political group meeting, but the views of constituents should be a relevant consideration in the minds of locally elected representatives.

The committee which determines planning applications cannot be the 'independent and impartial tribunal' of article 6 of the European Convention on Human Rights, for a number of reasons. It does not determine applications after hearing the views of both applicants and objectors. It does not give reasons for all of its decisions. Its members cannot be totally impartial as they have to consider their council's planning policies; and it is not independent of the Scottish Ministers who have the power to call in applications for decision and to whom refusals of planning permission can be appealed.

Following decisions in both the Scottish and English courts[1] it can be argued that there is sufficient judicial control over decisions of planning committees, by way of application to the Court of Session by an aggrieved person[2], to satisfy article 6 of the European Convention on Human Rights without the enforcement of the Code of Conduct's most stringent rules on local councillors.

In July 2004, the Standards Commission relaxed its guidance a little. It now states that it is appropriate for a councillor on a planning committee to make known what representations he or she has received from constituents about a pending application. The councillor is still prohibited from expressing a view in advance of the meeting.

1 *County Properties Ltd v Scottish Ministers* 2002 SC 79; *R (Holding and Barnes plc) v Secretary of State for the Environment, Transport and the Regions* [2001] 2 All ER 929.
2 Under the Town and Country Planning (Scotland) Act 1997, ss 238–9.

The operation of the Standards Commission for Scotland

7.34 The Ethical Standards in Public Life etc (Scotland) Act 2000 established the Standards Commission which is responsible for enforcing the Code of Conduct[1]. The members of the Commission, of whom there must be at least three, are appointed by the Scottish Ministers. Initially six members were appointed, only one of whom had direct experience of local government.

The members of the Commission are assisted by a Chief Investigating Officer (CIO) who is also appointed by the Scottish Ministers. The person first appointed was a former Director of Legal Services in a Scottish council. The members of the Commission cannot direct the CIO as to how to carry out investigations[2].

If an allegation is made, normally in writing and signed by the complainant, that a councillor has breached the Code, the CIO decides whether or not to carry out a confidential investigation. The CIO has power to require people to give relevant information and produce relevant documents and has the same powers as the Court of Session to enforce the attendance and examination of documents[3].

Once he has carried out an investigation, the CIO then decides whether to report the outcome of the investigation to the members of the Commission. If he concludes that there has been a contravention of the councillors' Code, he must send a copy of his proposed report to the councillor and the council concerned and give the councillor an opportunity to make representations before he submits his report to the Commission[4].

1 Ethical Standards in Public Life etc (Scotland) Act 2000, s 8.
2 ESPL(S)A 2000, ss 9, 10.
3 ESPL(S)A 2000, ss 12, 13.
4 ESPL(S)A 2000, s 14.

7.35   On receiving a report, the Commission may ask the CIO to investigate further, decide to hold a hearing or take no action. If a hearing is to be held, the councillor is entitled either to be heard in person or to be represented by a lawyer or some other person[1]. Hearings are normally to be held in public.

The Commission then states its findings in writing, giving copies to the councillor and the council concerned and to any other person the Commission considers relevant. Members of the public may request a copy on payment of a charge. The council concerned has to consider the findings of the Commission, normally within three months of receipt[2].

If the Commission finds that a councillor has contravened the Code of conduct, it must impose one of the following sanctions[3]:

- censuring, but otherwise taking no action against, the councillor;
- suspending, for a period not exceeding one year, the entitlement to attend one or more (but not all) of all meetings of the council; all meetings of one or more committees or sub-committees of the council; all meetings of any other body on which the councillor is representative or nominee of the council;
- suspending, for a period not exceeding one year, the entitlement to attend all meetings of the council and of any committee or sub-committee of the council and of any other body on which the councillor is a representative or a nominee of the council;
- disqualifying the councillor for a period not exceeding five years from being or being nominated for election or from being elected as a councillor.

A period of suspension which would continue until or beyond an ordinary election comes to an end at the beginning of the day on which that election is held.

1 Ethical Standards in Public Life etc (Scotland) Act 2000, s 17.
2 ESPL(S)A 2000, s 18.
3 ESPL(S)A 2000, s 19.

7.36   As discussed above, a councillor may become disqualified by failing to attend any meeting of the council, without good reason, over a six-month period[1]. However, the Local Government (Scotland) Act 1973 Act has been amended so that absence due to a period of suspension lasting for six months or more does not lead to disqualification.

It should be noted that suspension involves *entitlement to attend meetings* of the council, its committees and sub-committees and outside bodies to which he/she has been appointed by the council. In the case of a hung council where no party has an overall majority, the loss of the councillor's vote at such meetings may be significant but suspension does not prevent the suspended councillor from attending political group meetings (unless the group decides to impose its own sanction), or less formal working groups within the council. It does not prevent the councillor from carrying out the role of representing constituents by contacting relevant officials and it does not affect the councillor's basic remuneration. Nor does suspension prevent access to information relating to the council's activities. The 2000 Act[2] gives power to the Commission to issue guidance on the extent to which suspended members may engage in other council-related activities during a period of suspension but breach of such guidance is unlikely to form grounds for further action by the CIO or the Commission. Limited guidance was issued in July 2004, mainly relating to the cessation of payment of special responsibility allowances to suspended councillors. This guidance was updated in 2007 to take account of the changes in councillors' remuneration and recommends the cessation of Senior Councillor/Civic Head/Leader's remuneration where relevant.

Disqualification, on the other hand, has the effect of vacating that councillor's office. He or she ceases to be a councillor and is stripped of membership of all committees, sub-committees of the council, joint committees and joint boards and any other body on which the councillor is a representative or nominee of the council. Disqualification is a particularly draconian penalty, especially as it is imposed by what is in effect an unelected quango on an elected representative of the people; and it is difficult to see what act a councillor could commit which is so heinous as to merit that sanction which would not otherwise involve the criminal or election courts.

1 Local Government (Scotland) Act 1973, s 35. See ch 3.
2 Ethical Standards in Public Life etc. (Sc) Act 2000, s 6.

7.37   The Commission also has the power to impose renewable periods of interim suspension of up to three months at a time after receiving an interim report from the CIO. The Commission must be satisfied that the further conduct of an investigation is likely to be prejudiced if interim suspension is not imposed or that it is in the public interest to do so. There is no requirement for a hearing to be held but the councillor involved must be given the opportunity to make representations[1].

1 Ethical Standards in Public Life etc (Scotland) Act 2000, s 21.

7.38   The Scottish Executive initially did not intend there to be any appeal against the sanctions imposed by the Standards Commission but representations received during consultation on the draft Bill persuaded Ministers to support an amendment to the Bill to include an appeal to the sheriff principal and thereafter to the Court of Session[1]. An appeal can be made against a finding of contravention of the Code of Conduct, against a sanction (other than censure) and against interim suspension.

Normally, when a councillor is disqualified for any reason, a by-election must be held within three months. In the case of disqualification by the Standards Commission, the three-month period begins to run from the date of the determination of any appeal[2]. Thus a disqualification may not take effect quite as soon as the Commission might have wished.

1 Ethical Standards in Public Life etc (Scotland) Act 2000, s 22.
2 Local Government (Scotland) Act 1973, s 35 (as amended by ESPL(S)A 2000, s 29).

The operation of the Ethical Standards in Public Life etc (Scotland) Act 2000

7.39   At the time of writing, the Code of Conduct had been in operation for five years and the Commission had issued four annual reports. The number of complaints against councillors has risen from 138 in 2003/4 to 276 in 2006/7[1]. Some of these involved more than one councillor, so the number of cases dealt with each year is considerably smaller. For example, the number of cases dealt with in 2006/7 was 130, covering 276 complaints and in 2005/6 one case consisted of 99 individual but similar complaints on the same matter. In each year the majority of complaints relate to breaches of the key principles of the Code of Conduct and misconduct on individual applications, mostly planning applications.

The majority of complaints originate from members of the public but councillors also use the Standards Commission to complain about the conduct of colleagues. In 2003/4, 34 out of 139 complaints originated from councillors, (usually from a different political party). In 2006/7 this fell to 34 out of 284.

In 2006/7, 136 complaints (48%) were planning related and 99% of these came from members of the public with a material interest in a planning application, either as applicants or objectors. These are generally found to involve no breach of the Code.

Complaints completed in 2006/7 numbered 263 and a significant number of these (235) required some form of investigation, but only 5 (2%) resulted in a finding of a breach of the Code. One case resulted in a censure, the others in partial or full suspension. No councillor has yet been disqualified.

Most complaints were completed within 3 months of the commencement of the investigation and 95% within six months. None took more than nine months. However, some councillors against whom allegations were made have felt that the CIO or the Commission had taken an unacceptably long time in clearing them, leaving them with a cloud hanging over them for months.

1 The Standards Commission and Chief Investigating Officer Annual Report 2006/7.

7.40   The first case where a breach of the Code led to a hearing under the Ethical Standards in Public Life etc (Scotland) Act 2000, raised an important legal point. This case involved three SNP councillors of Renfrewshire Council who were accused by a Labour councillor of breaching the principles of respect and conduct in the chamber or in committee by disrupting a meeting of the council's Lifelong Learning and Work Policy Board in June 2003. The councillors' representative argued, amongst other things, that the Commission, in judging the case, would be acting incompatibly with article 6 of the European Convention on Human Rights, which guarantees in the determination of civil rights a fair and public hearing by an independent and impartial tribunal. The basis for this argument was the institutional relationship and working arrangements between the Commission and the Chief Investigating Officer. The Commission dismissed this argument on the grounds that the ESPL(S)A 2000 preserves the CIO's independence from the Commission by preventing the Commission from directing the CIO as to how he may carry out an investigation.

The Commission found that all three councillors had contravened the Councillors' Code of Conduct. It imposed the sanction of suspension from all meetings of the council, its committees and sub-committees for a period of six weeks in the case of two of the councillors and for a period of four weeks in the case of the third.

No appeal was made by any of the councillors, so the matter has not been judicially decided.

7.41   Councillors in general find the provisions of the Code of Conduct acceptable, with a couple of exceptions. The major reservation is what they and many council officers consider to be a failure to recognise the important representative role of councillors in relation to putting constituents' views forward on planning issues (see pages 139–140 above). Councillors are unhappy that they cannot take a full part in decisions on contentious local issues, while ordinary members of the public are puzzled that their elected representatives are unable to put forward their views and play a full part at planning committee meetings. Why, they ask, can their councillor speak and vote on, for example, the closure of a local school but not on the siting of an incinerator in their ward? One community council has submitted a petition to the Scottish Parliament's Petitions Committee, asking for some relaxation of the Code.

A more minor quibble is in relation to the guidance on the acceptance of gifts and hospitality[1]. While most of the guidance in this area is eminently sensible, the advice to refuse all gifts other than those of a trivial nature or inexpensive seasonal gifts such as calendars or diaries fails to distinguish between something offered as an inducement and something offered by way of genuine gratitude. It also fails to recognise the hurt or even insult that a constituent might feel if a large bunch of flowers or box of chocolates is declined. This is a difficult area in which to offer firm guidance and the councillor must decide for him or herself whether to accept a gift in the light of all the circumstances.

A longer period of operation of the Ethical Standards in Public Life etc (Scotland) Act 2000 is required before a proper evaluation can be carried out.

1 The guidance on gifts and hospitality is contained in paras 3.6–3.13 of the Councillors' Code of Conduct.

THE ROLE OF THE COURTS

7.42   The role of the courts in local government has been touched on in various chapters of this book, particularly in ch 4 in relation to the *ultra vires* rule. Here a more general look is taken at the various ways in which the courts can become involved in local authority business.

7.43   Each council has been established as a body corporate with a separate legal personality of its own. This means that a council can sue and be sued in the courts in the same way as a private individual or a private body. A local authority has a general statutory power to institute, defend or appear in any legal proceedings where it considers it expedient for the promotion or protection of the interests of the inhabitants of its area[1]. So a council may be sued (or sue) for breach of contract. A council is also liable in delict and is normally vicariously liable for any negligent action of its employees. Such actions will be raised in the normal way in the sheriff court or the Court of Session and ordinary remedies such as interdict, damages, payment and specific implement are available. Human rights issues can be raised against local authorities in any court or tribunal.

However, where a council has statutory powers and duties and a claim is made that it has caused damage or injury by, for example, encroaching on someone's property, then, provided that it has acted within its statutory powers, it will have that as a defence. In addition, local authorities can use the courts to implement and enforce their decisions such as the eviction of a tenant of council property or enforcement action under planning legislation.

1 Local Government (Scotland) Act 1973, s 189.

The sheriff court

7.44   Many of the Acts of Parliament which confer powers and duties on local authorities contain rights of appeal for people aggrieved by a local authority's decision. In some cases, the best known of which is the planning legislation, the appeal should be directed to the Scottish Ministers. In others, the right of appeal is specifically directed to the sheriff (or sheriff principal). The list of statutory appeals to the sheriff is enormous and only a few examples are given here. They include:

● decisions on applications for various licences – bookmakers, taxis, sex shops, cinemas, pet shops, window cleaners, street traders and many others;

- proceedings for the disqualification of councillors;
- the disposal of land belonging to the common good;
- school placing requests and attendance orders;
- local inquiries into the confirmation of byelaws;
- orders relating to public processions;
- permits for public charitable processions.

In some cases the sheriff's decision is final; in others there may be an appeal on a point of law to the Court of Session.

7.45   There is another interesting but little-used judicial remedy available from the sheriff court provided for in the Local Government (Scotland) Act 1973[1]. This is for use 'in cases of difficulty'.

Where:

- from failure to observe any of the provisions of the LG(S)A 1973 or from any other cause, a difficulty arises in carrying into effect any of the provisions of the Act; or
- a difficulty arises in carrying out Part 1 of the Local Government etc (Scotland) Act 1994 (local government reorganisation); or
- in any case a question arises as to the procedure to be followed; or
- any question arises in connection with the election of councillors; and
- no provision is made in the LG(S)A 1973 for dealing with the problem;

it is lawful for the local authority or seven local government electors for the area or the proper officer of the council or the returning officer (where appropriate) to make an application to the sheriff, setting out the circumstances. The sheriff must then, after any necessary inquiries, give such directions as he or she judges necessary to enable the Act to be complied with as far as possible or decide the question regarding the election of councillors.

The procedure was utilised by Kirkcaldy District Council in 1993 when it was discovered that all the councillors had failed to make the statutory declaration of acceptance of office within two months of their election in 1992. The sheriff's direction in this case prevented the expense of a mass by-election. The procedure was also used in 1998 by Dumfries and Galloway Council to determine whether the convener's letter of resignation was valid.

1 Local Government (Scotland) Act 1973, s 231 and the Local Government etc (Scotland) Act 1994, s 60.

The Court of Session

7.46   Some Acts of Parliament confer the right of appeal to the Court of Session but even where there is no right of appeal it is still possible for someone who is aggrieved by a decision of a local authority to apply to the Court of Session for judicial review of the decision. This is an important area of administrative law and simplified procedures were introduced in the Court of Session in 1985[1]. Some matters are excluded from judicial review, such as contractual matters relating to local government employees and tenants, and the procedure cannot generally be used if there is a statutory right of appeal. Nor should the procedure be used to challenge the merits as opposed to the legality of a decision.

1 For judicial review generally and the new procedures, see *SME Reissue* Administrative Law.

7.47   The three grounds for judicial review were neatly set out by Lord Diplock in the *GCHQ* case[1] as being illegality, irrationality and procedural impropriety. Lord Diplock did not intend this list to be definitive and he did not rule out proportionality being included as a further test in the future.

By 'illegality' he meant that a decision-making body did not have the power to act and that its decision was *ultra vires*. As discussed in ch 4, the rigour of the *ultra vires* rule was relaxed somewhat by the incidental rule, and the provision of the new power to advance well-being relaxes it even further. The number of cases on the *ultra vires* rule in this strict sense has never been high and will probably reduce as a result of the new power. However, 'illegality' may also include taking an irrelevant consideration into account, acting in bad faith or malice, using a power for an improper purpose, delegating decision-making to the wrong person, adopting a blanket policy which is applied regardless of the circumstances of individual cases and abdicating responsibility by failing to make any decision at all. So cases based on 'illegality' in the wider sense will continue.

By 'irrationality' Lord Diplock meant that a decision-making body had made a decision which was

> '... so outrageous in its defiance of logic or of accepted moral standards that no sensible person ... could have arrived at it ...'

or, in the words of an earlier judge[2], was

> '... so unreasonable that no reasonable authority could ever have come to it'.

This is sometimes called '*Wednesbury* unreasonableness'. This ground comes very close to challenging the merits rather than the legality of a decision and what is considered unreasonable can change with the times. For example, in the *Wednesbury* case, the judge quoted an earlier case in which it was stated that it was unreasonable to sack a teacher because she had red hair, yet in that case was the judges decided that it was not unreasonable to sack a woman teacher because she was married[3].

By 'procedural impropriety', Lord Diplock meant both the breach of procedural rules set out in Acts of Parliament and a breach of the general duty to act fairly and comply with the twin rules of natural justice. These rules are that the decision-maker should not be biased in any way and that both sides of a case should be heard. The courts have developed these rules to cover, for example, the presence at a decision-making process of a person who has an interest in the outcome and the need to give adequate notice of a hearing. Article 6 of the European Convention on Human Rights, which guarantees in the determination of civil rights a fair and public hearing by an independent and impartial tribunal, now comes into play in many cases.

'Proportionality' which Lord Diplock floated as a possible fourth ground for judicial review, has not yet been accepted by the English and Scottish courts as a separate ground of action, even although the concept is recognised in some European countries and in the European Court of Justice.

1 *Council of Civil Service Unions v Minister for the Civil Service* [1985] AC 374.
2 Lord Greene in the case of *Associated Provincial Picture Houses Ltd v Wednesbury Corporation* [1948] 1 KB 223.
3 The case was *Short v Poole Corporation* [1926] Ch 66. The Education Committee had decided that the duty of a married woman was primarily to look after her domestic concerns and regarded it as impossible for her to do so and act effectively and satisfactorily as a teacher at the same time. They sacked all their married women teachers. The judges did not disagree with their decision.

7.48   If a person wishes to challenge a local authority decision by way of judicial review, that person must have title and interest to sue. 'Title' means that a person must be party to some legal relation which gives him some right which the council against whom he raises the action either infringes or denies. Being a local council taxpayer is probably enough to confer title to sue. 'Interest' means that the person raising the action against the council has some personal concern in the outcome of the case.

The remedies available in judicial review include reduction (quashing the local authority's decision), interdict, an order for payment and declarator (a declaration of the legal position).

Chapter 8

Central–local relations post-devolution

INTRODUCTION

8.1   Local government is not free to do what it likes. It is constrained by various Acts of the UK Parliament and now, since 1999, by Acts of the Scottish Parliament and by regulations made by Ministers under the authority of Acts of both Parliaments. Local government is therefore subject to certain controls imposed originally by the UK Parliament and Ministers and, since devolution, mainly by the Scottish Parliament and by Scottish Ministers. The actual level of control will vary depending on the attitude of central government to local government. The relationship between central and local government is therefore both a constitutional and a political issue.

The amount of finance available for local government to spend on services is a crucial limiting factor. In chapter 6 it was seen that much of the finance available to local government is determined by Scottish Ministers and there was discussion about the controls which have been allocated by Scottish Ministers to the Accounts Commission for Scotland in auditing and monitoring not only the financial performance of Scottish local authorities but also their performance over the entire range of functions. Further, there was discussion of the penalties which, under an Act of the Scottish Parliament, can be imposed by the Accounts Commission on officers and members for failure to perform.

8.2   This chapter looks first at the development of relationships between the Scottish Parliament and Scottish Executive (later the Scottish Government)[1] and local government and then, more specifically, at other ministerial controls on local government. Most of these are in the hands of Scottish Ministers but some, relating to local government functions which are reserved to the UK Parliament, are in the hands of Ministers of the UK government.

1 The term Scottish Executive was used from 1999 to May 2007. When the Scottish National Party became the largest party in the Parliament following the election in May 2007, they announced (for political purposes) that the term Scottish Government should be used instead. However, Scottish Executive remains the legally correct term.

WHY HAVE MINISTERIAL CONTROLS?

8.3   It may be asked why central government, either at Scottish or UK level, should seek to regulate and control local government. Arguments put forward for controls include: the obligation of government to control public expenditure; the need for accountability to the Executive which provides much of local government finance by way of various grants; and the desire of central government to maintain, improve and possibly standardise standards of service in high-profile services such as education, housing and social work. Local authorities, on the other hand, argue that the essence of local government is that its councillors have been elected to provide local solutions to local problems and that councillors and local government officers are better able to gauge the needs of their areas and local public opinion than ministers or civil servants based in London or Edinburgh. Central government has won the argument (as it always will under our present constitutional set-up) and is unlikely to give up the controls it has. The use of them will depend on the relationship between central and local government generally and between central government and individual councils.

The Wheatley Report and central–local relations

8.4   The Wheatley Commission devoted a chapter in its Report to relations with central government[1]. Although the central government and local government to which Wheatley referred have changed dramatically since the Report in 1969, partly as a result of devolution to Scotland in 1999, much of what the Commissioners had to say is still relevant today.

The Commission recognised that, constitutionally speaking, since local government is not sovereign, central government has an undoubted right and duty ultimately to control the executive action of local government. However, local government with its elective basis and finance-raising powers has a constitutional status which should be matched by genuine local answerability. From a practical point of view, the kinds of control which can be exercised by central government can have a damaging effect on the independence and initiative of local government as an institution. What was at issue, the Commission believed, was how central government uses its undoubted powers. It should not feel obliged to use its powers as though it were running local services. Government departments should resist the temptation to rush in whenever they see things being done in a different way from that which they might have chosen. Local government should be trusted to get on with the job and, if so, a sense of responsibility would develop. Ministers should have sufficient powers to control the general lines of each service and its future development; but the duty of running (or providing) the service should be placed squarely on the local authorities themselves[2].

Wheatley viewed the proper relationship between central and local government as one of partnership with each respecting the other's individuality as a piece of the constitutional machinery of the country[3]. Unfortunately, a partnership such as Wheatley envisaged, can never be one of equals as local government is a creation of central government and its continued existence lies in the hands of central government.

In the years following the Wheatley Report, relationships between the two levels of government began to deteriorate, particularly during the period of Conservative government between 1979 and 1997 when financial controls were tightened, compulsory competitive tendering was introduced and emphasis was placed on the involvement of the private sector in the provision of local services. Local government was furthered weakened by the removal of some services including responsibility for further education in 1992 and, on reorganisation in 1995–96, responsibility for water and sewerage and for the Children's Reporter Service.

1 Report of the Royal Commission on Local Government in Scotland (Cmnd 4150) ch 32. For the Wheatley Commission, see ch 2.
2 Wheatley Report paras 1011–1020.
3 Wheatley Report para 1050.

Devolution and central–local relations

8.5   The Labour Party won the 1997 general election with a large majority. In its manifesto for that election, the Labour Party had included a commitment to establish a Scottish Parliament. Within weeks of the election the new government produced a White Paper entitled *Scotland's Parliament*. In relation to local government, the White Paper set out two very general principles: first that the Scottish Parliament should set the national framework within which local government should operate, and, second, that local authorities should be accountable to the Scottish people through local elections.

Some local authority members and officers saw (and to some extent continue to see) the establishment of a Scottish Parliament as a threat. As a result of the rather fragmented structure of Scottish local government caused by the reorganisation of 1995–96 and the plethora of joint arrangements which now exist, the fear was that the Scottish Parliament might want to take control of some local government services. From time to time, there has been discussion of a national police force and a national fire service. Structure planning, too, might be carried out on a national basis.

8.6   The government recognised that the relationships between the Scottish Parliament, the Scottish Executive and local government would be crucial to the good governance of Scotland and the provision of services to its people. In the White Paper it announced its intention to establish an independent commission to examine how to build the most effective relations between the Scottish Parliament, the Scottish Executive and strong and effective local government. The Commission on Local Government and the Scottish Parliament was established in 1998 by Donald Dewar, the Secretary of State for Scotland in the new Labour Government, and was chaired by Neil McIntosh who was the last Chief Executive of Strathclyde Regional Council prior to its abolition in 1996.

The Commission's remit was to consider the following:

- how to build the most effective relations between local government and the Scottish Parliament and Scottish Executive; and
- how councils could best make themselves more responsive and democratically accountable to the communities they serve.

The Commission was instructed to present its report to the First Minister when appointed.

THE REPORT OF THE MCINTOSH COMMISSION

8.7   The Commission consulted widely on the issues contained within its remit and its Report was published in June 1999, a month after the first election to the Scottish Parliament. Somewhat surprisingly, the actual relationship between the Scottish Parliament, the Scottish Executive and local government was dealt with in only eight pages. The remainder dealt with various other local government issues including the method of election to local councils, the conduct of council business and community councils. The Report, which was completed in a relatively short time, ranges widely over a number of matters which have given concern to local government members and officers over the years and reveals a considerable understanding of local government and its importance in the constitutional arrangements of Scotland. A number of its recommendations have already been implemented by the Scottish Executive/Government and the Scottish Parliament.

8.8   The Commission recognised that the establishment of the Parliament represented a fundamental change in the political landscape in which councils operate. Although each has a democratic base, it is the Parliament which has the ultimate power to determine what becomes of local government.

It identified two essential features of local government: the provision of a wide range of public services and representation of the community. Service provision brings local government into a direct relationship with central government; since devolution, largely with the Scottish Ministers. Ministers and Parliament have a proper concern with standards of service, while local government equally has a proper concern to respond to specific local needs, expectations and aspirations. This results in a tension between the two but it can be a creative tension if managed positively.

8.9   McIntosh believed that the principle of subsidiarity should be the key, that is that decisions should be taken by the tier of government which is closest to the people, consistent with good decision-making. The principle of subsidiarity underlies the Scotland Act 1998 which created the Parliament and should be equally applicable to the relationship between the Parliament and local government. If a greater centralisation of power were to be proposed, the onus of proof should be on those who propose centralisation to demonstrate that it will bring greater benefit to the public at large. The cardinal principle is that since both have a common democratic basis, relations between local government and the Parliament should be on the basis of mutual respect and parity of esteem. However, McIntosh asserted, that for local government to earn that parity of esteem, the Parliament would have to be convinced that it was dealing with local authorities which are as responsive to and as representative of their electorates as possible and which are ready and willing to embrace modernisation of their procedures and working practices.

Certain principles drawn from those laid down for the Scottish Parliament were set out:

- accountability to the public;
- accessibility, transparency, responsiveness and a participative approach to service planning and delivery;
- the need to promote equal opportunities for all.

These were further developed into the following:

- participation by the citizen by a variety of methods including community councils, decentralisation schemes, citizens' panels, local referenda etc;
- transparency in the conduct of council business so that it is intelligible to the general public;
- focus on the customer;
- delivery of quality and cost-effective services;
- partnership working with other bodies providing services in the area and with the local business community;
- improvement of the public image of local government;
- prom4otion of active citizenship and social inclusion especially among young people to improve participation in the election process.

Although many of these are to be found in local government at present, McIntosh warned that if local government did not deliver to the Parliament's satisfaction, the Parliament would look elsewhere – perhaps to quangos, accountable to ministers – and local government would find itself progressively stripped of functions and influence. Service in local government would become less attractive to able and ambitious people and councils would be denuded of talent. Local interests would have less and less of a voice and, in McIntosh's view, the people of Scotland would be the losers in the long run.

Relations between the Scottish Parliament and local government

8.10   The Report called for the Parliament and Scottish local authorities to commit themselves to a joint agreement or covenant, setting out the basis of their working relationship, and to set up a standing Joint Conference where MSPs and council representatives could hold a dialogue on the basis of equality[1]. A draft Covenant was included as an appendix to the Report, containing the following general principles:

- respect for each other's roles;
- partnership on strategic issues;
- genuine consultation prior to any major restructuring of local government;
- full pre-legislative discussion on local government issues;
- the provision of a sound financial base for local government;
- commitment to the principle of subsidiarity;
- commitment to openness and accountability;

- a recognition of councils' key roles in service provision and as strategic co-ordinators of service delivery.

McIntosh recommended that the Covenant should not be enforced through the courts nor by any other formal mechanism but by the political necessity of keeping to it. However, the Joint Conference should monitor its application and consider modifications from time to time.

McIntosh suggested a Joint Conference, rather than a committee of the Parliament, to handle the relationship with local government. The reasoning behind this was that a committee would be answerable to the Parliament alone and could not provide a basis on which the two could meet on an equal footing. The Joint Conference would be a separate body distinct from the Parliament.

It was recommended that the Joint Conference should consist of not more than 15 representatives each, of the Parliament (not ministers) and of local government. The Parliamentary representation should reflect the political balance of the Parliament while the local government representation should reflect the diversity of Scottish councils (urban, rural and islands) and their political structures. The chairmanship [*sic*] should alternate annually between the parliamentary and the local government sides. It should meet regularly, normally in public; and local government policy issues should be able to be placed on the agenda by either side. Any local authority or MSP should have the right to submit papers on agenda items. An important function of the Joint Conference should be the oversight of the relationship between local government and Scottish Ministers. Scottish Ministers might be invited and should be entitled to attend and speak. At least once a year all council leaders should be invited to attend. The Conference should work towards improved public service standards, provide an opportunity for the exchange of ideas, review policy and consider legislative proposals. It should produce an annual 'State of Local Government' report.

1 Report of the McIntosh Commission, para 34.

8.11   Unfortunately, these recommendations have yet to be implemented. Although a draft Covenant was drawn up and circulated by the Convention of Scottish Local Authorities (COSLA) for consultation, it has yet to be formally adopted. The Local Government Committee of the Parliament discussed the matter several times during the Parliament's first session (1999–2003) and concluded that there was little evidence of a desire by MSPs or the Scottish Executive to absorb the powers of local government. The Committee was also advised that a covenant could not alter the fundamental legal position that the Scottish Parliament could legislate on local government matters irrespective of the views of local government representatives or anyone else.

Councillors do not dispute this but feel that it would still be worthwhile to pursue this recommendation of McIntosh and that of a Joint Conference. Many feel that the status of local government should be strengthened and underpinned by statute.

Although the relationship between local government and central government in Scotland has improved considerably since devolution, many councillors believe that there is some evidence, during the first few years of the Scottish Parliament's life, of the undermining of local government. For example, responsibility for the Careers Service was transferred in 2002 from local government to a new body, Careers Scotland, aligned with the Scottish Enterprise network.

Relations between the Scottish Executive and local government

8.12   As to relationships between the Scottish Executive and local government, McIntosh recommended that an agreement should be established between local government and the Scottish Ministers similar to that which had been established between COSLA and the Ministers of the Scottish Office in 1997, prior to devolution. A draft was included as an appendix to the Report. The general principles in it are almost identical to those suggested for the Covenant. In addition, McIntosh suggested that the Scottish Ministers should commit themselves to consultation with COSLA, as the representative body of local authorities in Scotland, on policy issues affecting local government. COSLA should also be consulted during the pre-legislative phase on legislative proposals affecting local government. Sufficient time should be allowed, where possible, for a considered and representative response. Scottish Ministers should always convey public announcements directly concerning local government to COSLA no later than to the media and, where possible, in advance. COSLA should reciprocate in relation to announcements of relevance to Scottish Ministers. The First Minister and the Scottish Ministers responsible for major services should meet COSLA on a regular basis to exchange views. Either side should be able to request ad hoc meetings to discuss a specific subject. COSLA should be consulted on the appointment of local government representatives to other bodies.

McIntosh's recommendations were taken forward with the signing of a Partnership Framework between the Scottish Executive and the Convention of Scottish Local Authorities in May 2001.

Following the change of political control in the Scottish Parliament in 2007, the new SNP-led Scottish Government and the Convention of Scottish Local Authorities produced a similar partnership agreement, entitled a Concordat[1].

1 For more information on the Concordat, see para 8.41 below.

Miscellaneous recommendations of McIntosh

8.13   The second leg of the Commission's remit was to consider how councils might best make themselves responsive and democratically accountable to their communities. The Commission interpreted this widely and made a series of wide-ranging recommendations, the most significant of which are considered here along with the Scottish Executive's responses.

Local government finance

8.14   Although it was not included in its remit, the Commission examined the present system of financing local government. It had been told repeatedly during its consultation period that reform of local government finance was essential to ensure responsive and responsible local government and healthy central–local relations. The Commission examined the perceived short-comings of the present system[1] and became convinced that the proportion of finance raised locally should be substantially increased[2]. It recommended that an independent inquiry into local government finance should be instituted immediately. Unfortunately for local government, the Scottish Executive was not inclined to accept this recommendation at that time although a review was eventually conceded in 2004.

This review was conducted by a committee chaired by Sir Peter Burt. It concentrated mainly on local taxation, rather than the wider picture and recommended that a new local property tax, based on capital values, should replace the council tax[3]. However, Burt did recommend that urgent steps should be taken to clarify the relationship between central and local government and the financial systems that underpin the relationship[4].

1 For a discussion of the problems of the present system of local government finance, see ch 6.
2 The council tax raises approximately 20 per cent of council expenditure with the remaining 80 per cent coming from Scottish Executive grants and the nationalised non-domestic rate. However, since 2007, with the Scottish Government's insistence that councils should freeze council tax levels, the percentage raised by local government is reducing to around 18%.
3 A Fairer Way: Report of the Local Government Finance Review Committee, 2006, Section 14.
4 Ibid, Section 5.

A power of general competence

8.15   McIntosh also examined the restrictions of the ultra vires rule and the lack of a power of general competence[1] in local government in Scotland and concluded that, although legislation conferring such a power would require careful drafting to avoid ambiguities, it would provide significant benefits to local government, both symbolic and practical. It would, for example, give specific statutory form to the principle of subsidiarity between the Scottish Parliament and local government. It would be a way of expressing in statute the fundamental purpose of a council, to be the voice of its people and to promote their interests, and it would facilitate the process of community planning[2] by giving councils more freedom to form partnerships with other bodies to address particular issues.

The Scottish Executive consulted widely on the issue of a power of general competence. This power went through a couple of name changes during the consultation process, eventually emerging as 'a power to advance well-being'. Responses to the consultation exercises were generally favourable and the power to advance well-being is to be found in the Local Government in Scotland Act 2003[3].

1 For a power of general competence, see ch 4.
2 For community planning, see ch 4.
3 Local Government in Scotland Act 2003, ss 20–22. See also ch 4.

The term of office and the timing of local elections

8.16   McIntosh also recommended that the term of Scottish councils should be restored to four years from the three years provided for by the Local Government etc (Scotland) Act 1994. However, it was of the view that if local authority elections were held on the same day as the Scottish Parliament elections, national issues would dominate the elections and the democratic mandate of local government would be weakened. It therefore recommended that local elections should be held at the mid-point of the Scottish Parliament's four-year term. Again the Scottish Executive consulted on this and respondents were overwhelmingly in favour of a four-year term but divided as to the timing of the local government elections. The Scottish Executive opted for the synchronisation of the elections and the Parliament passed the Scottish Local Government (Elections) Act 2002 (SLG(E)A 2002). This extended the term of office of the councils which had been elected in 1999 to May 2003, when the second Scottish Parliamentary elections were due to be held, and provided that henceforth future local government elections should be held on the same day as the ordinary elections of the Scottish Parliament[1]. The SLG(E)A 2002 also gives local authorities the power, with the consent of the Scottish Ministers, to pilot new electoral procedures[2].

While the four-year term was welcomed by local government members and officers as providing increased stability and the chance to plan more effectively, there were mixed feelings about the synchronisation of elections. While synchronisation might increase the turnout for the two sets of elections[3], it is possible that voters will be influenced more by national rather than local issues in casting their votes. This could reduce the accountability of local councillors to their electorates rather than enhance it. In the synchronised elections of 2003, many local government candidates felt that local issues were indeed swamped by the national (UK) issue of war in Iraq. However, it is interesting to note that in some constituencies more votes were cast for the council candidates than for the candidates for the Scottish Parliament, indicating that some electors were more concerned with local rather than national issues.

The synchronised elections in 2007 seem to have brought matters to a head. The ballot paper for the Scottish Parliament had been redesigned and voters were required to vote for both constituency and regional candidates on a single ballot paper. In previous elections there had been separate ballot papers. In addition, a new electoral system (STV) was introduced for the local government elections. These two changes caused enormous voter confusion and many thousands of ballot papers, mainly for the Scottish Parliament, were rejected as spoiled[4]. A review team was appointed by the Electoral Commission to examine the various factors which had led to this, chaired by Ron Gould a well-known elections expert from Canada. On the issue of synchronised elections, the Review Team concluded that they were a disservice, not only to local councils and candidates but also to the electorate and recommended that the Scottish Parliamentary elections and local government elections should be separated, preferably by a period of about two years[5]. At the time of writing, it appears very likely that this recommendation

will be accepted and legislation put forward to decouple the elections before
the next elections due to be held in 2011.

1 Scottish Local Government (Elections) Act 2002, s 2.
2 SLG(E)A 2002, s 5.
3 The turnout at local government elections reached 50 per cent on only one occasion between
   1974 and 1996. In 1999, when the local government elections coincided with the first election
   to the Scottish Parliament, the turnout rose to 58.5 per cent. In the synchronised elections of
   2003, the average turnout in both was 49 per cent, only 5 per cent more than the average in the
   last council-only elections in 1995.
4 Around 147,000 ballot papers were rejected as spoiled.
5 The Gould Report, the Electoral Commission, 2007.

The local government electoral system

8.17   The McIntosh Commission also considered the First Past the Post
electoral system used in local government elections. It recommended that a
form of proportional representation should be introduced and that the issue
should be given urgent study with a view to legislation which could take effect
at the next council elections[1]. The Scottish Executive included this in the remit
of the Local Democracy Working Group[2] but legislation was not in place in
time for the 2003 elections.

The Local Governance (Scotland) Act 2004 replaced the First Past The Post
electoral system with the Single Transferable Vote and this new system was
used for the first time in the local government elections of 2007[3].

1 McIntosh Report, para 89.
2 For the *Report of the Renewing Local Democracy Working Group* and later developments, see
   below.
3 For the impact STV on local government, see para 8.35 below.

The conduct of council business

8.18   The Commission also examined the conduct of council business. The
traditional model for the organisation of local authority decision-making has
long been the committee system whereby the taking of most major decisions
is delegated by the council to committees and sub-committees composed of
councillors and organised along departmental lines (a Housing Committee, an
Education Committee and so on). In addition to the committees, varying levels
of decision-making are delegated to officers of the council. In most councils,
where councillors have been elected on a party political basis, the majority
group (if there is one) may form an informal executive committee which
recommends that decisions are taken at private party group meetings as to how
their members are to vote at committee and council meetings on particular
issues.

The Commission concluded that this traditional model failed to meet what it
saw as the guiding principles of accountability, accessibility, openness,
responsiveness and a participative approach. It was very critical of the
informal executive and party group arrangements, which the Commission saw
as stifling open debate and scrutiny of the actions of the council leadership and

making it difficult for the council as a whole to hold them to account for the decisions they reach.

It recommended that every council should carry out a review of the way in which it manages its decision-making at political level and publish its findings. The principal objective of such a review should be to ensure that policy proposals and matters for decision by councils are subject to open debate and that the actions of the leadership are capable of effective scrutiny by the council. McIntosh looked briefly at other models for the organisation of council business such as the so-called 'cabinet' model and the directly elected provost or leader[1]. Recognising that its consultation process had revealed little interest in either of these and that, in any case, both would require changes to existing legislation, the Commission went no further than to recommend that the latter option should be kept in mind in the light of developments elsewhere in Great Britain. It was strongly of the opinion, however, that the informal party executive should be put on a formal footing as a properly constituted committee of the local authority, open to the press and public[2].

Local authority leaders and councillors who were members of political groups were a little sceptical that such an arrangement would improve matters in the way which the Commission wished. They pointed out that the formal executive could hardly be prevented from meeting privately in advance of the public meeting to discuss the outcome of the business on the agenda and would want a private steer on policy issues from its group as a whole.

A review of the conduct of local authority business was the main remit given by the Scottish Executive to the Leadership Advisory Panel[3].

1 For more discussion of these models, see ch 5.
2 In terms of the statutory rules relating to access to information. See ch 5.
3 For the Leadership Advisory Panel, see below.

Electoral restrictions on council employees

8.19   McIntosh also considered whether there should be a change in the law which prevents council employees from being elected to the council which employs them[1]. It was recommended that, subject to certain safeguards, employees other than the most senior and those in politically restricted posts should be permitted to stand for election and serve as elected members. The Scottish Executive accepted this recommendation and amendments to the pre-existing law are included in the Local Governance (Scotland) Act 2004.

1 See ch 3.

Councillors' remuneration

8.20   McIntosh concluded that the present system of remuneration for councillors was unsatisfactory and recommended that a pay and conditions package should be drawn up, drawing on independent advice and including issues such as superannuation and childcare provision. This was taken forward by the Renewing Local Democracy Working Group[1]. There are provisions in the Local Governance (Scotland) Act 2004 for a new approach to members' remuneration which includes pension provision and the establishment of an independent Remuneration Committee to advise Ministers. These have now been implemented[2].

1 See below.
2 See Ch 3, paras 3.35–3.40.

The Scottish Executive's response to the McIntosh Report

8.21   Very soon after the publication of the McIntosh Report, in July 1999, the Scottish Executive announced its acceptance of the majority of its recommendations. Some of these, as seen above, have already been dealt with by Acts of the Scottish Parliament. Additionally, the Scottish Executive announced the establishment of a cross-party working group to further examine the widening of access to council membership, electoral reform and the remuneration of councillors. This working group was chaired by Richard Kerley, who had been a councillor in Edinburgh, and was known as the Renewing Local Democracy Working Group. It reported in June 2000.

At the same time, the Scottish Executive announced that all councils were to undertake a review of organisational structures and, in August 1999, an advisory panel was established to assist councils in their reviews. This panel was chaired by Alistair MacNish, a former council Chief Executive and became known as the Leadership Advisory Panel. It reported in April 2001.

In September 1999, the Scottish Executive published a fuller response and a consultation paper on various other issues raised by McIntosh including a power of general competence and the timing of local elections, directly elected council leaders, the election of local government employees to the council which employs them and politically restricted posts.

The responses of the Scottish Executive, issued so early in the life of the Scottish Parliament, gave an indication that the Scottish Executive and the Parliament seemed to be aware of the importance of local government and of the need for changes in the law in a number of areas. Councillors and local government officers alike generally gave a cautious welcome to what seemed to be a more positive attitude to local government which contrasted starkly with the attitude of central government to local government in the 1980s and 1990s, prior to devolution.

ETHICAL STANDARDS IN PUBLIC LIFE ETC (SCOTLAND) ACT 2000

8.22   The first Act of the Scottish Parliament relating to local government generally did not, however, arise out of any of the recommendations in the McIntosh Report. In November 1999, less than six months after taking its full powers, the Scottish Executive introduced the Ethical Standards in Public Life etc Bill into the Scottish Parliament. This legislation is dealt with in more detail elsewhere[1] and is only mentioned briefly here in the context of central–local relations.

Local government members were a little surprised that the first local government Bill to be tackled by the Scottish Parliament was a Bill relating to councillors' conduct, which was not a particularly major issue at the time. It transpired that, prior to devolution, the Scottish Office had been drafting such a Bill in response to the recommendations of the Nolan Committee on Standards in Public Life and civil servants suggested to the newly elected Scottish Executive that it might like to take this matter forward as one of their first Bills.

The Ethical Standards in Public Life etc (Scotland) Act 2000 was passed in June 2000 and established Codes of Conduct for councillors and for members of devolved public bodies (quangos), a Standards Commission for Scotland, the repeal of the prohibition on the promotion by local authorities of homosexuality 'as a pretended form of family relationship'[2] and the abolition of the penalty of personal surcharge for financial irregularities by councillors or officers.

Although councillors have some reservations about some of the guidance issued by the Standards Commission[3], the attitude of local government to the conduct provisions of the ESPL(S)A 2000 was fairly neutral, while the repeal of section 2A and the abolition of surcharge were generally welcomed.

1 See ch 7.
2 This prohibition was contained in the Local Government Act 1986, s 2A, but is better known as section or clause 28 which was the numbering of the clause in the Bill as originally published.
3 See further ch 7.

REPORT OF THE RENEWING LOCAL DEMOCRACY WORKING GROUP – THE KERLEY REPORT

8.23   The Working Group on Renewing Local Democracy was established as part of the Scottish Executive's response to the McIntosh Report (Neil McIntosh was a member of the Working Group). Its remit was to build on the recommendations of the McIntosh Report and consider ways in which council membership could be made more attractive to a wider cross-section of the community and councils could become more representative of the make-up of the community. It was also asked to advise on the appropriate number of councillors for each council and the most appropriate electoral system, taking account of proportionality, the councillor–ward link, fair provision for independent councillors, allowance for geographical diversity and a close fit between council wards and natural communities. The final part of the remit was to advise on an appropriate system of remuneration for councillors, taking account of available resources. (The reference to available resources was an unnecessary central restraint, bearing in mind that, while the Scottish Executive set the flat rate payments for councillors, it was left to each council to decide the Special Responsibility Allowances for its own councillors)[1].

1 For the current system of councillors' remuneration, see ch 3.

8.24   The Working Group reported in June 2000. It produced a package of proposals aimed at widening access to council members. These included recommendations that councils should review their business arrangements, partly to make it possible for most councillors to carry out their roles effectively on a part-time basis and partly to consider whether their arrangements contain factors which impact on women's participation. Councils were also urged to provide more training and better administrative support for their members. They recommended action by the political parties to review their procedures for selecting people to stand as candidates to ensure that both men and women are selected for winnable seats; COSLA and ethnic minority representatives were encouraged to draw up an action plan to persuade more people from ethnic minority backgrounds to participate in local government as councillors.

To encourage more participation by young people it was recommended that the age for standing for election should be brought into line with the right to vote and should be reduced from 21 to 18[1]. This would bring Scotland into line with most European democracies. This proposal has been adopted by the Scottish Executive and Parliament and amendment of the pre-existing law is included in the Local Governance (Scotland) Act 2004[1]. A number of teenagers took advantage of this change in the law and stood for election in 2007. Three candidates under 21 were elected.

1   Local Governance (Scotland) Act 2004, s 8.

8.25   The most controversial recommendation in the Kerley Report was that relating to the electoral system. Bearing in mind the criteria which had been set out in its remit, the Working Group examined various electoral systems and concluded (though not unanimously) that the system known as the Single Transferable Vote (STV) best met the requirements of its remit. Since STV requires multi-member wards it was recommended that ward sizes should be flexible – ranging from three to five-member wards except in sparsely populated areas, to allow natural communities to be maintained within wards. In sparsely populated areas, three to five-member wards would cover huge geographic areas and would result in some of the electorate being very remote from their councillors. Accordingly, the Working Group recommended that in such areas two-member wards might be appropriate.

The recommendation that STV be introduced as the electoral system for local government elections is controversial for a number of reasons. As a form of proportional representation, it removes the sometimes overwhelming dominance which First Past the Post can give to one political party and its results reflect more fairly the votes cast for candidates of different political parties. However, there is no doubt that multi-member wards weaken the member–ward link which councillors consider to be extremely important. Island and remote Highland communities may find themselves represented by councillors who have no connection with their communities. In wards which return councillors from various political parties, as the system is intended to do, tensions can arise between the councillors as they compete to represent their constituents and constituents play off one councillor against another in attempting to achieve their local objectives. (This is already apparent with MSPs who are elected by a mixed form of proportional representation, where list MSPs compete with those who have been elected by First Past the Post). More paperwork is generated as each councillor (possibly up to four in each ward) contacts relevant officials on behalf of their constituents. Furthermore, STV also makes it more difficult for any political party to achieve a majority in councils, leading to coalition agreements which might prove to be unstable and causing uncertainty amongst council officials as to what policy directions their council might take.

The Labour Party, whose candidates, particularly in the central belt, benefit from the First Past the Post system is also opposed to STV because it will lose seats. The smaller parties, on the other hand, support the system because under it they will win seats. Proportional representation is a policy particularly dear to the Liberal Democrat Party.

8.26   After the elections to the Scottish Parliament in May 2003 in which the Labour Party lost eight seats, it was forced to make certain concessions by the Liberal Democrats with whom a coalition agreement was being negotiated[1]. One of these was a commitment to introduce STV for the next local government elections (due in 2007). This is contained in the Local Governance (Scotland) Act 2004 and provides for wards of three or four councillors. COSLA, whose policy was to oppose the introduction of STV, was particularly enraged by this proposal as it was made without prior consultation with its members.

STV was the electoral system used in the elections in May 2007 and has changed the face of local government in Scotland[2].

1 The coalition agreement is *A Partnership for a Better Scotland* (2003).
2 For the impact of STV on local government in Scotland, see para 8.35 below.

8.27   Part of Kerley's remit was to advise on the appropriate numbers of councillors for each council. The numbers of councillors at present range from 79 in Glasgow City Council to 18 in Clackmannanshire Council. The diversity of Scottish local government, with densely populated urban wards and sparsely populated rural wards, made this no easy task. It was concluded, however, that the minimum number of councillors in any council should be 19 and the maximum 53. An exception was made in the case of Highland Council, where geography places unique travelling demands on members, and ten additional members were recommended for that council. It should be noted that these are odd numbers, not even. The reason for this is that Kerley considered that it was undemocratic to have fundamental decisions, such as the election of the provost, decided on the cut of a pack of playing cards after a tied vote[1].

Kerley then grouped councils into four bands on the basis of population density and settlement patterns, with the largest councils recommended to have between 49 and 53 councillors (plus 10 in Highland Council), the intermediate councils 39 to 43 or 29 to 33 and the smallest between 19 and 23 councillors[2].

The work done by Kerley on the number of councillors was, however, put on the backburner by the Scottish Executive which announced in 2002 that it was not planning to make wholesale reductions in the number of councillors in the foreseeable future, although individual council proposals for a reduction in numbers would be considered sympathetically[3].

1 This happened twice in Stirling Council.
2 Kerley Report, para 128.
3 Scottish Executive *Renewing Local Democracy: The Next Steps* March 2002 para 8.

8.28 The other major issue considered by Kerley was the remuneration of councillors, which has long been a thorny issue, particularly among those members who make service in local government a full-time job. As has been mentioned already, any recommendations had to take account of 'available resources'. Kerley was of the opinion that the system in place at that time was no longer workable. The basic payment, in 2000, of between £5,445 and £6,534 was too low and Special Responsibility Allowances (SRAs) were paid to too high a proportion of councillors (about two-thirds). There were inconsistencies in the allocation of SRAs across councils. It was recommended that the basic allowance should be raised to £12,000. In addition, the Working Group recommended that the leaders of the largest councils should be paid the same as MSPs, with other council leaders receiving similar remuneration on a proportional basis related to the population and financial turnover of the council concerned.

The Scottish Executive accepted some of the recommendations and a Scottish Local Authorities Remuneration Committee was established to advise Ministers on the remuneration of councillors. A new system of remuneration came into effect in 2007[1].

1 See paras 3.35–3.40 above.

REPORT OF THE LEADERSHIP ADVISORY PANEL – THE MACNISH REPORT

8.29 The Leadership Advisory Panel was established by the Scottish Executive in 1999 as part of its response to the McIntosh Report, chaired by Alastair MacNish who had previously been a Chief Executive in a Scottish local authority. The remit of the Panel was to advise councils on their review of their decision-making and policy review processes and the working practices which support those processes and to provide advice to Scottish Ministers on the outcome of councils' reviews. The Scottish Executive outlined the following core criteria against which the councils' plans could be measured by the Panel:

- openness in decision-making;
- effective scrutiny of the actions of the leadership;
- transparency in the use of the party whip; and
- the organisation of council business to allow a wider cross-section of the public to consider becoming councillors.

In carrying out its remit, the Panel visited each council at least twice to discuss existing organisational arrangements and the council's proposals for change.

The Panel reported in April 2001 and the bulk of the report consisted of a review, council by council, of proposals for change, tested against the criteria above. Three general categories of structures emerged: streamlined committee structures; executives; and devolved or partially devolved structures.

Streamlined committee structures

8.30 These generally involved a move by councils away from departmental committees to a more thematic approach which could better address cross-cutting issues, focused on the client and on outcomes. For example Children's Committees might take on part of the remits of Education and Social Work Committees while Community Services Committees could bring together issues such as safety and security, healthcare and criminal justice.

The Panel found that streamlined committee structures offered benefits in terms of a more strategic approach to policy issues, a reduction in the number of meetings and the volume of paperwork and a more efficient dispatch of business. By the time of the report 23 councils had adopted these.

Executives

8.31 In the executive structure, responsibility for most strategic decisions is devolved by the full council to a formal executive (committee), balanced by a separate scrutiny (committee or committees), sometimes chaired by a member of the opposition, whose task is to review and challenge, where necessary, the executive's decisions. By the time of the report, six councils had opted for this structure. The size of the executive varied from 13 members to five members. Some had allocated service-specific portfolios to executive members while others had cross-cutting policy briefs. All meet in public.

By 2007, eleven of the 32 Scottish Councils had adopted some form of the executive/scrutiny committee system.

Devolved and partially devolved structures

8.32 Three councils serving large and/or remote rural areas chose to shift some decision-making from the centre to the local level by enhancing the role of area committees, giving them more discretionary powers and some budgetary control.

An evaluation

8.33 Although critical of a small number of councils, the Panel's evaluation of the 32 councils' submissions was generally positive. It was found that most councils had engaged proactively in the process of review and that real progress had been made in reducing bureaucracy. However, the panel did emphasise that local authorities should take more seriously the importance of a genuine scrutiny role for backbench councillors in all of the new structures.

8.34 The attitude of the Scottish Executive towards the organisation of local government business contrasts very favourably with the attitude of ministers in England and Wales which has been much more prescriptive. There local authorities are required by the Local Government Act 2000[1] to choose one of the three following options for organising their business:

- an elected mayor and executive (or 'cabinet');
- an appointed leader and executive; or
- an elected mayor and council manager.

Only councils with a population of less than 85,000 were able to opt for a reformed committee structure.

Scottish local authorities welcomed the lightness of touch of the Scottish Executive in this area of reform and Scottish Ministers have not interfered further beyond encouraging councils which have not introduced scrutiny arrangements to do so[2]. What form that encouragement will take is not yet clear.

1 Local Government Act 2000, ss. 10, 11.
2 Scottish Executive *Renewing Local Democracy: The Next Steps* (March 2002) para 88.

Local Governance (Scotland) Act 2004

8.35 Reference has been made above to the Local Governance (Scotland) Act 2004 which was introduced into the Scottish Parliament by the Scottish Executive in 2003 and which began its progressed through the Parliament in 2004. Here we pull together the main provisions of this important Act[1].

They include:

- the replacement of First Past the Post electoral system with STV: section 2;
- the repeal of the law which prevents local government employees from standing for election to the council which employs them, replacing this with a requirement to resign only if elected: section 7;
- the reduction in the legal age for standing for election from 21 to 18: section 8;
- the removal of the political restrictions imposed on local authority employees by virtue of their salary level: section 9;
- the relaxation of the period during which a former councillor is ineligible to be appointed as a local government employee from 12 months to 3 months, except in the case of politically restricted posts: section 10;
- provisions for the remuneration of councillors, including, for the first time, provision for pension arrangements: section 11;
- the establishment of a Scottish Local Authorities Remuneration Committee (a quango) to advise Scottish Ministers on councillors' remuneration generally: section 13;
- provision to make severance payments to councillors who decide not to seek re-election: section 12[1].

1 The acceptance of a severance payment will render the recipient disqualified from standing for election ever again. It appears that severance payments will not be available after 2007.

THE IMPACT OF STV ON SCOTTISH LOCAL GOVERNMENT

8.36   STV is a form of proportional representation and is designed to offer voters the greatest range of choice. Candidates are successful when they win the necessary quota of votes required to be elected. The quota is determined by dividing the number of valid votes cast by the number of members to be elected plus one. Successful candidates are those who reach the quota, either outright on first preference votes or on the transference of second, third etc. preferences. The system enables smaller parties to stand a realistic chance of winning seats which they were unlikely to do under the First Past The Post system.

The Scottish local government election in May 2007 was the first occasion on which the Single Transferable Vote electoral system was used in a public election in Great Britain, although the system has been used in Northern Ireland for some time.

STV requires the formation of multi-member wards, each returning several councillors. At the ballot box, the voter expresses his or her preferences for candidates in numerical order, that is by marking 1, 2, 3 etc... against candidates' names The Local Governance (Scotland) Act 2004 requires three or four-member wards[1]. This was more restrictive than the Kerley proposals of two to five member wards[2] and caused the Boundary Commission some difficulty in drawing up proposals for the new wards, particularly in the Highlands and Islands[3].

Research carried out by Professor John Curtice of Strathclyde University[4], based on the results of the 2003 elections, predicted that the biggest losers would be the Labour Party, losing up to 99 seats, and the independents, losing 19 seats, while the gainers would be the Scottish National Party, the Conservative Party and the Scottish Socialist Party, gaining 110, 14 and 9 seats respectively. Ironically, the Liberal Democrats, who had demanded the introduction of STV as their price for forming a coalition with Labour in 2003, were predicted to lose up to 15 seats.

In 2007, the political climate in Scotland was very different from that of 2003. The Labour Government in Westminster was rather unpopular and disenchanted voters were turning to the Scottish National Party. In addition the Scottish Socialist Party had split into two, the Scottish Socialist Party and Solidarity.

The results of 2007 saw the Labour Party lose 161 seats while the SNP gained 182. The Conservatives gained 20 seats and the Liberal Democrats lost nine. The Green Party which had not contested the local elections in 2003, won 8 seats. The Scottish Socialist party and Solidarity won one seat each (although the defection of the sole Solidarity councillor to the Labour Party in Glasgow late in 2007 ended that party's representation in Scotland). Independents had a net loss of 40 seats with some suggestion that the nature of the STV system had allowed small "c" conservative independents to stand on the Conservative Party ticket.

As a result, the Labour Party lost control of eleven councils, retaining only Glasgow and North Lanarkshire Councils. Despite having the largest number of councillors (363), the SNP do not have majority control of any council, having lost control of Angus Council. They form a minority administration in Stirling. The Liberal Democrats lost majority control of Inverclyde Council and effective control in East Dunbartonshire. They are the largest single party in Aberdeen, Aberdeenshire and Edinburgh Councils but do not have enough members to form a majority administration. Independents, despite their losses, are in the majority in all three island councils.

So 27 of the 32 local authorities are in a situation where no one party is in overall control. In a very few, a single party attempts to run the council as a minority administration but in most there are coalitions formed from alliances of various parties and independents. These are inherently unstable and in the first 15 months following the elections in May 2007, at least three coalitions have fallen apart and new ones been negotiated.

In addition, almost half of the 1222 councillors elected in 2007 have no previous experience and are having to undergo extensive training.

STV has changed the face of local government in Scotland. It is a more representative system than First Past the Post and has brought about more proportionality in the political composition of local authorities. But the consequence of this is the decline in single-party administration and an increase in the likelihood of coalitions. The problem with this is the loss of stability, leading to difficulties in long-term planning.

1 LG(S)A, 2004, s 1.
2 See para 8.25 above.
3 Report and Analysis of the Local Authority Elections in Scotland, Electoral Reform Society, 2007, ch 9.
4 Reported in *The Scotsman*, 12 May 2004.

LOCAL GOVERNMENT AND DEVOLUTION: AN EVALUATION

8.37 The Scottish Parliament and Scottish Executive have been in existence only since 1999. Any evaluation of the impact of devolution on Scottish local government must, at this stage, be rather limited. However, at the end of the first two sessions of the Parliament, in 2007, the fears of local government that the Scottish Parliament would take over powers of local authorities had proved to be largely unfounded. Several changes to the law which local government members and officers had been requesting over many years, such as the abolition of surcharge and something akin to a power of general competence in the form of the power to advance well-being, had found their way to the statute book. The four-year term for councils had been restored. The Scottish Executive/Government had announced that there would be no enforced reduction in the number of councillors, had ruled out the upheaval of another reorganisation of local authority boundaries for the time being. Political restrictions on most council employees had been relaxed. A commitment had been given to changing the system of councillors' allowances and to establish some kind of pension provision, although councillors' joy over this was tempered by indications that the Scottish Executive was to be quite prescriptive about the number of Senior Councillors. Consultation processes appeared to be relatively fruitful in that the Scottish Executive was willing, on occasion, to introduce amendments to Bills during their process through the Parliament in response to issues raised by respondents[1]. The Scottish Executive's position regarding organisational and decision-making arrangements within individual councils had been less prescriptive than local government had feared.

1 For example, the consultation process on the Ethical Standards in Public Life etc (Scotland) Act 2000 resulted in the provision of an appeal to the courts against findings of the Standards Commission.

8.38   Early in its life the Scottish Parliament had established a Local Government Committee and its first convener was a former councillor, as were many of its initial members. The remit of the Committee (which has been renamed the Local Government and Communities Committee, with a wider remit) is to consider and report on matters relating to local government, including local government finance. The Committee undertakes the committee stage of Bills relating to local government, including the taking of evidence from interested parties on legislative proposals. The members' experience and understanding of local government has led it to take local government's 'side' on a number of issues. A prime example of this was the Committee's decision to undertake a comprehensive inquiry into local government finance, following the Scottish Executive's decision not to accept the McIntosh Commission's recommendation that an independent inquiry should be carried out.

On the negative side, there had been little progress in implementing the recommendations of the McIntosh Commission on Local Government and the Scottish Parliament that a Covenant should be agreed between the Scottish Parliament and the 32 local authorities and that a standing Joint Conference should be established.

A study on the impact of devolution on local government in the Parliament's early years found that, with the Parliament and the Scottish Executive being located in Edinburgh, ministers and MSPs were far more accessible than were the Scottish Office Ministers in pre-devolution days. The general feeling in local government was that ministers and civil servants were more open and responsive than in the past[1]. The views of councillors were mixed as to whether the Scottish Executive had diminished the importance of local government[2].

1 Bennett, Fairley and McAteer Devolution in Scotland: The Impact on Local Government (2002) ch 2.
2 Benett et al Devolution in Scotland ch 2.

8.39   However, relationships between local government and the Scottish Parliament deteriorated somewhat soon after the elections to the Parliament in 2003. Although the Labour Party remained the largest party in the Parliament, it was weakened by the loss of eight seats and, in the coalition negotiations with the Liberal Democrats, it was forced to make a number of concessions. One of these was the controversial commitment to introduce for the next local government election (due in 2007), the more proportional Single Transferable Vote system of election, discussed above. Moreover, the proposal was made without prior consultation with COSLA, the body which represents much of local government, which seemed to fly in the face of commitments by the Scottish Executive to consult before making announcements of proposals which would impact on local government.

8.40   Three other commitments in the coalition Partnership Agreement caused concern in local government circles because they appeared to be areas where the Scottish Parliament and Scottish Executive intended to take powers away from local government. The first of these was the proposal (now implemented in the Transport Act 2005) to set up a National Transport Agency with responsibility for delivering concessionary fare schemes and for co-ordinating public transport across Scotland. Public transport had previously been a local government function. The second was the proposal to establish a Single Correctional Agency which would remove from local government its current responsibilities for criminal justice social work services. However in this case, successful lobbying by local government resulted in the proposal being dropped. The third issue was the proposal to extend ministerial powers of intervention to deal with 'failing schools', which is now contained in the School Education (Ministerial Powers and Independent Schools) (Scotland) Act 2004. Local government argues that specific powers of intervention in schools already exist but have not been used in more that 20 years of their existence.

Local government members and officials have major concerns about the principle which seems to underlie these is, namely, that if services have to be improved, they have to be put under central government control. They believe that this undermines the principle of subsidiarity which underpins both the Scottish Parliament and Scottish local government. The taking of local government powers by Ministers threatens the legitimacy of councils as the elected local leadership.

On a more positive note, many of the provisions in the Local Governance (Scotland) Act 2004 referred to above implemented long-awaited changes to the law which local government councillors and officers have been arguing for over many years. The Scottish Executive also established an independent review of local government finance (the Burt Review Committee) which was completed by 2006, although it took no action on its proposals.

8.41   The Scottish Parliament elections of May 2007 caused a major upheaval in the governance of Scotland. The Scottish National Party emerged as the largest party in the Parliament with 47 seats, twenty more than they had achieved in 2003. The Labour Party won 46 seats, a net loss of four, while the Liberal Democrats and the Conservatives lost one seat each, leaving them with 16 and 17 seats respectively.

The majority of the SNP gains came at the expense of the so-called "minor parties" which had won seats in 2003. Only two Greens were elected in 2007, compared with seven in 2003. The Scottish Socialist Party lost six seats, thereby eliminating their representation in the Parliament, while the Scottish Senior Citizens Unity Party was similarly eliminated, losing the single seat it had won in 2003.

Since there are 129 seats in the Scottish Parliament, 65 MSPs are required to form a majority administration. As the largest party in the Parliament, the SNP signalled a willingness to enter into talks with other parties in order to form a coalition administration. However, both the Conservatives and the Liberal Democrats rejected these overtures. So the SNP decided to from a minority administration. They immediately announced that the term "Scottish Government" was to be used instead of "Scottish Executive", although the latter remains the legally correct term

Without a majority in the Parliament, the SNP Government has been forced to cut down its programme of legislation, citing the lack of a parliamentary majority as its reason for being unable to fulfil pre-election manifesto promises, such as eliminating student debt. At the time of writing, no Bills relating to local government had been introduced.

The Concordat

8.42   In November 2007, a partnership agreement, known as the Concordat, was reached between the Convention of Scottish Local Authorities and the Scottish Government. Although it has been signed by COSLA, it is not binding on individual local authorities.

In its own words, "the Concordat sets out the terms of a new relationship between the Scottish Government and local government, based on mutual respect and partnership". The Scottish Government is to set the direction of policy and the over-arching outcomes which the public sector in Scotland is expected to achieve and stand back from micro-managing delivery. Whether this turns out to be the case remains to be seen.

The Concordat consists of a package of measures, the main ones being:

- A commitment that the Scottish Government will not undertake structural reform of local government during the term of the Parliament;
- Announcement of the funding that local government can expect to receive over each financial year up to and including 2010–11;
- A reduction in the ring-fencing of government grants, enabling councils to allocate resources according to local priorities;
- Retention by local authorities of the full amount of any efficiency savings made;
- A move to a Single Outcome Agreement for each council, based on an agreed set of national outcomes;
- Delivery on a specified set of commitments including the freezing of the council tax at 2007–8 levels;
- Joint responsibility for monitoring the new partnership and for joint agreement on the handling of new pressures arising from policy development.

The Concordat has the potential for reducing bureaucracy and enhancing the flexibility of councils to allocate scarce resources to areas of local need. However, the necessity to freeze the council tax increases local government's dependence on central government funding.

The Scottish Government's intention to replace the council tax with a nationally set "local" income tax will increase that dependence and remove one of the key elements which entitles local government to be considered "government" rather than simply local administration.

8.43   As far as the public is concerned, the services delivered by local government affect them, literally, from the cradle (registration of births) to the grave (cemeteries and crematoria provision). Most Scots are educated in local authority schools, and many live in council houses. Leisure facilities, roads, refuse collection and disposal and many other services impinge on the life of every citizen. What is important to the public is the efficient and effective delivery of these services and value for the money they pay in council tax. What is also important is the local dimension. The delivery of services should take account of local needs. That is one reason why local government exists.

The old relationship between local government and the Scottish Office changed with the establishment of a Scottish Parliament and the Scottish Executive. It has changed again with the change of political control and the advent of a minority Scottish Government in 2007. It is important that the relationship between the two elected institutions is not one of rivalry, but of co-operation. The public will not be particularly interested in squabbles between the two, but they may become disenchanted with both if the results are less satisfactory services. A covenant as suggested by McIntosh, adopted early in the life of the Parliament and adhered to by both sides might well have put the relationship on a stable footing, but unfortunately that did not happen. The 'parity of esteem' recommended by McIntosh appears to be absent during the first two terms of the Scottish Parliament. Whether the Concordat agreed in 2007 will improve the relationship remains to be seen and only time will tell if local government will survive in its present form and with its present range of responsibilities.

Appendix

SPECIFIC MINISTERIAL CONTROLS

1   Local authorities are creatures of statute, established by Act of Parliament. Their existence is not guaranteed as they do not have any entrenched position in the constitution of the United Kingdom. They may be abolished by Act of Parliament and their powers transferred to other local authorities or bodies as Parliament so wills, as the regional and district councils were abolished in 1996[1]. The present 32 local authorities were established by an Act of the UK Parliament and functions and resources were allocated to them by Acts of Parliament. Various powers of regulation and control over local authorities were given to ministers by these Acts and until the establishment of the Scottish Parliament in 1999 most of these were vested in the Secretary of State for Scotland and the Scottish Office which was one of the central departments of the UK government.

However, since the establishment of the Scottish Parliament in 1999, it is the Scottish Parliament and the Scottish Executive which have the power to determine the structure, constitution and most of the functions of Scottish local government. Most of the powers of regulation and control previously exercised by ministers of the UK government have been transferred to the Scottish Executive. Therefore most references to the Secretary of State in Acts of Parliament relating to local government passed before the Scottish Executive assumed its powers in 1999 are to be read to include references to the Scottish Ministers. However, in certain areas which are reserved to the Parliament of the United Kingdom, local government carries out tasks on behalf of central government. Social security matters, for example, are reserved yet there are certain areas of social security, such as the administration of housing benefit, which are carried out in Scotland by local authorities. Immigration and asylum are also reserved to the UK Parliament and those Scottish local authorities which have agreed to take asylum-seekers into their areas are under the direction of the Home Secretary and the Home Office even in relation to their accommodation and the education of their children, which are normally devolved matters. Therefore there may be occasions when a reference in an Act of Parliament to a Secretary of State is still apt as the external regulation and control is exercised by a Secretary of State rather than by the Scottish Ministers.

1 Local Government etc (Scotland) Act 1994.

2   Several different categories of ministerial influence and control over local authorities exist, of differing status. Here we will concentrate mainly on the controls of the Scottish Ministers and it should be noted that the list below is not exhaustive.

173

Advice and guidance

3   The departments of the Scottish Executive provide local authorities with advice and guidance on their powers, duties and functions by issuing circulars and memoranda as the need arises. These will offer advice as to how legislation is to be implemented. Sometimes they are issued to fulfil a requirement in a particular statute that the local authority must exercise its powers under the guidance of the Scottish Ministers. For example, the Local Government in Scotland Act 2003 which gives local government the duty to secure best value, the duty of community planning and the power to advance well-being contains provisions which require local authorities to have regard to guidance issued by the Scottish Ministers[1]. Statutory guidance and advice notes were issued in 2004.

Such guidance, however, does not and cannot have the force of law and the Scottish Executive emphasises that the authoritative interpretation of legislation is a matter for the courts.

1 Local Government in Scotland Act 2003, ss 2, 18, 21.

Consents and approvals

4   Many proposals and actions undertaken by a local authority statutorily require the express approval of the Scottish Ministers. An example of this is the strategic development plans which councils, as planning authorities, are required to prepare and submit to the Scottish Ministers for approval in terms of the Planning etc (Scotland) Act 2006. Flood prevention schemes and compulsory purchase orders must also be confirmed by Scottish Ministers.

Powers of intervention

5   There are some situations where local authorities are free to formulate and carry out their own proposals without the express approval of the Scottish Ministers but where the appropriate statute makes provision for the intervention of the Scottish Ministers in certain circumstances. The formulation and adoption of local plans, for example, are primarily matters for the councils as planning authorities to deal with but section 18 of the Town and Country Planning (Scotland) Act 1997 (as amended by the Planning etc. (Scotland) Act 2006) gives the Scottish Ministers power to intervene by directing that a plan is not to have effect unless it is approved by them. It is unlikely that Scottish Ministers would become involved in the preparation of local plans unless an issue of national importance was involved or there was clear evidence that some statutory requirement had not been fulfilled. Under certain circumstances, Ministers also have the power to "call in" a planning application for their determination[1]. A particularly controversial example was the call in in 2008 of a planning application by an American developer Donald Trump for a golf course and associated developments in the area of Aberdeenshire Council.

1 Town and Country Planning (Scotland) Act 1997, s 46 as amended by the Planning etc. (Scotland) Act 2006.

Regulation-making powers

6 Many Acts of both Parliaments confer on the Scottish Ministers (or a Secretary of State) powers to prescribe or regulate in detail a wide range of matters incidental to the main legislation. For example, the Ethical Standards in Public Life etc (Scotland) Act 2000 provides that every council must set up, maintain and make available for public inspection a register of councillors' interests[1]. Councils must carry out this duty in accordance with regulations made by the Scottish Ministers.

~~Regulations made by statutory instrument have the force of law.~~

1 Ethical Standards in Public Life etc (Scotland) Act 2000, s 7.

Powers of veto

7 There are situations where a local authority is entitled to take action or incur expenditure without the prior approval of the Scottish Ministers, but where Scottish Ministers may subsequently direct the local authority to discontinue the action or stop incurring the expenditure. An example of this is to be found in the Housing (Scotland) Act 1987 which empowers local authorities to declare housing action areas in order to tackle the problems of substandard housing. Where the Scottish Ministers have received a draft resolution declaring a housing action area, they may, if they consider it appropriate and within a certain time limit, direct the local authority to rescind the resolution.

Confirmation of byelaws

8 As we have seen[1], all byelaws made by a local authority must be confirmed by the appropriate confirming authority specified in statute, normally the Scottish Ministers and the usual procedure for confirmation will be that laid down in the Local Government (Scotland) Act 1973[2]. If objections to the proposed byelaw are submitted to the Scottish Ministers, they may cause a public inquiry to be held to hear the case against the proposal. The Scottish Ministers will take into account the findings of the inquiry before deciding whether or not to confirm the byelaw.

1 In ch 4.
2 Local Government (Scotland) Act 1973, s 202.

Control of appointment and/or dismissal of certain officers

9 Local authorities can in general appoint such officers as they consider necessary to carry out local government functions. However, some statutes specify that a certain officer or officers must be appointed to carry out certain functions. For example, a local authority must appoint a chief social work officer who must hold an appropriate qualification in social work but who does not necessarily have to be the Director of the Department of Social Work.

Other officers who must be appointed, either by individual councils or by joint boards, are assessors (who deal with the valuation of properties for council tax and non-domestic rates purposes), chief constables, depute and assistant chief constables and firemasters. In certain cases such as those of chief, depute and assistant chief constables, statute requires that candidates must be approved by the Scottish Ministers before a shortlist is drawn up and appointment requires their express approval. The Scottish Ministers may require a police authority to ensure the compulsory retirement of a chief constable in the interests of the efficiency of the police force.

In the case of certain posts, for example assessors, the postholder may not be dismissed or required to resign by the local authority or joint board without the consent of the Scottish Ministers.

Appellate powers

10   There are some situations where a local authority has the power to make a decision without reference to the Scottish Ministers but where people affected by the decision may appeal to the Scottish Ministers who may uphold, modify or reverse the decision of the local authority. The best-known examples are certain appeals against the refusal of planning permission and appeals against planning enforcement action[1].

1 Town and Country Planning Act (Scotland) 1997, ss 47 and 130 as amended by the Planning etc. (Scotland) Act 2006.

Powers of inspection

11   In the case of certain local government services, central government is required by statute to appoint inspectors to ensure that the standards laid down in legislation are complied with by councils. Inspectors are usually appointed by the Crown but the onus of pursuing any shortcomings identified by inspectors lies with the Scottish Ministers. Examples of inspectorates include Her Majesty's Chief Inspector of Constabulary, Her Majesty's Inspectors of Fire Services and Her Majesty's Inspectors of Education.

Financial controls

12   The various financial controls over local government which Scottish Ministers possess are very significant and have been dealt with in more detail elsewhere in this book[1].

1 See ch 6.

Power to remove or relax controls

13   The Local Government (Scotland) Act 1973 contains a general power for the Scottish Ministers to make an order for the removal or relaxation of any controls which affect the exercise of any local authority functions[1].

1 Local Government (Scotland) Act 1973, s 209.

Power to order a local inquiry

14   The Local Government (Scotland) Act 1973 also gives Scottish Ministers the power to direct that a local inquiry should be held into the conduct of a local authority's business[1]. (This is different from the power to have an inquiry held prior to confirming a byelaw, mentioned above.) This power is intended to be used only in unusual circumstances. The person appointed by the Scottish Ministers to hold the inquiry is given powers to require the attendance of witnesses and the production of documents and books. Anyone who refuses to give evidence or suppresses documents and books is liable on summary conviction to a fine or a term of imprisonment.

An example of an inquiry held under these provisions was the inquiry carried out by Lord Clyde into childcare procedures in Orkney in 1992.

1 Local Government (Scotland) Act 1973, s 210.

Default powers

15   If a complaint is made to the Scottish Ministers that a local authority has failed to carry out its statutory duties, they may cause a local inquiry to be held into the matter[1]. If the inquiry reveals that there has indeed been such a failure, the Scottish Ministers can make an order declaring the authority to be in default and directing it to remedy the default. If the local authority fails to comply, the Lord Advocate may apply to the Court of Session for an order of specific performance.

This default power is rarely used and in practice is held in reserve to be used against a local authority which wishes to 'take on' central government as an act of political defiance. For example, Glasgow District Council was opposed to the Conservative government's legislation which gave council house tenants the right to buy their houses at discounted prices and attempted to thwart the legislation by inserting certain unlawful conditions into offers of sale. The Secretary of State for Scotland caused a public inquiry to be held which found that the council had failed to do what was required of them by law and a default order was made. The council continued to resist and a successful application was made by the Lord Advocate for an order of specific performance[2].

Other specific default powers are to be found in Acts dealing with particular functions, such as the Education (Scotland) Act 1980.

1 Local Government (Scotland) Act 1973, s 211.
2 *Lord Advocate v City of Glasgow District Council* 1990 SLT 721.

Enforcement directions

16   Some Acts confer on the Scottish Ministers the power to issue an enforcement direction to a local authority. For example, if it appears to the Scottish Ministers that a council is not complying with its duties in relation to best value, community planning or the publication of information about finance and performance or is exceeding its power of well-being[1], they may give the local authority such a direction requiring it to take specific action[2]. The School Education (Ministerial Powers and Independent Schools) (Scotland) Act 2004 confers powers on Scottish Ministers to give an enforcement direction in relation to recommendations made by HM Inspectors of Education.

1 For best value, community planning and the power of well-being, see ch 4.
2 Local Government (Scotland) Act 2003, ss 23–27.

Index

[All references are to paragraph number]

A

Abuse of process
ultra vires, and, 4.3
Acceptance of office
duties of councillors, and, 3.29
Access to information
data protection, 5.41–5.44
freedom of information, 5.36–5.40
generally, 5.29–5.35
human rights, 5.45
rights of councillors, and, 3.33
Access to meetings
generally, 5.29–5.35
Accounts Commission
best value, and, 4.17
Acquisition of land
local government powers, and, 4.38
Advancement of well-being
local government powers, and,
4.9–4.12
Aggregate external finance
council tax, and, 6.19
generally, 6.6–6.8
grant-aided expenditure, and, 6.5
meaning, 6.9
Allocation of council housing
voting restrictions, and, 3.31
Allocation of powers
structure of local government, and,
1.25
Allowances
remuneration of councillors, and, 3.38
Arms length external organisations
generally, 5.24–5.25
local government finance, and, 6.44
Arrears of Council tax
voting restrictions, and, 3.31
Attendance at meetings
rights of councillors, and, 3.32
vacation of office, and, 3.16

B

Best value
Accounts Commission, and, 4.17

Best value – *contd*
general duty, 4.13–4.17
generally, 6.40–6.43
publication of information, 6.48
Boundary changes
development of local government,
and, 2.34–2.37
Burghs
development of local government,
and, 1.1
Burt Report
local government finance, and, 6.24
Business rates
local government finance, and, 6.7
Byelaws
local government powers, and,
4.21–4.25

C

Cabinet
operation of councils, and, 5.21–5.22
Capital budget
local government finance, and,
6.25–6.29
Capital expenditure
local government finance, and, 6.3
Capping
local government finance, and, 6.21
Casual vacancies
councillors, and, 3.17
Central–local relations
codes of conduct for councillors and
members, 8.22
devolution, and, 8.5–8.6
evaluation, 8.36–8.42
introduction, 8.1–8.2
Kerley Report, 8.23–8.28
Leadership Advisory Panel Report,
8.29–8.34
Local Governance (Scotland) Act
2004, 8.35
MacNish Report
committee structures, 8.30
devolved structures, 8.32–8.34

Central-local relations – *contd*
  MacNish Report – *contd*
    executive structure, 8.31
    introduction, 8.29
    partially-devolved structures,
      8.32–8.34
  McIntosh Commission Report
    conduct of council business, 8.18
    councillors' remuneration, 8.20
    electoral restrictions on council
      employees, 8.19
    electoral system, 8.17
    generally, 8.7–8.9
    local government finance, 8.14
    miscellaneous recommendations,
      8.13
    power of general competence, 8.15
    relations with Scottish Executive,
      8.12
    relations with Scottish Parliament,
      8.10–8.11
    Scottish Executive's response, 8.21
    term of office, 8.16
    timing of local elections, 8.16
  Ministerial controls, 8.3–8.6
  Renewing Local Democracy Working
    Group Report, 8.23–8.28
  single transferable vote, and, 8.36
  Wheatley Report, and, 8.4
Code of Conduct
  background, 7.17–7.20
  central–local relations, and, 8.22
  conduct, 3.27
  declaration of interests, 7.24–7.29
  introduction, 3.26
  lobbying, 7.30
  Nolan Report, 7.19
  operation of statutory provisions,
    7.39–7.41
  planning applications, 7.31–7.33
  principles
    generally, 7.22
    summary, 3.26
  registration of interests, 7.23
  Standards Commission for Scotland,
    7.34–7.38
  statutory basis, 7.21
  Widdecombe Committee Report, 7.18
Committees
  appointment of councillors, 5.4
  membership, 5.12–5.13
  system, 5.6–5.11
Community charge
  local government finance, and, 6.12

Community councils
  structure of local government, and,
    2.30–2.33
**Community health and care
  partnerships**
  generally, 5.26
Community justice authorities
  generally, 5.27
Community planning
  local government powers, and,
    4.18–4.20
Compulsory competitive tendering
  best value, and, 4.13–4.14
Conduct
  See also CODE OF CONDUCT
  duties of councillors, and, 3.25–3.27
Conduct of council business
  McIntosh Commission Report, and,
    8.18
Contracts
  local government powers, and, 4.39
Controller of Audit
  And see LOCAL GOVERNMENT
    FINANCE
  best value, and, 6.41
  external audit, and, 6.34
  special reports, 6.35–6.39
Convenors
  generally, 3.19–3.21
**Convention of Scottish Local
  Authorities (COSLA)**
  joint arrangements, and, 2.29
Corporate governance
  operation of councils, and, 5.50
Council employees
  electoral restrictions, 8.19
Council manager
  operation of councils, and, 5.20
Council tax
  aggregate external finance, and, 6.19
  background, 6.10–6.12
  capping, 6.21
  collection, 6.22
  gearing, 6.23
  generally, 6.13–6.16
  grant-aided expenditure, and, 6.19
  problem areas, 6.23–6.24
  setting, 6.17–6.20
Councillors
  access to information, 3.33
  allocation of council housing, 3.31
  arrears of Council tax, 3.31
  Code of Conduct
    background, 7.17–7.20

Councillors – *contd*
  Code of Conduct – *contd*
    declaration of interests, 7.24–7.29
    lobbying, 7.30
    Nolan Report, 7.19
    operation of statutory provisions,
      7.39–7.41
    planning applications, 7.31–7.33
    principles, 7.22
    registration of interests, 7.23
    Standards Commission for
      Scotland, 7.34–7.38
    statutory basis, 7.21
    Widdecombe Committee Report,
      7.18
  convenors, 3.19–3.21
  depute convenors, 3.19–3.21
  disqualification, 3.9–3.14
  duties
    acceptance of office, 3.29
    conduct, 3.25–3.27
    declaration of interests, 3.28
    registration of interests, 3.28
  elections, and
    electoral system, 3.6
    right to vote, 3.2–3.3
    standing for election, 3.7–2.14
    timing, 3.4–3.5
  introduction, 3.1
  job description, 3.40
  Lord Provost, 3.20
  remuneration
    allowances, 3.38
    generally, 3.35
    McIntosh Commission Report, and,
      8.20
    new scheme, 3.37
    pensions, 3.39
    reimbursement of expenses, 3.38
    Remuneration Committee, 3.36
  requisition of council meetings, 3.34
  resignation from office, 3.15–3.18
  rights
    access to information, 3.33
    introduction, 3.32
    job description, 3.40
    remuneration, 3.35–3.39
    requisition of council meetings,
      3.34
  roles, 3.22–3.24
  standing for election, 3.7–2.14
  vacation of office, 3.15–3.18
  voting restrictions
    allocation of council housing, 3.31

Councillors – *contd*
  voting restrictions – *contd*
    arrears of Council tax, 3.31
    generally, 3.30
    widening access to membership,
      3.41–3.44
Councils
  introduction, 3.1
Court of Session
  role in local government, and,
    7.46–7.48
Courts' role
  Court of Session, 7.46–7.48
  introduction, 7.42–7.43
  sheriff court, 7.44–7.45
Crerar Report (2007)
  local government finance, and, 6.50

D
Data protection
  access to meetings, and, 5.41–5.44
Decentralisation
  development of local government,
    and, 2.16–2.18
Declaration of interests
  Code of Conduct, and, 7.24–7.29
  generally, 3.28
Depute convenors
  generally, 3.19–3.21
Devolution
  central–local relations, and, 8.5–8.6
Direct election of provost
  operation of councils, and, 5.19
Director of Finance
  local government finance, and, 6.1
Disposal of land
  local government powers, and, 4.38
Disqualification
  councillors, and, 3.9–3.14

E
Elections
  electoral system, 3.6
  McIntosh Commission Report, and,
    electoral system, 8.17
    restrictions on council employees,
      8.19
    timing, 8.16
  right to vote, 3.2–3.3
  single transferable vote system, 36
  standing for election
    disqualifications, 3.9–14
    generally, 3.7–3.8

Elections – *contd*
  standing for election – *contd*
    politically restricted posts,
      3.11–3.12
  structure of local government, and,
    2.34–2.37
  timing, 3.4–3.5
Electoral arrangements
  structure of local government, and,
    2.34–2.37
Excess of process
  ultra vires, and, 4.2
Executive and scrutiny committee
  operation of councils, and, 5.14
Expenses
  remuneration of councillors, and, 3.38
External audit
  local government finance, and,
    6.33–6.34

F
Fees and charges
  local government finance, and, 6.9
Finance
  And see LOCAL GOVERNMENT
    FINANCE
  arms length external organisations,
    6.44
  brief guide, 6.2–6.8
  capital budget, 6.25–6.29
  council tax, 6.10–6.22
  Crerar Report (2007), 6.50
  fees and charges, 6.9
  housing finance, 6.30
  introduction, 6.1
  problem areas, 6.23–6.24
  public accountability, 6.31–6.43
  significant trading operations,
    6.45–6.49
First meeting
  operation of councils, and, 5.3–5.4
Freedom of assembly and association
  operation of councils, and, 5.45
Freedom of information
  access to meetings, and, 5.36–5.40
Full council
  operation of councils, and, 5.5

G
Gaelic names
  structure of local government, and,
    2.38
General competence
  general power, 4.7

General competence – *contd*
  McIntosh Commission Report, and,
    8.15
  Scottish Parliament, and, 4.8
Government-supported expenditure
  local government finance, and,
    6.5
Grant-aided expenditure
  council tax, and, 6.19
  generally, 6.5

H
Homosexuality
  local government powers, and, 4.36
Housing
  local government finance, and, 6.30
Human rights
  access to meetings, and, 5.45

I
Incidental rule
  common law, at, 4.4
  statute, in, 4.5
  ultra vires, and, 4.2
Internal audit
  local government finance, and, 6.32
Investigations by Ombudsman
  annual report, 7.13
  complainants, 7.8
  enforcement powers, 7.12
  exempt decisions, 7.7
  introduction, 7.6
  miscellaneous, 7.13
  persons aggrieved, 7.8
  procedure, 7.9
  reports, 7.10
  special reports, 7.11

J
Job description
  rights of councillors, and, 3.40
Joint arrangements
  structure of local government, and,
    2.22–2.29
Judicial review
  ultra vires, and, 4.2–4.3

K
Kerley Committee Report
  access to council membership, and,
    3.41
  generally, 8.23–8.28
  remuneration of councillors, and,
    3.35

L

Leadership Advisory Panel Report
central–local relations, and, 8.29–8.34
Lobbying
Members' Code of Conduct, and, 7.30
Local Governance (Scotland) Act 2004
central–local relations, and, 8.35
Local government
boundary changes, 2.34–2.37
community councils, 2.30–2.33
constitutional position, 1.27–1.29
decentralisation, 2.16–2.18
electoral arrangement changes,
2.34–2.37
finance
And see LOCAL GOVERNMENT
FINANCE
generally, 6.1–6.50
functions, 2.19–2.21
historical development
generally, 1.1–1.16
Wheatley Commission, 1.17–1.26
joint arrangements, 2.22–2.29
name change, 2.38
powers and duties
And see POWERS AND DUTIES
generally, 4.1–4.38
reorganisation, 2.4–2.15
structure
changes, 2.34–2.38
community councils, 2.30–2.33
decentralisation, 2.16–2.18
evaluation of current arrangements,
2.39
introduction, 2.1–2.3
joint arrangements, 2.22–2.29
reorganisation, 2.4–2.15
Wheatley Commission, 1.17–1.26
Local government finance
aggregate external finance
council tax, and, 6.19
generally, 6.6–6.8
grant-aided expenditure, and, 6.5
meaning, 6.9
arms length external organisations,
6.44
best value
generally, 6.40–6.43
publication of information, 6.48
Burt Report, 6.24
brief guide
aggregate external finance, 6.6–6.8
capital expenditure, 6.3

Local government finance – *contd*
brief guide – *contd*
government-supported expenditure,
6.5
income sources, 6.4
revenue expenditure, 6.2
business rates, 6.7
capital budget, 6.25–6.29
capital expenditure, 6.3
capping, 6.21
community charge, and, 6.12
Controller of Audit
best value, and, 6.41
external audit, and, 6.34
special reports, 6.35–6.39
council tax
aggregate external finance, and,
6.19
background, 6.10–6.12
capping, 6.21
collection, 6.22
gearing, 6.23
generally, 6.13–6.16
grant-aided expenditure, and, 6.19
problem areas, 6.23–6.24
setting, 6.17–6.20
Crerar Report (2007), 6.50
Director of Finance, and, 6.1
external audit, 6.33–6.34
fees and charges, 6.9
government-supported expenditure,
6.5
grant-aided expenditure
council tax, and, 6.19
generally, 6.5
housing finance, 6.30
income sources, 6.4
internal audit, 6.32
introduction, 6.1
McIntosh Commission Report, and
generally, 8.14
introduction, 6.23
non-domestic rates, 6.7
performance indicators, 6.47
'poll tax', and, 6.12
Private Finance Initiative, and, 6.27
problem areas, 6.23–6.24
Prudential Code, 6.26
public accountability
best value, 6.40–6.43
external audit, 6.33–6.34
internal audit, 6.32
introduction, 6.31
special reports, 6.35–6.39

Local government finance – *contd*
   public private partnerships, and, 6.27
   publication of information, 6.47–6.49
   rates, and, 6.10
   revenue expenditure, 6.2
   revenue support grant, 6.8
   ring-fenced grants, 6.6
   Scottish Futures Trust, 6.28
   significant trading operations,
      6.45–6.49
   sources of income
      aggregate external finance, 6.6–6.8
      council tax, 6.10–6.22
      fees and charges, 6.9
      introduction, 6.4
      non-domestic rates, 6.7
      revenue support grant, 6.8
      ring-fenced grants, 6.6
   special reports, 6.35–6.39
   statutory framework, 6.1
Local government staff
   operation of councils, and, 5.46–5.49
Lord Provost
   councillors, and, 3.20

M
MacNish Report
   committee structures, 8.30
   devolved structures, 8.32–8.34
   executive structure, 8.31
   introduction, 8.29
   partially-devolved structures,
      8.32–8.34
Maladministration
   Ombudsman, and, 7.3
Management rules
   local government powers, and,
      4.26–4.28
McIntosh Commission Report
   conduct of council business, 8.18
   councillors' remuneration, 8.20
   electoral restrictions on council
      employees, 8.19
   electoral system, 8.17
   generally, 8.7–8.9
   local government finance
      generally, 8.14
      introduction, 6.23
   miscellaneous recommendations, 8.13
   power of general competence, 8.15
   relations with Scottish Executive, 8.12
   relations with Scottish Parliament,
      8.10–8.11

McIntosh Commission Report – *contd*
   role of political groups in decision-
      making, and, 5.17
   Scottish Executive's response, 8.21
   term of office, 8.16
   timing of local elections
      generally, 8.16
      introduction, 3.5
Ministerial controls
   And see CENTRAL–LOCAL RELATIONS
   generally, 8.3–8.6
   specific issues, Appendix

N
Name change
   development of local government,
      and, 2.38
Nolan Report
   Members' Code of Conduct, and,
      7.19
Non-domestic rates
   local government finance, and, 6.7

O
Ombudsman
   advice and guidance, 7.14
   evaluation, 7.14–7.16
   generally, 7.2–7.4
   investigation powers
      annual report, 7.13
      complainants, 7.8
      enforcement powers, 7.12
      exempt decisions, 7.7
      introduction, 7.6
      miscellaneous, 7.13
      persons aggrieved, 7.8
      procedure, 7.9
      reports, 7.10
      special reports, 7.11
   local authority requests, 7.13
   meaning, 7.3
   publicity for existence, 7.13
   statistics, 7.16
   statutory basis, 7.5
Operation of councils
   access to information
      data protection, 5.41–5.44
      freedom of information, 5.36–5.40
      generally, 5.29–5.35
      human rights, 5.45
   access to meetings, 5.29–5.35
   alternative forms of service delivery
      arms length external organisations,
         5.24–5.25

Operation of councils – *contd*
  alternative forms of service delivery –
      contd
    community health and care
        partnerships, 5.26
    community justice authorities, 5.27
  alternative models
    cabinet, 5.21–5.22
    council manager, 5.20
    direct election of provost, 5.19
    introduction, 5.18
  committees
    membership, 5.12–5.13
    system, 5.6–5.11
  corporate governance, 5.50
  executive and scrutiny committee,
      5.14
  first meeting, 5.3–5.4
  freedom of assembly and association,
      and, 5.45
  full council, 5.5
  introduction, 5.1–5.2
  local government staff, 5.46–5.49
  peaceful enjoyment of possessions,
      and, 5.45
  political groups, and, 5.15–5.17
  prohibition of discrimination, and,
      5.45
  public involvement, 5.28
  recent developments, 5.23
  right to fair trial, and, 5.45
  right to respect for private and family
      life, and, 5.45
  staff, 5.46–5.49

P
Parishes
  development of local government,
      and, 1.2
**Parliamentary Commissioner for
    Administration**
  generally, 7.3
Peaceful enjoyment of possessions
  operation of councils, and, 5.45
Pensions
  remuneration of councillors, and, 3.39
Performance indicators
  local government finance, and, 6.47
Planning applications
  Members' Code of Conduct, and,
      7.31–7.33
Political groups
  operation of councils, and, 5.15–5.17

Politically restricted posts
  elections, and, 3.11–3.12
'Poll tax'
  local government finance, and, 6.12
Powers and duties
  acquisition of land, 4.38
  advancement of well-being, 4.9–4.12
  best value, 4.13–4.17
  byelaws, 4.21–4.25
  community planning, 4.18–4.20
  contracts, 4.39
  disposal of land, 4.38
  general competence, 4.7–4.8
  incidental rule, 4.4–4.5
  introduction, 4.1
  management rules, 4.26–4.28
  private legislation, and, 4.29–4.31
  promotion of homosexuality, 4.36
  publicity, 4.32–4.35
  research of collation of information,
      4.37
  ultra vires, 4.2–4.6
Private Finance Initiative
  local government finance, and, 6.27
Private legislation
  local government powers, and,
      4.29–4.31
Prohibition of discrimination
  operation of councils, and, 5.45
Promotion of homosexuality
  local government powers, and, 4.36
Prudential Code
  local government finance, and, 6.26
Public accountability
  best value, 6.40–6.43
  external audit, 6.33–6.34
  internal audit, 6.32
  introduction, 6.31
  special reports, 6.35–6.39
Public private partnerships (PPP)
  local government finance, and, 6.27
Public Services Ombudsman
  advice and guidance, 7.14
  evaluation, 7.14–7.16
  generally, 7.2–7.4
  investigation powers
    annual report, 7.13
    complainants, 7.8
    enforcement powers, 7.12
    exempt decisions, 7.7
    introduction, 7.6
    miscellaneous, 7.13
    persons aggrieved, 7.8
    procedure, 7.9

Public Services Ombudsman – *contd*
investigation powers – *contd*
reports, 7.10
special reports, 7.11
local authority requests, 7.13
publicity for existence, 7.13
statistics, 7.16
statutory basis, 7.5
Publicity
local government powers, and,
4.32–4.35

R
Rates
local government finance, and, 6.10
Registration of interests
Code of Conduct, and, 7.23
generally, 3.28
Remuneration
allowances, 3.38
generally, 3.35
McIntosh Commission Report, and,
8.20
new scheme, 3.37
pensions, 3.39
reimbursement of expenses, 3.38
Scottish Local Authorities
Remuneration Committee, 3.36
**Renewing Local Democracy Working
Group (Kerley) Report**
access to council membership, and,
3.41
generally, 8.23–8.28
remuneration of councillors, and, 3.35
Reorganisation
structure of local government, and,
2.4–2.15
Requisition of council meetings
rights of councillors, and, 3.34
Research of collation of information
local government powers, and, 4.37
Resignation from office
councillors, and, 3.15–3.18
Revenue expenditure
local government finance, and, 6.2
Revenue support grant
local government finance, and, 6.8
Ring-fenced grants
local government finance, and, 6.6
Right to fair trial
operation of councils, and, 5.45
**Right to respect for private and family
life**
operation of councils, and, 5.45

Rights of councillors
access to meetings, and, 3.33

S
Scottish Executive
McIntosh Commission Report, and,
8.12
Scottish Futures Trust
local government finance, and, 6.28
**Scottish Local Authorities
Remuneration Committee**
remuneration of councillors, and, 3.36
Scottish Parliament
McIntosh Commission Report, and,
8.10–8.11
Scottish Public Services Ombudsman
advice and guidance, 7.14
evaluation, 7.14–7.16
generally, 7.2–7.4
investigation powers
annual report, 7.13
complainants, 7.8
enforcement powers, 7.12
exempt decisions, 7.7
introduction, 7.6
miscellaneous, 7.13
persons aggrieved, 7.8
procedure, 7.9
reports, 7.10
special reports, 7.11
local authority requests, 7.13
publicity for existence, 7.13
statistics, 7.16
statutory basis, 7.5
*Shaping the Future – The New
Councils* **(White Paper, 1993)**
joint arrangements, and, 2.25
structure of local government, and,
2.13
Sheriff court
role in local government, and,
7.44–7.45
Significant trading operations
local government finance, and,
6.45–6.49
Single transferable vote (STV)
central–local relations, and, 8.35
Special reports
local government finance, and,
6.35–6.39
Standards Commission for Scotland
And see MEMBERS' CODE OF
CONDUCT
generally, 7.34–7.38

Standing for election
councillors, and, 3.7–2.14
Stodart Committee Report
structure of local government, and, 2.3
Strathclyde Passenger Transport Authority
joint arrangements, and, 2.26
Structure of local government
changes, 2.34–2.38
community councils, 2.30–2.33
decentralisation, 2.16–2.18
evaluation of current arrangements, 2.39
introduction, 2.1–2.3
joint arrangements, 2.22–2.29
reorganisation, 2.4–2.15

U
Ultra vires
generally, 4.2–4.6
incidental rule, and
common law, at, 4.4
introduction, 4.2
statute, in, 4.5

Ultra vires – *contd*
Local Government (Contracts) Act 1997, and, 4.6

V
Vacation of office
councillors, and, 3.15–3.18
Voting restrictions
councillors, and, 3.30–3.31

W
Well-being
local government powers, and, 4.9–4.12
Wheatley Commission Report
allocation powers, 1.25
central–local relations, and, 8.4
community councils, and, 2.30
generally, 1.17–1.20
joint arrangements, and, 2.22
recommendations, 1.21–1.26
Widdecombe Committee Report
Members' Code of Conduct, and, 7.18